The Non-Canonical

C000172155

The Non-Canonical Gospels

Edited by

Paul Foster

t&t clark

Published by T&T Clark
A Continuum imprint
The Tower Building, 11 York Road, London SE1 7NX
80 Maiden Lane, Suite 704, New York, NY 10038

www.continuumbooks.com

All rights reserved. No part of this publication may be reproduced or transmitted in any form or by any means, electronic or mechanical, including photocopying, recording or any information storage or retrieval system, without permission in writing from the publishers.

Copyright © Paul Foster and Contributors, 2008

British Library Cataloguing-in-Publication Data
A catalogue record for this book is available from the British Library

ISBN-10: HB: 0-567-03301-5
PB: 0-567-03302-3
ISBN-13: HB: 978-0-567-03301-7
PB: 978-0-567-03302-4

Typeset by Newgen Imaging Systems Pvt Ltd, Chennai, India
Printed on acid-free paper in Great Britain by Cromwell Press, Trowbridge, Wiltshire

Contents

Preface

1. *The Selection and Collection of Texts*

As is familiar to those who study the New Testament, collections or groupings of texts are often arbitrary, or due to quirks of history, or they result from taxonomies of convenience. While it might potentially be more satisfying to lay afresh all the pieces of textual evidence on the table of academic enquiry and to regroup them along much more scientific lines, the weight of past history and ongoing faith commitments simply prevents such an endeavour. Moreover, even with the hope of scholarly objectivity it is unlikely that any consensus would be reached concerning appropriate groupings and the criteria that should be used to arrive at such decisions. As a result it is necessary to operate within the prevailing system of classifying gospel texts, while recognizing the artificial nature of the groupings. Thus one is left with a 'privileged' collection of four writings, Matthew, Mark, Luke and John – the canonical gospels, which at the latest by the end of the second century were recognized as an authoritative collection of texts for groups of emergent 'proto-orthodox' Christians. Around the year 180 CE, Irenaeus, bishop of Lyons, in his writings against Christians he described as heretics, was able to make the following elevated statements about the centrality of a fourfold gospel collection.

> It is not possible that the Gospels can be either more or fewer in number than they are. For, since there are four zones of the world in which we live, and four principal winds, while the Church is scattered throughout all the world, and the pillar and ground of the Church is the Gospel and the spirit of life; it is fitting that she should have four pillars, breathing out immortality on every side, and vivifying men afresh . . . He who was manifested to men, has given us the Gospel under four aspects, but bound together by one Spirit. (*Adv. Haer.* 3.11.8)

By contrast to this well-known and eventually official canonical collection of four gospels, a larger and more diverse range of gospel-like writings circulated in antiquity and into the Middle Ages. It is with this shadowy and often unknown set of writings and fragmentary texts that this book is concerned.

Unlike the New Testament, no systematic attempt to create a collection of non-canonical gospels is known in antiquity or the pre-Modern period. This stands in some contrast to the writings of the Apostolic Fathers where the *First* and *Second Epistles of Clement* stand together in Codex Alexandrinus, the *Epistle of Barnabas* and *the Shepherd of Hermas* in Codex Sinaiticus, and in codex Hierosolymitanus produced in 1056 CE, the *Didache, 1* and *2 Clement,* the *Epistle of Barnabas*, and the Longer recension of the letters of Ignatius had been collected together.[1] In fact, the earliest and most significant 'meeting' of two of the non-canonical gospel texts that can be documented prior to the modern period occurs in the Nag Hammadi writings where, in what is now conventionally numbered as codex II, the texts of the *Gospel of Thomas* and the *Gospel of Philip* stand alongside one another. Apart from this, the extant evidence suggests that the majority of the non-canonical gospels circulated in isolation from each other. (A notable exception is certainly found in some later Latin and Syriac manuscripts that try to piece together apocryphal 'lives' of Jesus by stringing together various infancy gospels and the *Gospel of Nicodemus* as well as sometimes the Dormition of Mary.) The reasons for the lack of cohesion in antiquity of these writings are numerous, and are due perhaps more to sociological and theological factors than relating to any concerns about literary style or genre. A number of the non-canonical texts were proscribed by some of the leading thinkers in proto-orthodox Christianity. Notwithstanding this, several of these texts appear to have been treasured by small conventicles of Christians, who sometimes lived in isolationist communities, but perhaps more frequently were embedded within emergent mainstream groups. However, such individuals or small groups lacked the hierarchy or organizational structure to collect, authorize and disseminate their own alternative texts. While this may lead to seeing such writings as marginal, perhaps it is better to recognize the resilience and survival of these texts despite voices opposing their perspectives. It is noteworthy that many of these texts which were perhaps written in the second century were still being read as authoritative documents by various individuals or communities of faith in the fourth and fifth centuries, and even beyond.

However, the fate of such marginal documents read by liminal communities in the face of a progressively more assertive and authoritarian Orthodox Church in the late antique and early medieval periods, meant that these texts eventually disappeared from the ecclesial landscape.[2] Apart from the occasional reference in the writings of early Christians given the stamp of legitimacy by later generations such as Irenaeus, Origen or Jerome, these texts became virtually forgotten, obscured by the mists of time and inaccessible because of their apparent non-survival. Consequently, often all that remained were lists of the names of proscribed texts, and occasionally one might be given a short quotation when an 'orthodox' writer, such as Irenaeus or Tertullian cited these writings usually for the purpose of refuting them.

1. For a discussion of this corpus see P. Foster (ed.), *The Writings of the Apostolic Fathers* (London: T&T Clark, 2007) vii–viii.

2. For a more strongly articulated presentation of this perspective see B.D. Ehrman, *Lost Christianities: The Battles for Scriptures and the Faiths We Never Knew* (Oxford: Oxford University Press, 2003).

The dry and desiccating climate of Egypt, combined with the archaeological expeditions of the late nineteenth century and further exploration throughout the twentieth century revealed a multitude of long forgotten texts. The vast majority of which were mundane: a tax receipt, a bill for agricultural produce, or a description of Roman roads. Some were important for revealing the social setting of the non-élitist classes: a letter from a son requesting more money from his father, or the arrangements of a fishing cartel based in Ephesus.[3] Hidden among these everyday documents, there were also a number of literary texts: fragments of the writings of Plato and other noted Greek authors. Yet there were also various religious texts, both Christian and non-Christian. Among the Christian texts were discovered important witnesses to the texts of the New Testament and other proto-orthodox writings (such as a fragment from Irenaeus massive work *Against Heresies*), but there also emerged a number of texts previously known by name or sometimes previously unknown. These revealed forms of Christianity that were vital and thriving, diverse and dispersed, élitist and complex, but that were definitely not of the form of known emergent orthodox Christianity. Instead for the first time it was possible to hear directly the voice of the competitors of proto-orthodoxy. The authors of these texts saw the message of Jesus in a very different manner to those who claimed to represent the continuation of the apostolic traditions. However, those writings that were unearthed in the Egyptian sands did not reveal a single uniform alterative, but a plurality of forms and expressions of faith and belief. The diversity of the various Christianities that existed in the earliest centuries of the movement had become apparent through the discovery of this range of new texts, especially the representations of Jesus presented in hitherto inaccessible alternative gospels.

It should be noted that among the texts covered in this book there is one notable exception to the tendency for these writings to become hidden or forgotten, and that text is the *Protevangelium of James*. Although never achieving canonical status, this text circulated widely, especially in eastern orthodoxy. It perhaps did not enjoy equal success in the west because it advanced the view that the siblings of Jesus were step-brothers and sisters from the widower Joseph's former marriage. This conflicted with the later idea which Jerome, a church father in the west, proposed, namely that Joseph was himself a perpetual virgin and that the 'brothers' were in fact cousins. Notwithstanding this perceived doctrinal weakness the contents of the *Protevangelium* were absorbed into other Christian writings that developed the evolving traditions concerning Mary and reflected the increase in Marian piety. Apart from the *Protevangelium of James* it should be mentioned that the *Infancy Gospel of Thomas* enjoyed

3. Peter Parsons, *City of the Sharp-Nosed Fish: Greek Lives in Roman Egypt* (London: Weidenfeld & Nicolson, 2007).

some wider circulation, although it was perhaps better known as a component of the later *Gospel of Pseudo-Matthew*.

So the texts covered in this book are reflective of the diverse forms of Christianity that existed during the movement's first few centuries. The attempt to bring these texts together in books such as this one needs to be recognized for what it is – a collection of convenience. Such a treatment is helpful as long as it is remembered that these texts do not represent a uniform perspective, in fact they are brought together so the very opposite phenomenon may be recognized, namely, the diversity and disparity of the various expressions of faith in Jesus. In this book the choice of texts is not exhaustive. There are various small fragments of non-canonical texts that have not been included – among these are Papyrus Oxyrhynchus 1224, the Strasbourg Fragment and Papyrus Merton 51. These have been omitted not only because of their fragmentary nature, but also because the form of these small snippets is extremely difficult to determine.[4] It is not impossible that such fragments are actually from rambling homilies (sermons that wander off the point are not a modern phenomenon!), and thus do not represent extracts from longer non-canonical gospels. Similarly, only two infancy gospels are included the *Protevangelium of James* and the *Infancy Gospel of Thomas*. Other related infancy texts such as the *Gospel of Pseudo-Matthew*, the *Arabic Infancy Gospel*, or the *History of Joseph the Carpenter* are expansionist retellings based on the two earlier infancy accounts that are covered in this book. The aim of this book is to provide a representative and scholarly overview of the earliest and most significant of the non-canonical gospels. The discussions enable readers to be brought up-to-date with the current range of scholarly debates, and to increase their understanding of the critical issues that surround these texts.

2. *The Discussions of the Texts in This Book*

There has been a flurry of recent interest in the non-canonical gospels – much of which has been generated by various conspiracy theories that have surfaced in a number of fictional works. The positive outcome, however, has been a growing interest in these often neglected as providing important windows into early Christianity usually from the second century onwards. As a number of the chapters will discuss, the significance of these texts for throwing light on the historical Jesus is much disputed. Perhaps the *Gospel of Thomas* alone has generated significant support among some scholars who see it as preserving either earlier forms of known Jesus sayings or even providing previously unknown authentic words of Jesus. At the other end of the spectrum the vast

4. Those wishing to find out more details about these fragmentary remains as well as other Christian texts from the first three centuries would be well advised to consult the web-based resource: www.earlychristianwritings.com (last accessed on 1 September 2007).

majority of critical scholars would see a text such as the *Protevangelium of James* as providing no independent historically reliable traditions concerning the birth of Mary or her son Jesus. Yet it is still a document with an important historical witness, but that witness is to the setting in which it was written and the piety which it reflects. Therefore, the aim of each of the authors in this book is to raise awareness and create a better appreciation of the non-canonical gospels, and to see these texts as reflecting the various forms of Christianity that existed in the early stages of the movement.

The book opens with a discussion of the significance of these non-canonical gospels as part of the wider phenomenon of the New Testament Apocrypha. This is an important insight, for it situates the narrower category of 'non-canonical gospel' against the larger backdrop of the trend in early Christianity to reflect upon existing traditions, to expand them and to fill gaps, and to creatively theologize about divine circumstances and motivations. Consideration of the context of the New Testament Apocrypha reveals that the Christian tradition has never been static. This perceptive introductory chapter has been written by J. K. Elliott who has wrestled with these texts for many decades and written numerous studies on the texts themselves and their influence in later art and literature. For those who wish to read the primary texts themselves (a more important task than reading the discussions in this book!) the standard and most accessible collection, *The Apocryphal New Testament*, is edited by Professor Elliott – and to everybody's relief is now available in an affordable paperback edition.[5]

Without any shadow of a doubt, the *Gospel of Thomas* is the one non-canonical text that has excited scholars as potentially casting fresh light on the historical Jesus. However, that issue may be ultimately unresolvable. Instead April DeConick focuses on more current trends in Thomasine scholarship. Her own work on *Thomas* has been prolific, especially in the area of tracing the composition history of the text. She conceives *Thomas* forming as a rolling corpus, not as separate redactions, but as an evolutionary process that occurred naturally in a communal setting where memory and orality dominated the modes of transmitting traditions. Here she draws heavily and astutely on wider work in the social sciences on social memory theory, and she deploys those insights with great creativity in probing the literary history of the text. She identifies a core, or kernel gospel, which was enriched and enlarged by the successive generations of the communities in which *Thomas* circulated. DeConick's treatment summarizes her own recent and technical research and

5. J. K. Elliott (ed.), *The Apocryphal New Testament: A Collection of Apocryphal Christian Literature in an English Translation Based on M. R. James* (Oxford: Clarendon Press, 1993; paperback edition, 2005).

in the process makes her theories available and accessible to a much wider audience.[6]

The *Gospel of Peter* has been another text at the centre of various controversies, especially concerning whether it or the canonical gospels preserve the earliest form of the Passion narrative. Here it is argued that this text, discovered in a monk's grave in Upper Egypt in 1886–7, is in fact later than, and derivative upon, the canonical gospels. In particular it is argued that there are demonstrable traces of Matthew, Mark and Luke in the *Gospel of Peter* and that when the text breaks off at its last preserved line it looks like it is about to recount a Johannine-type incident. Another contested issue has been the recent identification of a number of scraps of text from Oxyrhynchus (and elsewhere) as being much earlier fragments of the *Gospel of Peter*. This identification is questioned both here and in other scholarly articles.[7] The focus of the chapter concerns the theological outlook of this gospel text. It is seen to be popularizing in its presentation of the passion – the miraculous elements are more prominent and the anti-Jewish polemic is heightened. However, it is questionable whether the ancient concern that this was a docetic text can be sustained from what remains in the extant portion of the document.[8]

Following on from his recent critical edition of the *Gospel of Mary*, Christopher Tuckett presents here his main findings.[9] He argues that the *Gospel of Mary* gives little information about the historical Jesus, or for that matter the shadowy historical Mary Magdalene. The text is seen as originating from the early second century and as such provides a rare glimpse into the concerns of that period. Tuckett argues that if the characterizations of 'Peter' and 'Mary' in this text are representative of groups then they probably represent 'orthodox' and 'Gnostic' Christians. However, he notes the relatively mild tone of any 'polemic' and consequently suggests that this gives an indication that the text was written prior to any hardening of such boundaries. This chapter will whet the appetite of readers for Tuckett's fuller critical edition of this text and also in its own right provides an important contribution to scholarship on the *Gospel of Mary*.

'Jewish-Christian Gospels' may be another convenient label, which also lumps together a number of texts that may have been very different in form, structure and theological outlook.[10] In his discussion Andrew Gregory

6. A. D. DeConick, *Recovering the Original Gospel of Thomas: A History of the Gospel and Its Growth* (LNTS 286; London: T&T Clark, 2005); *The Original Gospel of Thomas in Translation, with a Commentary and New English Translation of the Complete* (LNTS 287; London: T&T Clark, 2006).

7. For example, P. Foster, 'Are There Any Early Fragments of the So-Called Gospel of Peter?', *NTS* 52 (2006) 1–28.

8. See also P. Foster, *The Gospel of Peter – An Introduction and Commentary* (Oxford: Oxford University Press, 2008).

9. C. M. Tuckett, *The Gospel of Mary* (Oxford: Oxford University Press, 2007).

10. A. F. Gregory, 'Hindrance or Help? The Category "Jewish-Christian Gospels"', *JSNT* 28.4 (2006) 387–413.

carefully sorts through the fragments that remain as citation in the writings of various Church Fathers. It is argued that at least two Jewish-Christian gospels can be identified, the *Gospel of the Ebionites* and the *Gospel according to the Hebrews*; however, it remains unclear whether the text known as the *Gospel of the Nazoraeans* is part of the *Gospel according to the Hebrews* or had a more separate existence. Unlike a number of the other texts treated in this book, which exhibit much creativity with the gospel tradition, the way Jewish-Christian gospels handle tradition is broadly congruent with the canonical gospels, especially the synoptic tradition. It is noted by Gregory that this proximity between the traditions contained in Jewish-Christian Gospels and the four gospels that later were included in the New Testament canon is reflected in the wide appeal these texts had before canonical boundaries were fully established.

The *Gospel of Philip* stands alongside the *Gospel of Thomas* in Nag Hammadi codex II; however, its contents are markedly different. It reveals a full-blown cosmological system and although the term 'Gnosticism' is now highly contested, it does represent many of the features one might expect in what would have traditionally been classified as a Gnostic text. The chapter dealing with this document notes some of the major theological themes and motifs that resurface throughout the gospel. There is also a discussion of whether the *Gospel of Philip* should be classified broadly as a 'Gnostic' text, or whether it should be seen more specifically as a Valentinian document, or even if it should be seen as an entity in its own right with no close connections to more widely known systems of thought.

The next two chapters are devoted to the most recently discovered text treated in this book, the *Gospel of Judas* – which only became publicly available in 2006. Perspectives on this challenging text are emerging and already competing stances are crystallizing. For this reason, as well as in order to provide a comprehensive treatment, two of the most important viewpoints are included by authors who have been quick to write on the text. First, Simon Gathercole presents a perspective which in many respects aligns with that of the original publication team.[11] He notes that the main focus is about the secret revelation that Jesus gives to Judas concerning the nature of the world and the true means of salvation. Gathercole is happy to apply the term 'Gnostic' to the *Gospel of Judas* and sees the document as representative of the gulf that had already developed between Gnostics and the 'great church' in the second century. He observes that this text delights in lampooning the supposedly simplistic views of proto-orthodox Christianity. The second chapter on *Judas* challenges the initial perspective, especially in relation to the characterization of the eponymous figure. Here, in line with her recently published critique of the initial

11. Gathercole's fuller treatment of the text can be found in S. J. Gathercole, *The Gospel of Judas* (Oxford: Oxford University Press, 2007).

interpretation,[12] April DeConick questions attempts to understand Judas as being positively portrayed in the text. Instead, she reads the narrative as a subversive attack on emerging mainstream Christianity and views Judas as linked into a tragically evil plan against Jesus from which there is no escape. In this sense Judas is not the one following his Master's will by betraying him, but in actual fact one entwined with evil cosmological forces from which he is also unable to break free. However, the destruction of the physical Jesus is not the ultimate reality and salvation is still possible for those who see beyond the physicality of material existence. While there is much common ground between Gathercole and DeConick, this central disagreement reveals a fundamental debate surrounding this text.

The next two chapters deal with 'gospels' that have a slightly different focus from those discussed above. They do not focus on events in Jesus' ministry neither do they record post-resurrection dialogues.[13] Instead they represent the genre of the Infancy Gospels. The two texts chosen here are the earliest surviving examples of the burgeoning interest in the early church that continued into the medieval period concerning the childhood and the prehistory of Jesus. These texts are treated in the chronological order assumed by their respective narratives. The first is the *Protevangelium of James*, which as this modern title that was applied to the document implies, is a text that recounts events prior to what are traditionally understood as true gospel events. Thus the text tells a tale that commences with the miraculous events of the birth of Mary, the mother of Jesus and ends with the death of Herod the Great soon after the birth of Jesus. The second of these chapters investigates the equally fascinating text known as the *Infancy Gospel of Thomas*. It can be confusing if one consults older works, since this text was often known simply as 'the Gospel of Thomas' until the more famous text bearing that name was discovered. This text narrates the unknown years of Jesus' childhood from the age of five until the incident in Luke's gospel when Jesus journeys to Jerusalem at the age of twelve. Tony Chartrand-Burke is one of the world's leading experts on this text. His doctoral dissertation meticulously researched questions surrounding the origins, transmission and various recensions of this text.[14] He also maintains a highly significant web-based resource dealing with this text.[15] The treatment in this book clarifies the complex issue of the various versions of the text that exist as

12. A. D. DeConick, *The Thirteenth Apostle: What the Gospel of Judas Really Says* (London: A Continuum imprint, 2007).

13. Examples of post-resurrection dialogues include probably *The Gospel of Mary* (see Chapter 4) and a text such as *The Book of Thomas the Contender*, where the risen saviour speaks directly with Judas Thomas.

14. Tony Chartrand-Burke, '*The Infancy Gospel of Thomas: The Text, Its Origins, and Its Transmission*' (Ph.D. Dissertation, University of Toronto).

15. www.tonychartrand-burke.com/infancy-gospel-of-thomas/ (last accessed on 1 September 2007).

well as describing the major themes and theological trajectories reflected in this text.

The final four chapters deal with a number of significant non-canonical texts that are in a more fragmentary or incomplete state than those dealt with in the earlier part of this book. These are important for various reasons. First, although incomplete, the material they preserve is important in its own right since such sayings and narratives transmit significant Jesus traditions. Secondly, such texts are illustrative of the scale of gospel-type writings and show that the phenomenon was widespread, not simply confined to the complete texts that survive due to the vagaries of manuscript preservation. Finally, the theological perspectives represented reveal an even fuller spectrum of diversity in the various groups that constitute the entire Jesus movement.

Discussing the text known as Papyrus Egerton 2 (+Papyrus Cologne 255), Tobias Nicklas notes that this is one of the earliest surviving Christian manuscripts – dating to around AD 200. Nicklas carefully documents the fragmentary nature of the text, and while there are three fragmentary leaves preserved it is noted that only two contain enough text to reconstruct at least a partially continuous narrative. Yet Nicklas points out that the Papyrus Egerton 2 is significant not only because of the text it carries, but also because of the physical features of the manuscript. In particular the fragments attest the early Christian preference for the codex and the manuscript provides one of the earliest examples of the practice of *nomina sacra*, the writing of certain words such as 'Lord', 'God', 'Jesus', 'Christ' etc. in contracted form with a supralinear stroke above the abbreviation. Nicklas brings erudition and clarity of explanation to this fascinating fragment. Building on his previous research into non-canonical texts, he makes an important contribution into further study of Papyrus Egerton 2.[16]

The next fragment to be considered is a scrap of text measuring approximately 4.3 by 3.5 cm, containing six partial lines of legible text and the remains on the seventh line of the tops of probably three letters. This text known as the Fay(y)ûm Gospel (or P.Vindob.G 2325) may be the first piece of textual evidence of a non-canonical gospel to be (re-)discovered in the modern era. While its exact provenance is unclear, this text was found in 1885 by G. Bickell in the papyrus collection of Archduke Rainer in Vienna; it parallels the story of the cock-crow of Mt. 26.30–35//Mk 14.26–31. It is uncertain whether this fragment is part of a larger non-canonical gospel, a free rendering of a canonical text, or simply a free-floating snippet of synoptic tradition. Thomas J. Kraus

16. Most recently see T. J. Kraus and T. Nicklas (eds), *Das Evangelium nach Petrus: Text, Kontexte, Intertexte* (Berlin: de Gruyter, 2007). Also T. J. Kraus and T. Nicklas, *Petrusevangelium und Petrusapokalypse* (Berlin: de Gruyter, 2004).

has previously produced a critical edition of this text,[17] and here delves more deeply into the meaning and theological trajectories of this text. He is also a contributor to the volume in the *Oxford Early Christian Gospel Texts* dealing with a number of the fragmentary non-canonical gospels.

The only book-length treatment of the fragment Papyrus Oxyrhynchus 840 has recently been published by Michael J. Kruger.[18] Here he summarizes that ground-breaking research, but further extends it with fresh ideas and reflection on the text. Kruger pays close attention to the physical features of the single surviving leaf of text. Written front and back, Kruger contends that this leaf is from a miniature codex, which was most likely written for personal use. He also argues that the story of a confrontation between Jesus and a Pharisee in the temple concerning the accusation that Jesus and his disciples are transgressing purity laws by viewing the temple vessels without having undergone ritual washings is historically plausible. This is quite a different claim from arguing that the incident took place. Instead Kruger suggests that there were occasions when visitors to the Temple could view the sacred vessels. In this chapter Kruger makes accessible an often forgotten text, and carefully analyses both the physical manuscript and probes the background to the incident and gives a brief commentary on the text. Along with Tobias Nicklas and Thomas Kraus, Michael Kruger is also a co-author of the book *Gospel Fragments* in the Oxford Early Christian Gospel Texts series.

The final text to be covered in this collection is the most controversial, and the decision to include it may be a mistake! A mistake that is, if claims that it is a forgery or hoax are true. The text known as *Secret Mark* was brought to light by Morton Smith who claimed to have discovered a previously unknown letter of Clement of Alexandria copied into the back of a seventeenth-century book in the library of Mar Saba in Palestine. This letter claims to know of the existence of an expanded form of Mark's Gospel read by the Carpocratians. Clement cites two incidents from the expanded gospel. The first and longest tells a story which has certain parallels with the raising of Lazarus. The deviations are, however, equally striking with the raised young man making a nocturnal visit to Jesus. The second shorter addition describes Jesus meeting the sister of this young man and a companion Salome. Recently the authenticity

17. T. J. Kraus, 'P.Vindob.G 2325: Das sogenannte Fayûm-Evangelium – Neuedition und kritische Rückschlüsse', *ZAC* 5 (2001) 197–212. See also T. J. Kraus, '*P.Vindob.G 2325*: Einige Modifikationen von Transkription und Rekonstruktion', *ZAC* 10 (2007) 383–385; and T. J. Kraus, '*P.Vindob.G 2325*: The So-Called Fayûm-Gospel-Re-Edition and Some Critical Conclusions', in T. J. Kraus (ed.), *Ad fontes: Original Manuscripts and Their Significance for Studying Early Christianity. Selected Essays* (TENT 3; Leiden-Boston: Brill, 2007) 69–94.

18. M. Kruger, *The Gospel of the Savior: An Analysis of P.Oxy. 840 and Its Place in the Gospel Traditions of Early Christianity* (Leiden: Brill, 2005).

of this text has been strongly defended,[19] as well as stridently opposed.[20] The final chapter looks at what is at stake in this polemical debate.

3. *The Value of the Non-Canonical Gospels*

Measuring the worth of an ancient text is of course a subjective business. One recent writer on the *Gospel of Judas*, perhaps best left unnamed, recently saw this text as virtually without value since it was not the 'real gospel' as represented by the four canonical texts. Without wishing to draw attention to the circularity of such reasoning, it needs to be recognized that such an argument starts with a fairly closed definition of what constitutes a gospel and then allows no other textual evidence to encroach on that hermetically sealed definition. Such an approach is not followed by the contributors to this book. Instead they start with texts rather than theories, and pursue open discussion rather than clinging to closed definitions. For some the danger of this method is that it will challenge tightly drawn boundaries; for others the hope is that it will enlarge horizons of understanding.

The texts themselves are diverse and are brought together for convenience and ease of reference. However, it would be a fundamental mistake to assume that the act of collecting implies uniformity of genre, purpose, outlook, origin or theological concerns. Yet it is in the recognition of this very diversity that the true value of the non-canonical gospels can be found. They represent the varied currents that flowed in the formative centuries of the Jesus movement. They challenge any idea that there existed a pure source of 'orthodoxy' from which other perspectives deviated. Rather these documents reveal that there was a plurality of understandings, and these became highly contested. It is, nonetheless, possible to extrapolate too much from such textual diversity. It is not possible to determine the numerical strength of the various groups that read these texts, or to know precisely the circumstances of their origin. The majority of these texts do in fact appear to be derivative on the traditions contained in the canonical accounts. The writers of these texts no doubt thought such theological developments and reflections were valid (if not in fact spiritually revealed) insights into the true meaning of Jesus' teachings. It is also apparent from the documents themselves and the writings of Church Fathers that the second century was a period of highly contested theological views. Perhaps the fundamental contributions of the non-canonical gospels to modern understandings of formative Christianity are twofold. First, they allow direct access to the

19. S. G. Brown, *Mark's Other Gospel: Rethinking Morton Smith's Controversial Discovery* (ESCJ 15; Ontario: Wilfred Laurier, 2005).

20. S. C. Carlson, *The Gospel Hoax: Morton Smith's Invention of Secret Mark* (Waco: Baylor, 2005); P. Jeffery, *The Secret Gospel of Mark Unveiled: Imagined Rituals of Sex, Death and Madness in a Biblical Forgery* (New Haven: Yale University Press, 2007).

thought and theology of various groups that had alternative understandings of Christianity (although it is debatable whether all these groups would have applied the term 'Christian' to themselves). Secondly, such a range of texts correct false understandings of a monolithic view Christianity existing from the second century onwards. Although later Church Fathers may wish us to believe this, it is, as these texts make patently clear, demonstrably false. The non-canonical gospels should be read and appreciated as being some of the earliest literary remains of the vibrant and diverse movements that linked their spiritual understandings to the person of Jesus.

While texts such as the *Gospel of Thomas* may preserve some authentic Jesus material, the vast majority of these non-canonical gospels were written in the second century and later. This does not mean that they have no historical value, rather they give an insight on a period later than the events they purport to record. With the dominance of what became 'orthodox Christianity' in the fourth century and later, many of the alternative expressions of Christian faith were suppressed and these often small groups of believers in Jesus were written out of the historical narrative of the Great Church, or if mention was made of these groups it was only to lambaste them as heretics and deviants from the truth. Even inside the Christian movement the winners have shaped the authorized historical understandings of the growth and emergence of the movement.

The non-canonical gospels have offered a unique, if at times partial opportunity to reclaim those long silenced and marginalized voices suppressed for many long centuries. What they reveal is a diverse rather than a homogeneous movement. They illustrate a pluriformity of expressions of faith in Jesus. However, this should not be taken as some golden age of open and tolerant exchange of ideas. There was strong opposition and polemical rejection of alternative positions as is illustrated in a text such as the *Gospel of Judas*. While these texts offer highly significant insights into the world of second-century Christianity outlandish claims that they offer a reliable picture of the historical Jesus should be treated with great caution. Critical scholars working with the four canonical gospels have long recognized the difficulty in recovering the deeds and words of Jesus from these sources. The problems surrounding the use of non-canonical gospels for historical Jesus research are frankly even greater.

Therefore, these texts do not offer an easy path to the genuine message of Jesus, nor do they offer the prospect of repristinating Christianity by taking readers back to irenic golden age. Instead they allow a 'warts and all' view of the diverse expressions of the Jesus movement in the second century and later. For those who can live with an unsanitized history of Christianity, the non-canonical texts provide a vibrant and vital insight into the early phase of the movement.

4. *Reading the Texts*

The primary goal of this volume is that the treatments of the various texts may assist readers in reading the texts of the non-canonical gospels themselves.

Thus, the individual chapters have outlined the major critical issues that attend the respective texts; they have discussed the contents of the various writings, and highlighted the theological contribution that each text makes. For those who wish to read the actual texts in English translation both print and online resources exist. Perhaps the most complete and readily accessible collection of texts in English translation is:

> J. K. Elliott, The Apocryphal New Testament (Oxford: Clarendon Press, 1993; first paperback edition 2005).

An ever-expanding online resource for early Christian texts including the non-canonical gospels is:

> www.earlychristianwritings.com

Between them, these two databases of texts present various English translations of the texts covered in this volume. The online resource also has links to original language versions of some of the texts. Let the reader see these texts with their own eyes and touch them with their own hands!

PAUL FOSTER
Feast of St Thomas
3 July 2007

Abbreviations

Primary Texts

Abr.	Philo, *Abraham*
Acts Jn	*The Acts of John*
Acts Pet.	*The Acts of Peter*
AF	The Apostolic Fathers
Adv.Haer.	Irenaeus, *Adversus Haereses*
Arab. Gos. Inf.	*Arabic Infancy Gospel*
Arm. Gos. Inf.	*Armenian Gospel of the Infancy*
Barn.	*Epistle of Barnabas*
B. Metropoleos *MS gr.*	Samos, Bibliothek Metropoleos, *Ms graecus 54*
Bologna *Univ.*	Bologna, *Biblioteca universitaria 2702*
1 Clem.	*1 Clement*
2 Clem.	*2 Clement*
Cod. A 95	*Codex A 95*
Cod. Atheniensia gr.	Athens, Ethnike Bibliotheke, *Codex Atheniensia graecus 355*
Cod. hist. gr.	Vienna, Österreichische Nationalbibliothek, *Codex historicus graecus 91*
Cod. Lavra Θ 222	Mount Athos, M. Megistes Lauras, *Codex Lavra Θ 222*
Cod. Sabait.	*Codex Sabaiticus*
Cod. Sinait. gr.	Mount Sinai, *Codex Sinaiticus graecus*
Cod. theol. gr.	Vienna, Österreichische Nationalbibliothek, *Codex theologicus graecus 123*
Cod. Vatopedi	Mount Athos, *Codex Vatopedi 37*
Comm. Ezek.	Jerome, *Commentary on Ezekiel*
Comm. John	*Origen, Commentary on John*
Comm. Matt.	Origen, *Commentary on Matthew*
de Carn. Christi	Tertullian, *De Carne Christi*
de Cibis	Pseudo-Tertullian, *de Cibis*
De Princ.	Origen, *De Principiis*
de Trin. et Incarn.	*of Trinity and Incarnation*
De vir.	Jerome, *De viris illustribus*
Dial.	Justin, *The Dialogue with Trypho*
Did.	*Didache*
Did. Ps.	Didymus, *expositio in Psalms*

Did. Zech.	Didymus, *fragmenta in Zechariah*
Diog.	*Epistle to Diognetus*
Dresden *A*	Dresden, Sächsische Landesbibliothek, *A 187*
Ep.	*Epistle*
Ep. Apos.	*Epistle of the Apostles* (a.k.a. *Epistula Apostolorum*)
'Erub.	*Eruvin*
Gos. Bart.	*Gospel of Bartholomew*
Gos. Egy.	*Gospel of the Egyptians*
Gos. Jud.	*The Gospel of Judas*
Gos. Mary	*The Gospel of Mary*
Gos. Nic.	*The Gospel of Nicodemus*
Gos. Pet.	*The Gospel of Peter*
Gos. Phil.	*The Gospel of Philip*
Gos. Thom.	*The Gospel of Thomas*
H.E.	Eusebius, *Historia Ecclestiastica*
Hist.	*Historiae*
Hist. Jos. Carp.	*History of Joseph the Carpenter*
Hipp. *Ref.*	Hippolytus, *Refutations*
Hom. Jo.	*Homiliae in Joannem*
Hom. vi in Luc.	Origen, *Homily six on Luke*
I.Eph.	*The Epistle of Ignatius to the Ephesians*
IGT	*Infancy Gospel of Thomas*
I.Mag.	*The Epistle of Ignatius to the Magnesians*
Inst.	*Institutio oratoria*
I.Philad.	*The Epistle of Ignatius to the Philadelphians*
I.Poly.	*The Epistle of Ignatius to Polycarp*
I.Rom.	*The Epistle of Ignatius to the Romans*
I.Smyr.	*The Epistle of Ignatius to the Smyrnaeans*
I.Trall.	*The Epistle of Ignatius to the Trallians*
Jos. *Ant.*	Josephus, *Antiquities*
M.Pol.	*The Martyrdom of Polycarp*
MS G 50	*manuscript G 50*
Pan.	Epiphanius, *Panarion*
Paris *A. F. gr.*	Paris, Bibliothèque nationale, *Ancien fond graecus 239*
P.Lit. Lond.	Papyrus Literary London
Poly. *Phil.*	Polycarp, *Epistle to the Philippians*
P.Oxy.	Papyrus Oxyrhynchus
Prot. Jas	*Protevangelium of James*
P.Ryl.	Papyrus Rylands
Ps.-Tert. *Ag. Haer.*	Pseudo-Tertullian, *Against Heresies*
Pseud. Clem.	*Pseudo-Clementines*
P.Vindob.G	*Papyrus Vindobonensis Graecus*
Šeqal.	*Sheqalim*
SH	*The Shepherd of Hermas*

Mand.	*Mandates*
Sim.	*Similitudes*
Vis.	*Visions*
Sib.Or.	*Sibylline Oracles*
Strom.	Clement of Alexandria, *Stromateis*
Sus	*Susannah*
Tert.	Tertullian
Vat. lat.	*Vaticanus latinus*
Vat. *Palat. gr.*	Rome, Biblioteca Apostolica Vaticana, *Palatinus graecus 364*
Vat. *syr.*	Vaticanus *syriacus*
Vienna *Phil. gr.*	Vienna, Österreichische Nationalbibliothek, *Phil. graecus 162*
Vit. Poly.	Pionius, *Life of Polycarp*

Secondary Sources

ABD	*Anchor Bible Dictionary*
ABR	*Australian Biblical Review*
ABRL	Anchor Bible Reference Library
AELAC	Association pour l'étude de la littérature apocryphe chrétienne
AGAJU	Arbeiten zur Geschichte des antiken Judentums und des Urchristentums
AnBoll	*Analecta Bollandiana*
ANRW	Aufstieg und Niedergang in der römischen Welt
ASE	*Annali di storia dell'esegesi*
AsiaJT	*Asia Journal of Theology*
ATR	*Anglican Theological Review*
BAR	*Biblical Archaeology Review*
BCNH	Bibliothèque Copte de Nag Hammadi
BETL	Bibliotheca Ephemeridum Theologicarum Lovaniensium
BIFAO	*Le Bulletin de l'Institut français d'archéologie orientale*
BiTS	Biblical Tools and Studies
BR	*Biblical Research*
BW	*Biblical World*
CAH	*Cambridge Ancient History*
CBQ	*Catholic Biblical Quarterly*
CCSA	Corpus Christianorum Series Apocryphorum
Coni. Neotest.	*Coniectanea Neotestamentica*
EDNT	*Exegetical Dictionary of the New Testament*
EPRO	Études préliminaires aux religions orientales dans l'Empire romain
ESCJ	Studies in Christianity and Judaism/Études sur le christianisme et le judaïsme

ETL	*Ephemerides theologicae lovanienses*
ExpT	*The Expository Times*
FFF	*Foundations and Facets Forum*
GCS	Die Grieschischen Christlichen Schriftsteller
Gr.P.	Greek Papyrus
HNT	Handbuch zum Neuen Testament
HSCL	Harvard Studies in Comparative Literature
HTR	Harvard Theological Review
ICC	International Critical Commentary
IEJ	*Israel Exploration Journal*
JA	*Journal asiatique*
JAC	*Journal of Ancient Christianity*
JBL	*Journal of Biblical Studies*
JEA	*Journal of Egyptian Archaeology*
JECS	*Journal of Early Christian Studies*
JQR	*Jewish Quarterly Review*
JSNT	*Journal for the Study of the New Testament*
JSNTSS	Journal for the Study of the New Testament Supplements Series
JSOTSS.	Journal for the Study of the Old Testament Supplements Series
JTS	*Journal of Theological Studies*
LCL	Loeb Classical Library
LHH	Lightfoot-Harmer-Holmes
LNTS	Library of New Testament Studies
MThSt	Marburg Theological Studies
MtS	Marburger Theologischer Studien
NG	National Geographic
NHC	Nag Hammadi Codex
NHMS	Nag Hammadi and Manichaean Studies
NHS	Nag Hammadi Studies
NKZ	*Neue kirchliche Zeitschrift*
NovT	*Novum Testamentum*
NovTSup	Novum Testamentum Supplements
NTS	*New Testament Studies*
OECGT	Oxford Early Christian Gospel Texts
PO	*Patrologia Orientalis*
PSI	Dai papiri della Società Italiana
PTS	Patristische Texte und Studien
QD	*Quaestiones disputatae*
RB	*Revue Biblique*
RHE	*Revue d'histoire ecclesiastique*
RHPhTh	*Revue des sciences philosophique at théologique*
RHR	*Revue de l'histoire des religions*
SBL	Society of Biblical Literature

SC	Sources Chrétiennes
SecCent	*Second Century*
SHR	Studies in the History of Religions
SPCK	Society for the Propagation of Christian Knowledge
StPatr	*Studia Patristica*
TDNT	Theological Dictionary of the New Testament
TENT	Texts and Editions for New Testament Study
ThZ	*Theologische Zeitschrift*
TLZ	*Theologische Literaturzeitung*
TU	Texte und Untersuchungen zur Geschichte der altchristlichen Literatur
VC	*Vigiliae Christianae*
VCSupp	Vigiliae Christianae Supplements Series
VT	*Vetus Testamentum*
WUNT	Wissenschaftliche Untersuchungen zum Neuen Testament
ZAC	*Zeitschrift für antikes Christentum*
ZKTh	*Zeitschrift für katholische Theologie*
ZNW	*Zeitschrift für die neutestamentliche Wissenschaft*
ZPE	*Zeitschrift für Papyrologie und Epigraphie*
ZWT	*Zeitschrift für wissenschaftliche Theologie*

List of Contributors

Tony Chartrand-Burke is Assistant Professor in the School of Arts and Letters of the Atkinson Faculty of Liberal and Professional Studies at York University, Canada.

April D. DeConick is the Isla Carroll and Percy E. Turner Professor of Biblical Studies at Rice University, Houston, Texas.

J. K. Elliott is Honorary Professor of New Testament Textual Criticism in the Department of Theology and Religious Studies at the University of Leeds.

Paul Foster is Senior Lecturer in New Testament Language, Literature and Theology in the School of Divinity at the University of Edinburgh.

Simon J. Gathercole is Lecturer in New Testament Studies and Fellow of Fitzwilliam College at the University of Cambridge.

Andrew Gregory is Chaplain of University College and a member of the Faculty of Theology at the University of Oxford.

Thomas J. Kraus holds a Ph.D. from the Universität Regensburg, Katholisch-Theologische Fakultät and is now a private scholar teaching at a German grammar school and participating in several research projects.

Michael J. Kruger is Associate Professor of New Testament at Reformed Theological Seminary, Charlotte, North Carolina.

Tobias Nicklas is Professor of New Testament Exegesis and Hermeneutics at the University of Regensburg.

Christopher M. Tuckett is Professor of New Testament at Pembroke College and in the Faculty of Theology at the University of Oxford.

Chapter 1

The Non-Canonical Gospels and the New Testament Apocrypha: Currents in Early Christian Thought and Beyond

J. K. Elliott

Although the texts discussed in this collection are non-canonical Gospels they belong to a wider body of writings, now commonly known as the New Testament apocrypha. These Gospels share many characteristics and themes with other apocrypha of a different literary genre, and all may be considered together. Although casual readers may dismiss these non-canonical writings as peripheral to the early literature of Christianity, in fact their contents reveal much about the piety and beliefs of their writers and original audiences; many insights into early Christian theology may be found in them. More importantly, these writings had a huge influence on Christian practice and belief.

1. *The Concept of a New Testament Apocrypha*

The title 'The Apocryphal New Testament' is the (less than ideal) name given to that amorphous collection of early, non-canonical Christian writings, dating from the second century onwards, which purports to tell us about the main personages of the New Testament and the deeds of the founding apostles of various churches. It is a collection largely written in imitation of the genres of literature that are found in the canonical New Testament – gospels, acts, epistles, apocalypses – but not entirely so. Speaking, as we are, of literature that began life before the canon of the New Testament was finally fixed means that my use of terms like 'canonical', 'apocryphal' and 'orthodox' here is anachronistic, of course, but I hope is understandable.

The Apocryphal New Testament is the body of writings that includes the *Infancy Gospel of Thomas*, when Jesus behaves like an *enfant terrible* killing those who vex him, or, to change our language, a *Wunderkind* confounding his teachers, stretching planks or causing clay birds to fly. This is the body of literature that has Peter in the *Acts of Peter* revive a dead tunny fish; that has John rebuke bedbugs which disturb his sleep in the *Acts of John*; that has a parricide who castrates himself and a protracted story that ends in an attempted necrophiliac rape, both also from the *Acts of John*; that has Paul baptize a lion in the *Acts of Paul*.

Good, entertaining stuff of course, but just how influential were these writings on subsequent generations? How enduring was (or is) it? Our initial instincts are to dismiss their importance and to relegate them as uncritical, magical, superstitious. But before we dismiss the relevance of the texts on those grounds we need to recall that it is in the canonical *Acts of the Apostles* that we have stories in which Peter's shadow is sufficient to effect healings; where scarves touched by Paul are similarly efficacious; where Peter and later Paul escape from gaol through miraculous means; where the supernatural deaths of Ananias and Sapphira are reported; not to mention the stirring sea yarn at the end, or the conversion of Cornelius or Saul's blindness. We may also recall some of the nature miracles in the New Testament gospels: the multiplication of the bread and fish, the walking on the water, the stilling of the storm as well as the transfiguration of Jesus, to see that the apocryphal writings do not have a monopoly of incredulous legends and are in effect building on and within a tradition.

We may, on intellectual grounds, choose to overlook the apocryphal literature, preferring instead to concentrate on the rigorous theology of the Fathers and schoolmen. And until the twentieth century it was the fate of these writings to be simply ignored by scholars and the clerical intelligentsia. Montague Rhodes James in England, Edgar Hennecke in Germany, Helmut Koester in the USA, and François Bovon and his Francophone teams responsible for the Corpus Christianorum series of critical editions of the Christian apocrypha, the French pocket book translations in Brepols' series *Apocryphes* as well as the founding of the journal *Apocrypha* all helped turn the tide. Their efforts have drawn New Testament scholars' attention to the existence and importance of this long-neglected corpus.

The distaste for the apocryphal literature was, however, not one shared by centuries of early Christians, particularly the ordinary worshippers in the pew. This body of literature was the popular reading matter, the basis for much folk religion and popular piety. The apocryphal writings were also known and referred to by many patristic authors. According to Eusebius, Bishop Serapion in the second century knew of a church in Rhossos that read and used the *Gospel of Peter*. Tertullian in *De Baptismo* 17 implies that the example of Thecla as an apostle, preacher and woman baptist found in the *Acts of Paul* was known and was influential. Mainly of course the fathers refer to these apocryphal texts to condemn them. Augustine, Epiphanius and Turribius all warn about the heterodoxy of the *Acts of Thomas*. Eusebius deemed the *Acts of John* heretical; he also denounced the *Acts of Andrew*.

Comments by the fathers and early canonical lists such as the Gelasian Decree, the List of the Sixty Books or the Stichometry of Nicephorus provide evidence of the general and widespread use and knowledge of these writings. In one sense the existence of apocryphal writings and other contemporary writings produced by Gnosticism and Manichaeism acted as catalysts for those wishing to establish an authorized canon of Christian writings that had to be not only apostolic and old but also universally used and accepted by the church.

2. *Reclaiming Rejected Texts*

Our concern now is with those books that were rejected. The censoring of books and the placing of certain books on a black list always perversely have the opposite effect to the one intended. In the case of the Christian writings castigated as non-approved many survived, some admittedly in clandestine or catholicized versions. The apocryphal Acts in particular were heavily rewritten, frequently revised or epitomized – M. R. James called these rewritings *réchaufés*. For example, Gregory of Tours rewrote the ancient *Acts of Andrew*, setting out, as he put it, to avoid verbosity and to omit 'all that bred weariness'. In fact those of us who have tried to edit the apocryphal Acts find that the stories of the deaths of the eponymous heroes (typically martyrdoms) survived relatively intact, but that little of their earlier careers has. The modern editor has to work back from fragments and from the expurgated rewritings to try to establish the second-century form. What is important to realize is that these stories continued to circulate for centuries in one form or another.

Some of our texts are known from only a few manuscripts or even only a single copy sometimes of quite recent discovery. Although antiquity refers to a *Gospel of Peter*, it was only in 1886–7 that a portion of this gospel came to light. At the same archaeological dig a section of the *Apocalypse of Peter* also emerged – the first Greek portion of that apocryphon known to modern scholarship. The *Gospel of Thomas* – that now famous sayings document – was discovered among the Nag Hammadi Library found in 1945–6. Early in the twentieth century a Coptic text of the *Acts of Paul* helped reunite a text which hitherto was known only in disconnected portions.

However, in contrast to these sparse remains, it is remarkable that for several apocryphal texts many manuscripts survive. The *Protevangelium of James*, for example, is extant in Greek – its original language – in over 100 manuscripts today. And not only do so many manuscripts exist that may be dated from differing centuries, thus betraying the ongoing appeal of the writings, but translations also survive – in the case of *the not Protevangelium* these are in Syriac, Coptic, Georgian, Armenian, Slavic and Arabic. Versions of other apocrypha in the ancient Christian languages also exist. This indicates their continuing and widespread popularity.

3. *Theological Influences of Non-Canonical Texts*

But let us now turn to specific areas in which these texts were influential. First and foremost they helped shape Christian theology. We may unwisely dismiss these books as untheological and turn in preference to the weightier patristic writings of similar age, but the apocryphal texts represent the popular reading matter of the leisured classes. The writings reflected but also fuelled popular piety and practice, and much of this concerns Mary.

Mary's role in the New Testament is surprisingly minimal outside the Nativity story. Her family, her upbringing, her death are not related. Such gaps in her biography gave rise to curiosity and the imaginative reconstructions that lie behind many an apocryphal text's origins. The second-century Protevangelium became one of the most popular of all the apocryphal texts. In it Mary's parents appear, her birth is described, her presentation in the Temple (which was not only a popular scene in many later paintings but was an incident that influenced those churches which celebrate the Presentation of Mary as one of the Twelve Great Feasts), her childhood as a ward of the Temple where she is succoured by an angel, and the selection of Joseph as her guardian are all related here. The end of her life is reported in various dormition stories (among which are the Homily of Evodius, the Twentieth Discourse of Cyril of Jerusalem, the Discourse of St John the Divine concerning the Falling Asleep of the Holy Mother of God and the Narrative of Pseudo-Melito). Here her bodily reception into heaven eventually gave rise to the doctrine of the Assumption but from the earliest times these stories helped emphasize Mary's uniqueness. This is most prominent in the emphasis on her continuing virginity. The story of Salome, the midwife, and the withering of her hand is intended to prove Mary's virginity post-partum. The exaltation of Mary as a virgin par excellence gave rise not only to devotion to her as 'ever-virgin' but also helped foster the church's extolling of virginity and chastity as virtues.

Celibacy is a virtue found in the New Testament, but in the apocryphal literature this theme is dominant. The extreme asceticism and encratite views in early Christianity encouraged, and were themselves encouraged by, literature such as the apocryphal Acts, the theme in many of which is the conversion of a pagan woman to Christianity. As a consequence of the apostle's ascetic teaching, the convert forsakes her husband's bed. The spurned husband, usually a prominent citizen, then arranges for the arrest and death of the apostle whose teachings have stolen his wife. Jesus disguised as Thomas in the *Acts of Thomas* in a sermon to a couple of newlyweds urges them to devote themselves to chastity. In the *Acts of Thomas* 12 is contained a denunciation of begetting children. John gives thanks that he was prevented from marrying (*Acts of John* 113). Peter is praised for allowing his daughter to remain a paralytic rather than be a temptation to men. It is no wonder that encratite and apotactite groups found teachings such as these congenial.

This asceticism is allied to poverty. In the *Acts of Thomas* 20 we are presented with Thomas as a model that would influence Christian monasticism thereafter: John 'continually fasts and prays and eats only bread with salt, and his drink is water, and he wears one coat . . . and he takes nothing from anyone but gives to others what he has'. Such teaching is paralleled by sermons denouncing wealth, beauty and possessions (for instance *Acts Pet.* 17, 30–31; *Acts Jn* 43–47).

Other teaching influenced Christian piety and devotion to Mary. Mary as interlocutor in Christian tradition may be traced back to the apocrypha. In the *Arabic Infancy Gospel* in many scenes the Lady Mary's intercession effects cures and miracles. We are thus well on the road to Mary's description as

Mediatrix of All Graces or Co-Redemptrix. Intercession by saints is also a part of Christian tradition and that too owes much to the apocryphal Acts where frequently the apostle is prayed to and where he then effects a miracle or healing in his role as the alter ego of Christ. The saint as representation of the absent Christ is dramatically depicted in many of the apocryphal Acts, for example, *Acts of Thomas* 11 or 39 where Judas Thomas, the twin of Christ, and the reappearing Jesus himself are indistinguishable, or the *Acts of Andrew* 28 where Jesus and Andrew are identical.

Particular apostles seem to be associated with particular places. One common theme in the apocryphal Acts is the dividing of the universe into sections to be evangelized by an individual apostle. Thus Thomas is selected by lot to preach in India. Similarly, John is chosen to serve in Ephesus. Another commissioning occurs in the later *Acts of Philip*. Here we see the origin of the tradition of patron saints, that is, apostles associated with a particular geographical area, and venerated locally as a founding father.

Anti-Jewish sentiment may be nascent in the New Testament proper, where it can be seen that the blame for Jesus' arrest and crucifixion is increasingly pinned on the Jews en bloc thereby exonerating the Romans, despite the reluctant constitutional role they were obliged to play. But in the apocryphal literature that theme is dominant. In the *Gospel of Peter* the motive for not proceeding with the plan to expedite Jesus' crucifixion by breaking his legs is Jewish malevolence – they want his death to be prolonged and painful. The Jews are responsible for the crucifixion in *Gospel of Peter* 3 and in the Descensus (*Gospel of Nicodemus* part 2). In the Letter of Pilate to Claudius, found, among other places, in the *Gospel of Nicodemus*, the Jews are reported as plotting the crucifixion 'out of envy'. In the story of Mary's dormition her bier is desecrated, significantly by a Jew, during her funeral procession. Again, we detect that a minor theme in the New Testament becomes distorted and exaggerated in the later non-canonical writings. Doubtless it was literature like this that fuelled medieval anti-Semitism and justified it.

The Christian interest in the veneration of relics may also be traced to the apocrypha. The efficacy of a saint's remains as a panacea – a belief which became an important aspect of medieval piety and still has an influence on many Christians' devotion today – may have originated in the *Acts of Thomas* where dust from his tomb is taken away to effect a healing. The virgin's girdle is venerated at Prato in the Cappella del sacro cingelo. The story behind this is the Narrative of the Assumption by Joseph of Arimathea where the ascending Mary throws Doubting Thomas her belt. The origin of the written story of Veronica's kerchief, which captured Christ's facial image, occurs in the *Vindicta Salvatoris* and in the *Mors Pilati*: the kerchief itself is venerated in Rome. The incident is commemorated in the sixth Station of the Cross.

The obscure reference in 1 Pet. 3.19 is in itself probably insufficiently strong to have promoted Christian belief in Christ's descent to Hades. It was the expansion of that tantalizingly imprecise reference that led to a fully fleshed out drama in the *Gospel of Nicodemus* part 2 which popularized the idea that Christ released from death the faithful who had died before the crucifixion; and it was that popularization which influenced Christian teaching and led to the credal formula 'He descended into Hell'.

4. *Non-Orthodox Ideas in Non-Canonical Texts*

So far I have been concerned with influences that may be called orthodox. And it needs to be emphasized that, despite their naivety and uncritical stance, most of the apocrypha are not heretical, as conventionally defined. However, possible unorthodox influences may be pointed to. The *Acts of John* 101 occurs within a section of the reconstructed Acts (*Acts Jn* 87–105) found in only one manuscript. In it Jesus reports to John that his death was only the symbolic crucifixion of a phantom body. *Acts Jn* 89–91, 93 recalls the earthly Jesus' differing guises, some of which are non-corporeal.[1] The *Gospel of Peter* 4 could be translated so as to imply that Jesus was physically incapable of feeling pain at the crucifixion. The Arundel Infancy Gospel is perhaps the most docetic of all the apocrypha in describing Jesus' birth as the appearance of a light that gradually assumed human form as a midwife looks on, although we may perhaps prefer to see that scene as poetic, as a dramatization of the belief that Jesus was the Light of the World.

However, given the fact that most of these writings originated in the syncretistic world of the second–third century, it would be surprising if docetic, Gnostic or other heretical ideas had *not* permeated them. (Again, we need to remember that terms like 'heretical' are anachronistic when used of these early texts.) Perfectly orthodox views on corporeality counterbalance the examples just given. The child Jesus in the *Infancy Gospel of Thomas*, to which we alluded at the beginning, clearly has a Jesus who (however possessed to have power over the life and death of others) is a normal child described in anti-docetic terms.

5. *Influence of Non-Canonical Texts in the Arts*

5.1 *Painting and the Plastic Arts*

It is in the field of painting and the plastic arts where the influence of the apocryphal traditions is most obviously and strongly felt. Visitors to galleries or to many churches are often confronted by mosaics, sculptures, frescoes, stained glass or canvases where the artist has found inspiration not only from the Bible itself but also from the post- or extra-Biblical themes that we know independently from the apocryphal New Testament. The following are popular iconic

1. See P. Foster, 'Polymorphic Christology: Its Origins and Development in Early Christianity', *JTS* 58 (2007) 66–99, esp. 85–90.

themes: the inverse crucifixion of Peter; the many scenes including the female apostle Thecla; the inverse crucifixion of Philip. All these come from the apocryphal Acts. Peter's water miracle, where he is a new Moses, is found in written form in Ps-Linus, *Martyrium beati Petri apostoli* 5. The image of Christ's face on Veronica's sudarium; the scene of the date palm bowing at the infant Jesus' command during the rest on the flight into Egypt; John and the poisoned chalice (as in El Greco's famous picture in Madrid); the water trial of Joseph and Mary (as in the ivory plaque on Maximilian's throne in Ravenna); the numerous scenes of Mary's death and assumption – all these are found in the Christian apocrypha.

In a recent book David Cartlidge and I have analysed the parallels between art and literature and have been scrupulous to avoid suggesting that the iconic representation is always dependent on a written source.[2] We allow that the reverse may sometimes be the case. A written description of Jesus as in the *Letter of Lentulus* may well be based on an actual image before the writer's eyes. The well-known inclusion of an ox and an ass in nativity scenes is found in the *Gospel of Ps-Matthew* 14 of the eighth century, but the earliest representation of this scene is on a sarcophagus lid now in Milan that is two centuries earlier. The detail may have come into the elaboration of the Christmas story in oral form, and it was that which influenced the carver; only later was that story written in a source behind *Pseudo-Matthew*.

However, where there is a sequence of scenes illustrating the life and death of an apostle then there we may legitimately look to the priority of the rhetorical form which a later artist has illustrated. The story of St John in the splendid Trinity College, Cambridge, Apocalypse illustrates very vividly scenes known to us from the *Acts of John* and the *Virtutes Iohannis* attributed to Abdias. Cartlidge and I include several examples from this manuscript in our book, but it is unfortunate that we were obliged to print only monochrome plates as the original colours, especially the gold, are still dazzling in their freshness and brilliance. The Mary cycle, and the Thomas cycle in Chartres; the John cycles at Bourges, Chartres and St Mark's, Venice; scenes of the deaths of the apostles at St Mark's, Venice – all these and many more have parallels in the apocryphal New Testament.[3] Scenes of the annunciation to Mary that take place at a well parallel a similar setting for this episode in *Prot. Jas* 11. In this context we may ask: Do the many depictions of the Heavenly Jerusalem as a circular city derive from the Apocalypse of Paul 23 (in contrast to the foursquare city of Rev. 21.16)?

2. David R. Cartlidge and J. Keith Elliott, *Art and the Christian Apocrypha* (Routledge: London and New York: Routledge, 2001).

3. A database (*apocicon*) of these images may be accessed online at www.maryvillecollege.edu/cartlidge/homepage.htm (last accessed on 15 April 2007).

The famous frescoes by Giotto in Padua are to be seen in the Scrovegni Chapel; among the scenes that decorate the entire chapel are a sequence of the life of the Virgin's parents, Joachim and Anna, and a sequence of the Virgin's early life. Again, those scenes parallel comparable episodes in the written apocryphal infancy gospels. Also in the Scrovegni Chapel on its west wall is a large fresco depicting the fate of the damned and the elect. Among the scenes in Hell are horrors that seem to owe their inspiration to the vivid descriptions found in the many written apocalypses in the apocryphal New Testament such as *Apoc. Pet.* 26, 27, 31. If we find these depictions or descriptions familiar and commonplace it is because the written texts were of continuous popularity. The apocryphal apocalypses and the *Acts of Thomas* 51–61 contain tours of heaven and hell – popular stories of earlier centuries that were kept alive and which eventually fuelled the medieval mind. It is said that Dante around, 1300 knew the *Apocalypse of Paul* written in the third century, and possibly refers to it in *Inferno* Canto 2.28. Certainly his vivid depictions of punishments in Hell owe much to the apocrypha.

5.2 *Literature, Drama and Music*

Claudio Zamagni of Lausanne is collecting an extensive collection of allusions to the New Testament apocrypha in Dante's *Divine Comedy*. He is in the process of compiling a comprehensive study on the topic, but already has co-authored a survey that indicates just how extensive were Dante's borrowings from the *Apocalypse of Paul*.[4]

In some cases the medieval writer and artist may have become familiar with the apocryphal stories from their retelling in the popular *Golden Legend* by Jacob of Voragine, but behind the *Golden Legend,* the *Lives of the Saints* or Pseudo-Bonaventura's *Meditations* lie the apocrypha of many centuries earlier. The filtering process which the original apocrypha went through is part of the fascination of this field of study (however frustrating it may be to editors wishing to plot the literary history or establish that elusive 'original' form) and clearly shows that these writings had an influence and ongoing relevance for centuries.

As we have now entered the world of literature, it is worth noting that Milton too was imbued with the same medieval world view of life in the otherworld that owed much to the popularization of such imagery found in our New Testament apocryphal texts. The German poet Herder in his *Saint John* includes from the apocrypha the story of the partridge, now sometimes printed as Chapters 56–57 of the *Acts of John*.

In drama too the apocryphal story of the descent of Jesus to the underworld to release the faithful dead in the period between Good Friday and Easter found

4. Reviewed in the journal *Apocrypha* 12 (2001), 297–298.

first in the fifth–sixth century *Gospel of Nicodemus* emerges in the mystery plays. These medieval plays were performed in the streets to audiences by members of trade guilds as they processed on carts through English cities. The Harrowing of Hell, as that story is often labelled, was performed by the saddlers' company in the York cycle. That scene (often painted too) has Jesus breaking down the gates of Hell and extending his hand to awaken Adam or a Patriarch.[5] Another medieval mystery cycle, known as the N-Town plays,[6] shows an even greater debt to the apocryphal New Testament. Its nativity scene, for example, includes the physical examination of Mary by the midwives after Jesus' birth, and the withering of Salome's hand. The two animals are present and there is a reference to the bowing cherry-tree (a parallel to the bowing date-palm in the apocryphal tale of the Flight to Egypt). The N-Town plays include the Presentation of Mary in the Temple, the Trial of Joseph and Mary, a trial before Pilate that owes much to the *Gospel of Nicodemus*, and a scene about Joachim and Mary, as well as the episodes of the Harrowing of Hell and the Assumption of Mary. These and other details show just how influential our New Testament apocrypha were in the Middle Ages.

Even Hollywood in the epic *Quo vadis?* draws on and elaborates a story found originally in the *Acts of Peter* when Peter, escaping punishment, meets the risen Christ and asks him 'Quo vadis, domine?'

The English composer, Gustav Holst, wrote a choral work in the 1920s for the Three Choirs Festival titled 'The Hymn of Jesus'. The libretto for this was the Dance of Jesus found in the *Acts of John* 94–95. The New Testament apocrypha may therefore be seen to have influenced even the world of music too!

5.3 *Archaeology*

No one can doubt the influence that these apocrypha had on the arts or on theology. An area that has a less obvious link with the apocrypha is archaeology. A few years ago James Charlesworth of Princeton asked me to investigate links between the New Testament apocrypha and archaeological sites.[7] At first this looked unpromising, but it does appear that the existence of certain burial sites allegedly of, say, Thecla in Seleucia or of John in Ephesus, or of Thomas in India owes something to the legends about these saints popularized in and by the apocrypha. The canonical New Testament tantalizingly says nothing about the deaths of Peter or of Paul. The apocryphal traditions have both men die in

5. This well-known story, with its quasi-humorous exchanges between Satan and a personified Hades, has been imaginatively and cleverly rewritten in Fredrick Buechner's novel, *Lion Country*.

6. Edited by Stephen Spector in the Early English Text Society series for Oxford University Press in 1991.

7. My results appeared as a contribution to a collection of essays: J. K. Elliott, 'The Christian Apocrypha and Archaeology', in J. H. Charlesworth (ed.), *Jesus and Archaeology* (Grand Rapids: Eerdmans, 2006) 683–691.

Rome and it is in Rome where archaeologists try to locate their actual tombs, St Peter's in the Vatican being the better known example.

A not unrelated area is that of the origin of place names. Old Testament scholars are familiar with such legends. One such New Testament example concerns Paul in Rome. The apocryphal story of Paul's death by decapitation gave rise to the origin of the church near the E.U.R. in Rome called S. Paolo Tre Fontane because a subsequent legend said that his head bounced three times on the earth, and at each place a spring erupted – hence the three fountains!

5.4 *Textual Criticism*

Another less obvious area is the possible influence of the apocrypha on the textual criticism of the New Testament. I have checked to see how far, if at all, wording (usually of sayings of Jesus) in the apocryphal tradition may have influenced scribes of New Testament manuscripts. I was stimulated to start this investigation after having noted that two Pauline manuscripts, 181 and 460, add to the text of 2 Timothy. At 2 Tim. 3.11 the manuscript 181 adds words from the *Acts of Paul*. 181 and 460 similarly add to 2 Tim. 4.19 from this same apocryphon. Also, I noted that the Nestle-Aland Greek New Testament bizarrely includes a reading from the apocryphal Papyrus Egerton 2 in its apparatus at Jn 5.39 as if this manuscript were a witness to the textual tradition of the Fourth Gospel.

As a result of my survey, I contend that there is no evidence that the apocryphal tradition had any significant influence on scribes of the New Testament. I have set out my findings, negative though they are, in the specialist journal *Apocrypha*.[8] Suffice it here to note two examples:

1) In the *Gospel of the Ebionites* quoted by Epiphanius there is a passage parallel to Mk 3.31–35. There is no mention of Jesus' sisters in the parallel to verse 32. Our Greek testament shows a division in the manuscripts of Mark at this verse between those that refer to the sisters and those that do not. I conclude that the shorter reading at Mark could have come about through homoioteleuton or by assimilation to the synoptic parallels, rather than because a scribe of Mark had been influenced by the wording in an apocryphon.
2) The so-called *Fayyum Fragment* parallels Mk 14.27–30 and agrees with the variant in Mark that refers to the twofold cockcrow. The direction of influence seems to be from a version of Mark towards the text found in this apocryphal fragment, rather than the reverse. (Nestle-Aland included this

8. J. K. Elliott, 'The Influence of the Apocrypha on Manuscripts of the New Testament', *Apocrypha* 8 (1997) 265–271.

witness in its apparatus to Mk 14.28, but that evidence was, properly, omitted in the 27th edition.)

The place where there are most parallels between the New Testament and an apocryphal text is in the logia of the *Gospel of Thomas*. Many modern editions of the synoptic gospels show the parallels with this apocryphal gospel. But these belong to the area of source criticism and to redaction. As far as I can see, the often differing wording in a dominical saying in the *Gospel of Thomas* is not found in even a single manuscript of the New Testament gospels. Elsewhere too I have negative conclusions. In P.Oxy. 1224 a form of a saying close to Mt. 9.10–13; Mk 2. 15–17; Lk. 5. 27–32 adds the word 'priests': surprisingly, that (arguably understandable) addition is not replicated in any Greek New Testament manuscript I am aware of. Although apocryphal traditions add names to characters nameless in the New Testament, such as the centurion with the spear at the crucifixion, or the criminals crucified alongside Jesus, those names are not then found as variants in the New Testament manuscripts. We would need evidence of longer insertions or significant variants that parallel the exceptional cases in 181 or 460 to see wholesale influence. I suggest such examples do not exist.

6. *Concluding Observations*

The non-canonical writings have played their part in moulding Christian thought; they reflected and influenced popular piety and devotion; their influence can be seen in art and the arts. They seldom aspire to great literature, although the occasional purple passage stands out; but in many cases they tell a racy tale, encapsulate a well-turned phrase, even recall a *bon mot* of Jesus – one which may even be among his *ipsissima verba* – and certainly they provide the researcher plotting the history of Christianity with a rich seam that only nowadays is being recognized as the origin of much that is firmly fixed in its traditions.

Bibliography

Collections of Texts

A. E. Bernard (ed.), *Other Early Christian Gospels: A Critical Edition of the Surviving Greek Manuscripts* (LNTS 315; London: T&T Clark – A Continuum imprint, 2006).

J. K. Elliott (ed.), *The Apocryphal New Testament: A Collection of Apocryphal Christian Literature in an English Translation Based on M. R. James* (Oxford: Clarendon Press, 1993; paperback edition 2005).

M. R. James (ed.), *The Apocryphal New Testament* (Oxford: Clarendon Press, 1924; corrected edn 1953).

J. M. Robinson (ed.), *The Nag Hammadi Library in English* (4th rev. edn; Leiden: Brill, 1996).

W. Schneemelcher (ed.), *New Testament Apocrypha*, Eng. trans. R. McL. Wilson (2 vols; Louisville: Westminster John Knox, 1991, 1993).

www.earlychristianwritings.com (last accessed on 1 September 2007).

General Introductory Works

D. R. Cartlidge and J. K. Elliott, *Art and the Christian Apocrypha* (New York and London: Routledge, 2001).

J. H. Charlesworth, 'Research on the New Testament Apocrypha and Pseudepigrapha', *ANRW* II.25.5 (1988) 3919–3968.

B. D. Ehrman, *Lost Christianities: The Battles for Scripture and the Faiths We Never Knew* (Oxford: Oxford University Press, 2003).

P. Jenkins, *Hidden Gospels: How the Search for Jesus Lost Its Way* (Oxford: Oxford University Press, 2001).

H.- J. Klauck, *Apocryphal Gospels: An Introduction*, Eng. trans. B. McNeil (London: T&T Clark – A Continuum imprint, 2003).

H. Koester, *Ancient Christian Gospels: Their History and Development* (London/Philadelphia: SCM/TPI, 1990).

Chapter 2

The *Gospel of Thomas*

April D. DeConick

If there is one early Christian gospel that has a career both famous and infamous, it is the *Gospel of Thomas*. It has been called a 'direct and almost unbroken continuation of Jesus' own teaching – unparalleled anywhere in the canonical tradition'[1] as well as 'perversion of Christianity by those who wanted to create Jesus in their own image'.[2] It has been understood as an early Jewish Christian document, preserving independent Jesus traditions older than the New Testament gospels, as well as a late Gnostic gospel entirely dependent on the canonical gospels. On the one hand it has been lauded as the 'fifth gospel', while on the other it has been dismissed as 'heretical'. What are we to make of this enigmatic gospel containing 114 known and unknown sayings of Jesus?

1. *Discovery of the* Gospel of Thomas

The *Gospel of Thomas* was found in the 1945 in Nag Hammadi, Egypt. The story of its discovery was eventually traced by a young American scholar of the New Testament and early Christianity, Professor James Robinson, in 1975 when he personally followed up a lead recorded in Arabic in the acquisitions log of the Coptic Museum in Cairo, a lead which stated that 70 leaves of an ancient Christian Coptic manuscript were purchased by the Museum for 250 pounds from Raghib Andarawus on 4 October 1946.

The story that Professor Robinson recovered is quite fantastic, even legendary now. It all started with a young peasant by the name of Muhammad Ali and his two brothers who were searching near the village Hamrah Dum for fertilizer to use on their crops and fuel their family's cooking fires. Muhammad's brother, Khalifah, dug up a large clay pot. At first Muhammad Ali was afraid to open the pot, for fear that a jinn, an evil spirit, might reside in the old pot.

1. H. Koester, 'GNOMAI DIAPHOROI', in *Trajectories through Early Christianity* (ed. James M. Robinson and Helmut Koester; Philadelphia: Fortress Press, 1971) 139.

2. Robert Grant and David Noel Freedman, *The Secret Sayings of Jesus: The Gnostic Movement Which Challenged Christianity and Its 'Gospel of Thomas' Recently Discovered in Egypt* (Garden City: Doubleday, 1960) 20.

But curiosity and lust for coin took the better of him and he regained his courage and smashed open the jar. When his mallet broke the pot, tiny bits of golden particles littered the air, papyrus fragments floating away on the wind like flakes of snow. Inside the jar was a cache of old leather books. He gathered them up and took them home. When he arrived in his yard, he dumped the papyri books on the ground next to his mother's baking oven. His mother later confessed to Professor Robinson that she used the torn books and covers to start the fires to bake her bread![3]

The books found their way into the hands of various antiquities dealers and private individuals, including Carl Justav Jung, after whom the Jung Codex is named. Eventually, all of the books were tracked down and gathered by the Egyptian authorities. By the late 1950s, all came to be housed together in the Coptic Museum in Old Cairo.

UNESCO assembled an international team of scholars to photograph the manuscripts and publish a facsimile edition. The team was also responsible for transcribing, translating and publishing the books as quickly as possible. Professor Robinson led the team. The first English translation of the entire Nag Hammadi collection was published in 1979, 34 years after the original find. In 1988, a completely revised edition of the translation was made available to the public. In total, there are 13 separate leather-bound books containing 40 *previously unknown* texts from the early Christian period, literature written almost 2,000 years ago and lost for the past 1,600 years. The *Gospel of Thomas* is among them, written in Coptic as are the rest of the texts in the collection.

Early transcription work on the *Gospel of Thomas* made clear that another papyrus hoard from Oxyrhynchus, Egypt in the 1890s was related to the *Gospel of Thomas*.[4] In the late 1800s, Professors Brenard Grenfell and Arthur Hunt from Oxford University had excavated one of the chief centres of early Christianity in Egypt, the city of Oxyrhynchus. It is located about 120 miles south of Cairo on the edge of the desert. They unearthed the old town dump where they found scores of papyri, mainly in Greek, which had been discarded with the rubbish. The papyri they found dated from the first to the eighth century, and embraced the very subject that one might expect to find discussed by the inhabitants of a flourishing Roman city.

There was quite an enthusiastic reaction in the academic world to the original publication by Professors Grenfell and Hunt of the 'lost sayings' of Jesus preserved by P. Oxy. 1, 654 and 655. It wasn't until 1952 that the French scholar Henri-Charles Puech made the connection between these fragments and the Coptic *Gospel of Thomas* found at Nag Hammadi.[5] While in Cairo with

3. James M. Robinson, *Nag Hammadi Library in English* (San Francisco: Harper, 1988) 22–25.

4. B. P. Grenfell and A. S. Hunt, *Sayings of Our Lord from an Early Greek Papyrus* (London: The Egypt Exploration Fund, 1897); B. P. Grenfell and A. S. Hunt, *New Sayings of Jesus and Fragment of a Lost Gospel from Oxyrhynchus* (London: The Egypt Exploration Fund, 1904).

Professor Quispel examining some of the Nag Hammadi texts gathered at the Coptic Museum, he realized that the Oxyrhnychus fragments were pieces of the *Gospel of Thomas*. This was quite significant because it meant that the Coptic was a translation from an earlier Greek version of the Gospel, and since one of the Greek papyri had been dated to 200 CE, this meant that there was manuscript evidence of this Gospel 150 years older than the Coptic. Since Professors Grenfell and Hunt had argued from internal evidence, however, that the original composition of this Greek fragment could be dated to the late first or early second century – no later than 140 CE – suddenly the *Gospel of Thomas* became very interesting to scholars of early Christianity. A gospel containing lost sayings of Jesus could be contemporary with some of the writings that ended up in the New Testament.

2. *Initial Scholarly Interpretations of the* Gospel of Thomas

2.1 *Old Jewish Christian Gospel*

Professors Quispel and Puech had been invited to the Coptic Museum in the early 1950s by the successor to Toga Mina as the Museum's director, Mr. Pahor Labib. Together, they examined the Nag Hammadi manuscripts and began to form an initial opinion about the *Gospel of Thomas* – its provenance and theology. Professor Quispel in his first publications on the Gospel in the late 1950s was convinced that the *Gospel of Thomas* was based on an old lost gospel that had been used by Jewish Christians, either the *Gospel of the Hebrews* or the *Gospel of the Nazoraeans*.[6] He argued that the sayings in the *Gospel of Thomas* have no literary connection with our Greek New Testament Gospels, but represent an independent early tradition of sayings associated with James the leader of the Jerusalem Church and probably known in Aramaic. This appeared reasonable given the linguistic work that Professor Antoine Guillaumont had been doing on the *Gospel of Thomas*.[7] Professor Guillaumont had joined Quispel in

5. H. -Ch. Puech, 'Une Collection de Paroles de Jésus Récemment Retrouvée: L'Évangile selon Thomas', *Comptes rendus des séances – Academie des inscriptions & belles-lettres* (1957) 146–166.

6. Gilles Quispel, 'The Gospel of Thomas and the New Testament', *VC* 11 (1957) 189–207; 'Some Remarks on the Gospel of Thomas', *NTS* 5 (1958/1959) 276–290; 'L'Évangile selon Thomas et les Clémentines', *VC* 12 (1958) 181–196; 'L'Évangile selon Thomas et le Diatesssaron', *VC* 13 (1959) 87–117; 'The "Gospel of Thomas" and the "Gospel of the Hebrews"', *NTS* 12 (1966) 371–382; 'The *Gospel of Thomas* Revisited', *Colloque International sur les Textes de Nag Hammadi. Québec, 22–25 août 1978*, BCNH 1 (ed. B. Barc; Québec, 1981) 218–266.

7. A. Guillaumont, 'Sémitismes dans les logia de Jésus retrouvés à Nag-Hammâdi', *JA* 246 (1958) 113–123; A. Guillamont, 'Les 'Logia' d'Oxyrhynchus sont-ils traduits du copte?', *Mus* 73 (1960) 325–333; A. Guillaumont, 'NHSTEUEIN TON KOSMON (P. Oxy. 1, verso, 1.5–6)', *BIFAO* 61 (1962) 15–23; A. Guillamont, 'Les sémitismes dans l'Évangile selon Thomas: Essai de classement', in R. van den Broek and M. J. Vermaseren (eds), *Studies in Gnosticism and Hellenistic Religions Presented to Gilles Quispel on the Occasion of His 65th Birthday*, EPRO 91 (Leiden: E. J. Brill, 1981) 190–204.

his study of the text as they prepared with three other colleagues the first English translation of the Gospel. Guillaumont's linguistic analysis of the Coptic in commentary-like articles he published in the late 1950s had been building the case for an Aramaic or Syriac substratum for the Thomasine sayings. Although Professor Quispel referred to some linguistic arguments, the main case he made for his position came from his training as a Source Critic – he tried to determine the earliest literary sources upon which the *Gospel of Thomas* was based. He attempted to do so by identifying sayings in the *Gospel of Thomas* that had reasonable – but not exact – parallels in other extra-canonical gospel documents.

2.2 *Late Gnostic Gospel*

By the early 1960s, however, scholars weren't absolutely convinced by Professor Quispel's theory, mainly because his arguments relied on fragmentary evidence from Jewish Christian Gospels composed in Greek, not Aramaic. The versions of the sayings and the thematic parallels he identified in the Jewish Christian sources varied enough from their parallels in the *Gospel of Thomas* to posit some doubt in the minds of most scholars at the time. So scholars turned to a more colourful, even exotic explanation, developing the opinion that the *Gospel of Thomas* was a Gnostic gospel and therefore late and literarily dependent on our New Testament Gospels.

Scholars who first thought that the *Gospel of Thomas* was a Gnostic gospel set out to prove that it belonged to a specific Gnostic group by comparing sayings found in the Gospel with information that we have about certain Gnostics preserved in the writings of the Church Fathers and Bishops of the early Church. The two most influential scholarly opinions were that it was written by either a Naassene Gnostic[8] or a Valentinian Gnostic.[9] These theories were worked out by several international scholars in the early 1960s including Professors Grant, Freedman, Schoedel, Smyth, Cornélis, Cerfaux, Garitte and Gärtner. Once it was recognized, however, that the theology of the *Gospel of Thomas* did not cohere to either Naasene or Valentinian forms of Gnosticism, scholars tried another angle. 'Could the *Gospel of Thomas* represent a generic form of

8. The opinion that the *Gospel of Thomas* emerged out of Naasene Gnosticism was developed by several international scholars in a variety of early publications: Robert Grant, 'Notes on the Gospel of Thomas', *VC* 13 (1959) 170–180; Robert Grant and David Noel Freedman, *The Secret Sayings of Jesus*; William Schoedel, 'Naasene Themes in the Coptic Gospel of Thomas', *VC* 14 (1960) 225–234; Kevin Smyth, 'Gnosticism in "The Gospel according to Thomas"', *Heythrop Journal* 1 (1960) 189–198; E. Cornélis, 'Quelques elements pour une comparison entre l'Évangile de Thomas et la notice d'Hippolyte sur les Naassènes', *VC* 15 (1961) 83–104.

9. The origins of the *Gospel of Thomas* in the Valentinian Gnostic tradition was pioneered by three scholars: L. Cerfaux and G. Garitte, 'Les paraboles du Royaume dans L'Évangile de Thomas', *Muséon* 70 (1957) 307–327; Bertil Gärtner, *The Theology of the Gospel of Thomas* (trans. Eric J. Sharpe from the Swedish original; London: Collins, 1961).

Gnostic religiosity?' asked scholars like Wilson, Bauer, Roques, Montefiore, Vielhauer, Schrage, Säve-Söderbergh, Ménard and Haenchen. If so, perhaps the Gospel represented the premier example of an ancient religion which scholars called 'Gnosticism', a relatively modern term coined to describe an ancient possibility. Scholars went so far as suggesting that the very existence of 'Gnosticism' was proven by the existence of the *Gospel of Thomas*, a circular argument if ever there was one! This interpretation of the *Gospel of Thomas* became standard (and dismissive of the Gospel) even though no scholar could account for the fact that the text does not even hint at the demise of Sophia or point to the role of the Demiurge. If the text were truly Gnostic, why did it not refer in any way to unique features or terminology characteristic of Gnostic mythology?

2.3 *A Proto-Gnostic Gospel*

To account for the Gnostic 'silence' in the *Gospel of Thomas*, some scholars started to think of this Gospel as a 'precursor' to what they began to call 'full-blown' Gnosticism. It was a text in transition, on its way to becoming a Gnostic gospel, but not-quite-there-yet. The champions of this highly influential position were Helmut Koester and James Robinson (and later their students, including Steven Patterson, Marvin Meyer, Ron Cameron and Phil Sellew) whose works systematically explore the connection between the proverbial tradition and the *Gospel of Thomas*.

According to this school of thought, the *Gospel of Thomas* was a Gnostic gospel, not in the sense of a fully mature Gnostic system, but in some proto-Gnostic sense. However, it was not dependent on the New Testament or composed late because the genre of the *Gospel of Thomas* was earlier and more primitive than the New Testament gospels.[10] The *Gospel of Thomas* did not develop out of an interest in evangelizing Jesus' passion and resurrection. So it does not represent the latest end of the written gospel trajectory with its interest in recording a narrative about Jesus' death and its salvific agenda. Rather, from the perspective of genre, it is a collection of sayings very similar to the earlier written sources that the authors of the New Testament gospels relied on when they created their narratives about Jesus' ministry and death. It has affinities with Q.

Professor Koester recognized several different types or 'forms' of sayings in Q and the *Gospel of Thomas*. Present were sayings in the form of pronouncements on legal issues, prophetic sayings, blessings and curses, parables and apocalyptic sayings. But it was the proverbs or 'wisdom sayings' – sayings that are admonitions from a teacher and general expressions of truth – that he focused on and argued determined the nature of this collection of sayings.[11]

10. Robinson and Koester, *Trajectories*, 158–204.

11. Professor Koester refers to examples in *Gos. Thom.* of general truths (31–35, 45, 47, 67, 94) and admonitions (26, 39, 92, 93).

This study led Koester to argue that the *Gospel of Thomas* presents Jesus not as a prophet, but as a sage who speaks with the authority of the heavenly Sophia. Through his words, Jesus grants salvation to those who hear his words and understand them.[12] He admonishes people to recognize themselves, particularly their inner divinity and destiny, in order to overcome death. The Kingdom, far from being a future end-of-the-world or 'eschatological' experience, is present in the person of Jesus and the believer. Renunciation of the world is preached, along with liberation of the soul from the body.

But what about the large number of sayings found in the *Gospel of Thomas* that appear much more esoteric than the proverbial system can account for? In the *Gospel of Thomas*, Jesus does not simply teach 'everyday' wisdom to the common folk. He is characterized as a 'living' mystagogue, a hierophant, teaching 'hidden sayings' and 'mysteries' to a chosen few. Koester said that this 'spiritualization' of the wisdom sayings – when the author goes beyond the traditional usages of Jewish proverbs to Gnostic conceptions – is a 'natural progression' towards Gnosticism, an idea dependent on the research of Professor Robinson.[13]

If it were the case that the *Gospel of Thomas* is a collection of proto-Gnostic sayings, then they cannot represent early Christian traditions. Or could they? Professor Koester insisted that, even though *Thomas'* sayings are 'Gnostic' as they are preserved in this Gospel, there is still an 'almost unbroken continuation of Jesus' own teaching' taking place, a continuity 'unparalleled anywhere in the canonical tradition'.[14] He noted that, when compared with variants of the sayings in the New Testament Gospels, the versions of the sayings in the *Gospel of Thomas* often lacked secondary interpretations and developments. This led him to conclude that the author of the *Gospel of Thomas* probably had access to a very old collection of Jesus' sayings, a collection that also was incorporated into Q. So *Thomas* contained sayings that predated our earliest sources for the New Testament Gospels, Q.

It is this unresolved tension between 'primitive tradition' and 'Gnosticism' that complicates his theory. He seems to be aware of this, admitting that the 'natural' progression makes it difficult to sort out what sayings belong to the 'original composition' and what are 'later additions'. But even so, he goes on to argue that it is quite likely that an early version of the *Gospel of Thomas* was composed around the year 50 CE, in the area of Palestine or Syria since a few of the sayings from this Gospel and its 'wisdom theology' are known to the Corinthian community.[15]

12. Helmut Koester, *Introduction to the New Testament: History and Literature of Early Christianity* (vol. 2; Walter de Gruyter: Berlin, 2nd edn, 2000) 154–158.

13. Robinson and Koester, *Trajectories*, 71–113.

14. Robinson and Koester, *Trajectories*, 139.

15. 1 Cor. 1–4.

If the sayings in the *Gospel of Thomas* represent very early versions of the words of Jesus when compared with their parallels in the New Testament Gospels, how did they compare with Q? Professor Koester noticed one striking difference. All the sayings in Q which speak about the so-called Son of Man were absent from the *Gospel of Thomas*. Professor Koester concluded from this that the Gospel was based on a collection of sayings older than Q, *before* Jesus was identified with the Son of Man.

This meant to him that the non-apocalyptic sayings in the *Gospel of Thomas* represented an early version of Christianity in which Jesus appears as a wise sage whose words bring salvation to the believer. This version of Christianity did not know about the Cross, nor an interpretation of Jesus' death steeped in atonement ideology, nor did it anticipate the imminent End of the world. It was a form of Christianity unaware of traditional theology and based authentically on Jesus' own message. He thought that Thomas' gospel developed these original sayings of Jesus along a Gnostic trajectory, while Q along an apocalyptic one.

Koester's assessment of Q and the *Gospel of Thomas* has worried more than a few scholars. One of the most vocal, perhaps, has been Professor James Dunn. He said in response to Koester's theory, 'I do not think that the apocalyptic elements of Jesus' teachings can be sloughed off quite so readily', because 'Q is almost certainly earlier and nearer to Jesus' emphasis than any non-apocalyptic version of the Jesus-tradition'. More to the point, he noted that a large number of sayings in the *Gospel of Thomas* look much more like 'de-eschatologized tradition rather than pre-apocalyptic tradition'.[16]

Another factor in some scholars' resistance to Koester's position has been his uncritical reliance on Robinson's identification of the 'sayings of the wise' genre. Although Robinson's 'trajectory' might represent a possible development of sayings traditions in the case of the Gnostic *Gospel of Philip* or *Pistis Sophia*, it certainly does not represent the 'only' or the 'natural' one. In the case of the *Dialogue of the Savior* and the *Book of Thomas the Athlete*, the sayings traditions are reused in an encratic context, a context honouring the celibate lifestyle at the expense of the married. The *Teachings of Silvanus* and the *Sentences of Sextus* show a continued interest in the sayings genre among the 'orthodox' Christians in Alexandria, who recycle the sayings for their own purposes.

So some scholars began emerging in the late 1970s and 1980s who have been reluctant to describe the *Gospel of Thomas* in terms of proto-Gnosticism. Professor Stevan Davies explored the theology of the Gospel as an expression

16. Professor Dunn refers to sayings 1, 3, 8, 11, 19, 21, 35, 37, 51, 59, 76, 103, 109, 111, 113. James Dunn, *Unity and Diversity in the New Testament: An Inquiry into the Character of Earliest Christianity* (Philadelphia: Westminster Press, 1977) 286.

of the Jewish wisdom tradition with no reference to Gnostic thought.[17] The French Sister and pupil of Jacques Ménard, Margaretha Lelyveld, alternatively found that the *Gospel of Thomas* is not a proverbial or Gnostic collection at all.[18] Rather it is an oracular collection of prophetic sayings that opens in terms similar to Deuteronomy, 'These are the words that Moses spoke to all Israel.'[19] Because oracular collections include prophetic sayings, apocalyptic pronouncements, legal rulings, and so forth, this appeared to her to allow for a better genre comparison with the *Gospel of Thomas* than a proverbial collection alone allows.

I myself deeply question scholars' continued reliance on proto-Gnostic or Gnostic traditions to explain the esotericism in the *Gospel of Thomas*, precisely because there is no distinctive feature of Gnostic mentality to be had among these sayings. I also am deeply concerned that scholars so easily jump to locate esotericism outside of mainstream Christianity, labelling it dismissively 'heretical' or 'gnostic', as if esotericism cannot be found within 'orthodoxy' as well. The impulse toward mysticism is very strong in early Judaism and Christianity – I would even argue 'foundational'.[20] It is this form of religiosity that I myself turn to in order to explain the esotericism preserved within the *Gospel of Thomas*.[21] I think that such an interpretative move is necessary to carry us beyond the Gnostic stalemate to a more historically astute perspective.

3. *Compositional History of the* Gospel of Thomas

If we have any chance of rediscovering the meaning of the *Gospel of Thomas*, we must first solve the great mystery of its history. Where did it come from? How did it come into its present form? Why did it develop the way it did? These questions may seem to have easy and obvious answers. Did someone not sit down with a pen in hand and write it, perhaps relying on written sources like the New Testament Gospels? This type of answer reveals the enormous distance between ourselves and the ancient people, between our world of information technology and their world of memory and story. Their culture was one dominated by memory and orality, punctuated only by occasions of reading and writing.

17. Stevan L. Davies, *The Gospel of Thomas and Christian Wisdom* (New York: The Seabury Press, 1983).

18. Margaretha Lelyveld, *Les Logia de la Vie dans L'Évangile selon Thomas* (NHS 34; Leiden: Brill, 1987) 5, 134–135.

19. Deut. 1.1.

20. April D. DeConick, 'What Is Early Jewish and Christian Mysticism?', in *Paradise Now: Essays on Early Jewish and Christian Mysticism* (edited by April D. DeConick; Symposium 11; Atlanta: SBL, 2006) 1–24.

21. April D. DeConick, *Seek to See Him: Ascent and Vision Mysticism in the Gospel of Thomas* (VCSupp 33; Leiden: Brill, 1996).

3.1 *Oral Consciousness and Rhetorical Culture*

For the most part people in the ancient world did not know how to read or write, nor did they have ready access to people who could read and write. What they knew, they knew because they had heard it from someone, and what they could teach, they taught by retelling it from their memories. This means that when we are trying to understand the transmission of traditions among the first Christians, we are dealing for the most part with oral mentalities, not a process imagined by us in familiar literary terms. Even the process of writing was approached by those who were literate from the perspective of an oral consciousness rather than the literate consciousness that dominates our culture today. Like literacy which has its own mentality, orality has its own consciousness. It is an organic consciousness with distinct tendencies.

What are these tendencies? We are fortunate enough to have the results of studies conducted by folklorists and anthropologists in the early 1900s, at a time when there existed pocket cultures whose consciousness was dominated by orality. From these studies as well as more recent ones, we can begin to see how the oral world was characterized by markedly different presuppositions and thought patterns from our own.[22] Oral thought is commonly aggregative, adding details and new material to the base information. Oral thought provokes redundancy in a way that writing does not, since the orator frequently repeats parts of his story and cannot go back and erase. Oral thought demands a reliance on memory with little to no dependence on external sources of information. Oral thought is controlled by its situation, who the audience is, what they wish to hear, how long they might remain, who might interrupt, what questions might be posed, and so on. Oral thought is dynamic, fluid and plastic in ways that written texts are not.

One can imagine what this meant practically for the early Christians. An orator might have stood in front of a crowd and began to speak from his own memory of Jesus, or from his memory of what he had heard about Jesus. The moment of his oration was the moment of composition, when he provided the listeners with his own understanding of the traditional material he had learned from Jesus or some other teacher. This oration would never have reproduced

22. M. Parry, *The Making of Homeric Verse: The Collected Papers of Milman Perry* (ed. A. Parry; Oxford, 1971); A. Lord, *Singer of Tales*, HSCL 24 (Cambridge: Harvard University Press, 2nd edn, 2000); E. A. Havelock, *Preface to Plato* (Cambridge: Harvard University Press, 1963); W. J. Ong, *Orality and Literacy* (New York: Routledge, 1982, 2000); W. J. Ong, *The Presence of the Word* (New Haven: Yale University Press, 1967); W. J. Ong, *Rhetoric, Romance, and Technology* (New York: Cornell University Press, 1971); E. A. Havelock, *Origins of Western Literacy*, The Ontario Institute for Studies in Education, Monograph Series 14 (Toronto, 1976); K. O'Brien O'Keeffe, *Visible Song: Transitional Literacy in Old English Verse*, Cambridge Studies in Anglo-Saxon England 4 (Cambridge: Cambridge University Press, 1990); J. M. Foley, *Immanent Art: From Structure to Meaning in Traditional Oral Epic* (Bloomington: Indiana University, 1991);J. M. Foley, *The Singer of Tales in Performance* (Bloomington: Indiana University, 1995).

the 'original' story or speech because he would not have memorized it 'word for word' in the sense that we literates understand the 'word'. Professor Ong, an expert on orality, has explained that the way verbal memory works is very different from what literate people imagine. In a literate culture, we memorize words verbatim by referring to a text as often as possible to perfect and test our mastery.[23] This was not the case among peoples controlled by oral mentalities.

Does this mean that the orator or performer was completely free with the traditions and could remake them in any way he chooses? Absolutely not. Kenneth Bailey has studied orality in modern Middle Eastern villages for over 20 years.[24] He found that certain types of traditions have more flexibility in their retelling than others. Poems and proverbs had very little room for adjustment and were retained conservatively in the tradition. Parables and narratives had more room for play, while jokes and casual news the most. He unequivocally found that the audience acts as a 'control' for the performer so that the traditions do not become unpredictable or disconnected from the community's memory and experience.

3.2 *Communal Memory*

The community's control on its repository of traditions highlights for us the communal nature of traditions, that the ideas, stories, sayings, texts, rituals, myths, creeds, liturgies, and so on, are attached to specific groups of people, in specific locations and regions. This observation helps to check any faulty impression that ancient texts represent the imagination and opinions of an isolated author, when they more likely represent the communal memory of living religious groups of people.[25]

Understanding the tendencies of communal memory is essential to understanding how and why the ancient Christians passed on and recorded information in the ways they did. Social memory, or communal memory as I prefer to call it, is the dimension of remembering that we share in common with each other. It is a group's 'remembered history', transcending the individual person.[26] It is dependent on shared frames of reference within a culture, and makes little sense outside these frames.

One of the most important tendencies we must understand regarding the nature of communal memory is that the memory of the group is not a factual

23. Ong, *Orality and Literacy*, 57–58.

24. K. Bailey, 'Informal Controlled Oral Tradition and the Synoptic Gospels', *AsiaJT* 5 (1991) 34–54; K. Bailey, 'Middle Eastern Oral Tradition and the Synoptic Gospels', *ExpTim* 106 (1995) 363–367.

25. For a good introduction to social memory theory, see B. Zelizer, 'Reading the Past against the Grain', *Critical Studies in Mass Communication* 12 (1995) 214–239.

26. B. Lewis, *History: Remembered, Recovered, Invented* (Princeton: Princeton University Press, 1975) 11–12.

recounting of previous events or ideas. The formation of communal memory is not a simple matter of the retrieval of past traditions and history. Sociologists and anthropologists have demonstrated again and again that the memory of the group is dominated, even controlled by the present experience of the group. This means that the past is remade into memories with contemporaneous meaning. It is the group that attributes significance to certain details from its past. It is the group that is responsible for continually renewing and reviving the memories of the community's origins and other landmark events in its history. Each community actually weaves together what Professor Y. Zerubavel calls its 'master commemorative narrative' which each new generation realigns with its own present experiences.[27]

Here we circle back to Professor Bailey's observation that the community really controls the adaptation of the tradition, not the individual performer. It is the community that keeps the memories of its past from being invented out of nothing or grossly distorted by a contemporary whim or ideology. True, its memories are emerging out of the past in the contemporary moment, but this does not mean that the orator or performer can do anything he wishes with his material. At the same time, issues like historical accuracy or authenticity are accommodated to other issues of community concern, be it social identity, political authority, religious orthodoxy, and so forth.

3.3 *A Rolling Corpus*

So what comes to the forefront for us is not the question of how accurately a collection like the *Gospel of Thomas* depicts what Jesus actually said, but why a particular group of Christians constructed its memories in this particular way at some particular time. That the sayings were preserved at all in written format is highly significant and is connected to the group's desire to retain and retrieve its memory. This means that written texts like the *Gospel of Thomas* served as memory aids, which were used by the community as permanent sites for the storage and future dissemination of its contents.

So the *Gospel of Thomas* emerges as a written document under the weight of its past and the needs of the community to make sense of changing historical circumstances. The Gospel we have represents a long history of transmission, perhaps 'beginning' as a simple written gospel of some of Jesus' sayings. As new needs arose in the community, is it not plausible that additional sayings would have accumulated in this collection in order to address these needs? As new converts joined the community, is it not reasonable that they would have brought with them new ideas and interpretations? As the Christians in this community welcomed wandering preachers, is it not likely that they would

27. Y. Zerubavel, *Recovered Roots: Collective Memory and the Making of Israeli National Tradition* (Chicago: University of Chicago, 1997) 4, 7.

have learned 'new' Jesus sayings from them, and added these to their gospel performances?

If this is the case (and I think it very probable), it would mean that the sayings in the *Gospel of Thomas* represent different moments in its history and might be read as memoirs of practices and conflicts that arose over time within the community. An aggregate text like this likely would have been the result of its recitation and explication during community gatherings when the written sayings of Jesus were orally reperformed probably as homilies or instructions for proselytites. We can imagine that the developing traditions were rescribed at crucial moments in the history of the community, when members feared the loss of their traditions or when pressure within the group demanded significant reinterpretation. The version of the *Gospel of Thomas* that we have before us would represent a scribing of one of these later recitations, or a memory of it.

So the text we possess is an aggregate text, a text that accumulated traditions and their interpretations over time. It began as an old core, or as I call it, a Kernel gospel, which was expanded to include new sayings and opinions that worked to align the new experiences of the community with its remembrance of its past. This expansion would not have been a conscious rewriting of the old traditions, as if a Christian sat down one day with a pen in hand and added new sayings and erased others, but a result of the community's memory seamlessly adapting their past to make sense of the present, mainly (although not exclusively) within the field of oral performance.

So the *Gospel of Thomas* is a 'rolling' book, containing memories of the words of Jesus over the entire life of the community, until such a time when the book began to be considered 'sacred' and preserved by copyists, instead of orators who had enjoyed more flexibility with the 'text'.

4. *Theological Perspectives in the* Gospel of Thomas

Of course, a big question emerged for me in the course of my study of the *Gospel of Thomas* from this compositional perspective.[28] How is it possible to distinguish earlier Kernel sayings from later ones that may have accrued during a later performance of the Kernel Gospel? How can we identify and separate the later accretions from the earlier traditional material?

The starting point for me is the identification and examination of sayings where we see obvious signs of secondary development: when interpretative clauses have been appended to older sentences; when sayings have been reshaped into rhetorical question-and-answer units; and when retrospective

28. This is thoroughly laid out in my two volume work: April D. DeConick, *Recovering the Original Gospel of Thomas: A History of the Gospel and Its Growth* (LNTS 286; London: T&T Clark, 2005); April D. DeConick, *The Original Gospel of Thomas in Translation, with a Commentary and New English Translation of the Complete Gospel* (LNTS 287; London: T&T Clark, 2006).

dialogues have reclaimed older sayings. Once these accretive units are identified, they can be examined in order to further identify vocabulary and themes characteristic of the accretive material. Only after the characteristic vocabulary and themes have been demarcated, can they be used to expose additional accretions by searching the remaining sayings for coherence to the cited vocabulary and themes. The remaining sayings are determined to be the oldest, the sayings which likely were part of the original Kernel.[29]

An analysis of the Kernel sayings reveals a speech gospel that is quite old. It appears to have contained five speeches of Jesus and has affinities with Q. The contents of the speeches point to their origin in the Jerusalem mission prior to 50 CE. All five speeches are organized around the imminence of the eschaton, emphasizing how urgent the time is, how near judgement, and what this means to discipleship, exclusivity to Jesus and his cause, and the inaugurated Kingdom. The Christology in the Kernel is strikingly early, pre-dating even Q. In the Kernel, Jesus is God's Prophet who exclusively speaks God's truth. He is also thought to be an exalted Angel of Judgement, casting fire upon the earth and selecting the faithful from the unfaithful for the Kingdom.

All of these descriptors are commonly associated with the theology of early Christian Judaism from Jerusalem, a tradition of Christianity that travelled east and was embedded in later texts written in eastern Syria like the *Pseudo-Clementines.* I think it worth noting that it is in the *Pseudo-Clementine* correspondence that we hear that Clement was commissioned by James to write down the words and instructions of the true Prophet as Peter taught them to his audiences. This speech record was to be sent to James for use in proselytizing (*Rec.* 1.17; 1.21; *Hom. Epistle of Peter to James* 2). It is also of great value that it is in the *Pseudo-Clementine* material that we find only references to distinctive parallels of sayings from the Kernel. The clusters, sequencing, and hermeneutics of many of these sayings also follow the Kernel rather than the sequencing or interpretation provided by the Synoptics.[30] This is highly suggestive of a written Kernel known to the author of the *Pseudo-Clementines* or his sources.

So the original *Gospel of Thomas* was urgently and imminently eschatological in its orientation, and may provide us with some valuable information about the theology of the Jerusalem church during the 'dark age' of early Christianity, the years 30–50 CE. It appears that this old speech gospel was taken by the missionaries east into Syria where it was left with the Christian community there. Over the years in this new environment, it was adapted to the changing

29. For a complete listing of the Kernel sayings and the accretions, see DeConick, *Original Gospel of Thomas in Translation*, 10. Pages 25–31 contain an English translation of the Kernel, while pages 32–42 contain an English translation of the complete gospel with accretions in italics.

30. DeConick, *Original Gospel of Thomas in Translation*, 242–243.

needs, demands and theology of the Christians in Syria. Accretions gradually developed within the collection, working to reconfigure and reinterpret the older sayings and hermeneutics once they became a liability or irrelevant to the present experience of the Syrian Christians. This shift in the gospel can be traced linguistically as well as theologically, since there is evidence for an older Aramaic substratum beneath the Kernel sayings, while a Syriac one beneath the accretions.[31]

The theology of the accretions develops the apocalypticism of the Kernel in the sense that it shifts from the eschatological dimension to the mystical. The main experience (but not the exclusive one!) which led to the reconfiguration of the Kernel was the Non-Event – when the contemporary experience of the Christians in Syria did not match their expectations for world dissolution and Judgement. When the Kingdom did not come, they responded by reinterpreting Jesus' sayings in their small speech book. The external imminent eschaton was collapsed into the internal immanent *visio dei.* So the accretions describe a mystical form of Christianity in which the believer worked not just to understand God, but to 'know' him in the most immediate and the most direct sense.

For the Christians who reconfigured the gospel, the first step in this mystical transformation was to achieve the body-without-passions. So many of the sayings encourage an encratic praxis, honouring the life of the solitary or single person above all else. These Christians took seriously the call to celibacy, believing that sexual renunciation would serve to recreate their bodies in Adam's image before the Fall (*Gos. Thom.* 4.1, 4.3, 11.2–4, 16.4, 21.1–4, 21.6–9, 22, 23.2, 27.1, 37, 49, 64.12, 75, 85, 101, 105, 106, 110, 111.2, 114). They taught each other that it was necessary to renounce the world, to fast from the world, and to guard against temptations and worldliness (*Gos. Thom.* 21.6–8, 27, 110). Imitation of Jesus conquering his passions at his crucifixion was encouraged (*Gos. Thom.* 55, 56, 58, 80, 87, 112). Participation in the eucharist appears to have aided in the person's transformation since the gospel mentions on several occasions the power of divine food and drink to render the person 'equal' to Jesus (*Gos. Thom.* 13, 61, 108).

Once the body had been conquered and Jesus imitated, the believer was encouraged to study and meditate on the words of Jesus (*Gos. Thom.* 1). Through this praxis, they sought revelation and vision. This mystical apocalypse included journeys into the heavenly realms to see Jesus (*Gos. Thom.* 37) and worship before God's throne (*Gos. Thom.* 15). Knowledge of the passage through the heavenly realms was memorized (*Gos. Thom.* 50) so that the believer could gaze upon God before death in order not to die (*Gos. Thom.* 59). In heaven, the believer would meet his or her divine twin, the lost image, the

31. DeConick, *Original Gospel of Thomas in Translation*, 11–15, 19–21.

true Self (*Gos. Thom.* 84). The Christians who participated in this praxis believed that the immediate and direct vision of God would result in their full transformation into their original bodies of glory, so that they would no longer 'die'. This praxis results from a fusion of early Jewish mystical traditions about the heavenly Man, the loss of the radiant Image and its recovery with the Hermetic story about the fallen soul and its recovery through Self-knowledge and vision. It is a praxis that appears to have been developed in tandem and dialogue with Christianity in Alexandria in the late first and early second centuries.

All in all, the accretions tell the story of a Christian community in Syria whose members are no longer waiting for death or the eschaton in order to enter the Kingdom or achieve immortality. Instead of waiting for heaven to come to them, they are invading Eden, sincerely believing that the eschatological promises of God are fulfillable in the present. Their apocalyptic expectations have collapsed, shifting their theology away from hopes of an imminent eschaton to mystical pre-mortem experiences of God. They were already Adam and Eve in Paradise. So the Non-Event became for them the fulfilment of the Event. Jesus' promise of the imminent End had been actualized within the boundaries of their community.

5. *The Thomasine Community*

This reading of the *Gospel of Thomas* places it squarely within early orthodoxy rather than outside. The *Gospel of Thomas* does not represent the voice of some late generic Gnostic heresy or some early unique sapiential Christianity. Rather it is quite cogent with early Syrian Christianity as described in the oldest literature from the area. So any recovery of 'community' is really the recovery of the Christian community in Syria, with the knowledge that the community experienced shifts within its membership during the time that the gospel itself was composed, particularly an increase in Gentile converts and a shift to accommodate their interests (*Gos. Thom.* 6.1, 14.1–3, 14.5, 27.2, 43, 52, 53, 60).

Arthur Vööbus taught us long ago that Christianity in eastern Syria in the first couple of hundreds of years demanded celibacy and asceticism for admission into the Church. The literary evidence from Nag Hammadi, the apocryphal Acts, the *Pseudo-Clementines*, the records of the Church Fathers, point to a form of Christianity in Syria which was encratic, honouring the solitary life over the marital. The larger Catholic Church particularly in the West did not favour this position, so our historical memory of these people is that of sectarians and even heretics. But they were neither. For these Christians, baptism followed by daily washings and renunciation of the body extinguished desire and made it possible for them to begin to restore their souls to the glorious Image of God. This position on the solitary life appears to me to have shifted with Aphraates, whose writings show us that the demands of celibacy were eventually relaxed, reserved for the privileged class of the Syrian Church, the 'sons and daughters of the covenant'.

What is the religiosity of our earliest Syrian sources? In this literature, the human being regains a lost Paradise through his or her own effort of righteous living as revealed by Jesus, not through some act of atonement on Jesus' part. Over and over again, through story after story, the Christian is taught that he or she must become as self-controlled as possible, overcoming desire and passions that lurk in the soul. He or she is taught through discourse and example that marriage should be abandoned in order to achieve the prelapsarian conditions of 'singleness'. When this is done, gender difference is abolished and the believer can be united with his or her divine double in the 'bridal chamber'. This divine double, the person's new spouse, is in fact Jesus himself. It is Judas Thomas, Judas the Twin, who becomes the metaphor for all believers since Jesus is described as his very own Twin.

So I am completely convinced that the *Gospel of Thomas* theologically and practically is an infant of eastern Christianity, particularly as it was practiced in Syria. It is one of our earliest, if not our earliest text showcasing a very old form of 'Orthodox' thought. As such, it is very at home in the Syrian environment and represents old Syrian religiosity. It is a precursor to eastern Orthodoxy, as even a superficial reading of that catechism reveals. Eastern Christianity is about a mysticism of the heart and the progressive transformation of the soul into its glorious Image. In the West, the Augustinian position reigns, so that we know about 'original sin' severing us from our true Image, leaving us lost and helpless and damned. In the West, the lost are saved through grace and atonement which is completed in the eucharist, a sacrificial meal. In the East, the glorious Image is not lost, but only diminished or stunted by Adam's decision. It can be recovered in part through our own orientation and action. In the East, the eucharist is the ingestion of the divine body, aiding the transformation of the soul into the glorious Image. In Orthodoxy, the believer is called to self-knowledge, renunciation of the body through temperance in marriage or the hermitic life, spiritual warfare and purification of the passions, the path of virtue, imitation of Jesus and contemplation. This leads to a gradual glorification – a transformation due to 'gnosis' and 'theoria' – and ultimately the Taboric vision of God as light.

The mystical tradition in the *Gospel of Thomas* is very old, and emerges out of connections with apocalyptic thought. Once the eschatological story did not manifest as expected, these Christians remodelled the familiar sayings of Jesus by shifting their focus to the mystical dimension of Jesus' sayings. The theology that they developed shares the megastory of the earliest Christianity in Syria, and ultimately should be recognized as an early 'Orthodox' Syrian Gospel.

I think that the 'place' of the *Gospel of Thomas* within early Christianity has been wrongly identified in the past, not because it represents a type of Christianity unfamiliar to the canonical tradition or deviant from it. I think it has been wrongly identified for the simple reason that our categories, particularly in regard to mysticism in this period, could not contain it. That Western religiosity has controlled the discourse on this Gospel has not helped matters, since this Western discourse did not possess the conceptual framework to explain it.

Bibliography

S. L. Davies, *The Gospel of Thomas and Christian Wisdom* (New York: The Seabury Press, 1983).

A. D. DeConick, *Seek to See Him: Ascent and Vision Mysticism in the Gospel of Thomas* (VC Supplement 33; Leiden: Brill, 1996).

A. D. DeConick, *Recovering the Original Gospel of Thomas: A History of the Gospel and Its Growth* (LNTS 286; London: T&T Clark, 2005).

A. D. DeConick, *The Original Gospel of Thomas in Translation, with a Commentary and New English Translation of the Complete Gospel* (LNTS 287; London: T&T Clark, 2006).

F. T. Fallon and R. Cameron, 'The Gospel of Thomas: A Forschungsbericht and Analysis', *ANRW* II.25.6 (New York, 1988) 4195–4251.

B. P. Grenfell and A. S. Hunt, *Sayings of Our Lord from an Early Greek Papyrus* (London: The Egypt Exploration Fund, 1897).

B. P. Grenfell and A. S. Hunt, *New Sayings of Jesus and Fragment of a Lost Gospel from Oxyrhynchus* (London: The Egypt Exploration Fund, 1904).

B. Layton, *Nag Hammadi Codex II, 2–7, NHS* 20 (Leiden: E.J. Brill, 1989).

M. Lelyveld, *Les Logia de la Vie dans L'Évangile selon Thomas* (Nag Hammadi Studies 34; Leiden: Brill, 1987).

J. -E. Ménard, *L'Évangile selon Thomas, NHS 5* (Leiden: E.J. Brill, 1975).

M. Meyer, *The Gospel of Thomas: The Hidden Sayings of Jesus* (San Francisco: Harper San Francisco, 1992).

S. Patterson, 'The Gospel of Thomas and the Synoptic Tradition: A Forschungsbericht and Critique', *FFF* 8 (1992) 45–97.

S. Patterson, *The Gospel of Thomas and Jesus* (Sonoma: Polebridge Press, 1993).

J. Robinson and H. Koester (eds), *Trajectories through Early Christianity* (Philadelphia: Fortress Press, 1971).

R. Uro (ed.), T*homas at the Crossroads: Essays on the Gospel of Thomas* (Edinburgh: T&T Clark, 1998).

R. Uro, *Thomas. Seeking the Historical Context of the Gospel of Thomas* (London: T&T Clark, 2003).

Chapter 3

THE *GOSPEL OF PETER*

Paul Foster

Interest in those gospels not included in the canon of the New Testament continues to fascinate those who do, or do not claim attachment to Christianity. Often discovery of such texts is accompanied by claims that they contain insights into radically different versions of early Christianity, or that their perspectives on the historical Jesus overthrow orthodox beliefs. Behind such claims lies the assumption that the group that came to dominate in the early church suppressed equally valid, if not more primitive forms of Christianity in favour of a more hierarchical organization, and that down through the centuries the church leadership (usually in the form of the Vatican) has concealed the true origins of the Jesus movement. Such claims often appeal to the corpus of non-canonical gospels for support, but infrequently cite passages from these texts to support such assertions.[1] While the existence of these non-canonical gospels has been known through their mention in the writings of the Church Fathers, for most of the history of Christianity the actual texts have been lost. Admittedly a number of infancy gospels such as the *Protevangelium of James* or the *Infancy Gospel of Thomas* have survived, along with some post-resurrection accounts such as the *Gospel of Nicodemus* and the *Acts of Pilate*. However, it was not until the manuscript discoveries of the late nineteenth century onwards that scholars began to unearth in the dry and desiccating sands of Egypt, texts that contained additional or alternative narratives depicting the life and ministry of Jesus.

1. *The Discovery of the* Gospel of Peter

With so much recent interest focusing on the *Gospel of Thomas* and the *Gospel of Judas*, it is usually forgotten that the first non-canonical text to be

1. The edition of the *National Geographic* which announced the disclosure of the text known as *The Gospel of Judas* claims that '[i]n ancient times, some of these alternative versions may have circulated more widely than the familiar four Gospels' (p. 88). The article suggests suppression of such texts by the powerful alliance of the emperor Constantine and the Orthodox Church, '[b]y the end of the fourth century, though, it was unwise to possess such books' (p. 92). Despite such claims, relatively few passages are cited from the text, perhaps only a few extracts from about half a dozen enigmatic sayings. See 'The Gospel of Judas', *National Geographic* (May, 2006) 78–95.

rediscovered, which deals with events from the life of Jesus, was the so-called *Gospel of Peter*. This text was discovered by a team of archaeologists from the *Mission archéologique française au Caire* during the winter season dig of 1886–1887 at Akhmîm in Upper Egypt. Because of the sheer volume of artefacts and texts unearthed by the archaeological team there was a delay in the publication of this codex, so its contents did not become known to the wider scholarly world until 1892.[2] Apart from the skeletal remains, the grave in question contained a small codex (or book) consisting of 33 leaves, with papyrus sheets glued on the inside of both covers. The tomb itself is dated in the range from eighth to twelfth century. The small book is dated probably around the eighth century on the basis of palaeographical analysis (handwriting style). Providing page numbers for the unpaginated codex enables the following table of contents to be formed.

Page	Contents
Inside Front Cover	Blank
1	Decoration, religious in nature, including Coptic crosses
2–10	The *Gospel of Peter*
11–12	Blank
13–19	Apocalypse of Peter (but pages stitched the wrong way round and upside down, so they must be read in the order 19–13).
20	Blank
21–66	Two fragments from 1 Enoch
Inside Back Cover	Martyrdom of St Julian

Both the quality of handwriting and the amateurish compilation of this codex lead to the suspicion that the text was not produced in a professional scriptorium, but was rather the product of a relatively unskilled individual, perhaps even the same monk in whose grave the book was interred.

Identification of the first document in the codex as the *Gospel of Peter* was suggested in the initial publication report, and followed by other scholars writing on the subject.[3] There are two major pieces of evidence that suggest this identification – one internal, the other external. The internal indicator is that on two occasions in the text breaks into first person narrative. The first of these is

2. The *editio princeps* was published under the title, U. Bouriant, 'Fragments du texte grec du livre d'Énoch et de quelques écrits attribués à saint Pierre', dans *Mémoires publié par les membres de la Mission archéologique française au Caire* (t. IX, fasc. 1; Paris 1892) 93–147.

3. In his important edition of the text with accompanying notes Swete states, 'There is no reason to doubt that the Akhmîm fragment was rightly assigned by M. Bouriant to the lost Gospel of Peter.' See H. B. Swete, *The Akhmîm Fragment of the Apocryphal Gospel of St Peter* (London: Macmillan and Co., 1893) xii.

not particularly revealing, for it only shows that the voice of one of the disciples is used to relate events:

> But I with my companions grieved, and being wounded in mind we hid. For we were being sought by them as evildoers and as those wishing to burn the temple. But through all of these things we were fasting and sat mourning and weeping night and day until the Sabbath. (*Gos. Pet.* 7.26–27)

The more important piece of first person narration occurs in the final verse of the surviving portion of the text, where Peter is explicitly identified as the narrator. 'But I, Simon Peter, and Andrew my brother, taking our nets went to the sea, and there was with us Levi the brother of Alphaeus, whom the Lord . . .' (*Gos. Pet.* 14.60). The external evidence comes from two statements recorded by Eusebius in regard to a document that circulated under the title of the *Gospel of Peter* in the late second century. First, discussing writings attributed to the name of Peter, Eusebius states that catholic tradition does not accept 'the Gospel named according to him'. (*H.E.* 3.3.2). Secondly, relating information concerning Serapion, bishop of Antioch (AD 191–211), Eusebius outlines the contents of one of his writings titled *Concerning the So-Called Gospel of Peter* (see *H.E.* 6.12.1–6). According to the source, Eusebius claims to be citing, during a pastoral visit to the church of Rhossus, without examining its contents, Serapion initially permitted the reading of the *Gospel of Peter*. Upon returning to Antioch, after being informed of the contents of this document, he reversed his decision.

> But since I have now learnt, from what has been told me, that their mind was lurking in some hole of heresy, I shall give diligence to come again to you; wherefore, brethren, expect me quickly. But we, brethren, gathering to what kind of heresy Marcianus[4] belonged (who used to contradict himself, not knowing what he was saying, as you will learn from what has been written to you), were enabled by others who studied this very Gospel, that is, by the successors of those who began it, whom we call Docetae (for most of the ideas belong to their teaching) – using the materials supplied by them, were enabled to go through it and discover that the most part indeed was in accordance with the true teaching of the Saviour, but that some things were added, which also we place below for your benefit. (see *H.E.* 6.12.3–6)

Unfortunately Eusebius does not replicate Serapion's list of added elements. What these convoluted sentences appear to communicate is not that this Gospel was itself docetic (although unspecified elements had been added), but rather that it was used by those labelled as being docetic to support their own

4. In the Armenian version of the Ecclesiastical History, the name Marcianus, Μαρκιανός, is replaced by that of the better known heretic Marcion. It may be more likely that this identification represents an error on the part of the Armenian tradition, since elsewhere, when Eusebius is referring to Marcion, the name is spelt Μαρκίων.

teachings. Notwithstanding this distinction, part of the early scholarly treatment involved identifying features of the text which were seen as aligning with Docetism.[5]

The contents of the text were disseminated through the published transcription of Urbain Bouriant, a member of the French archaeological team and the editor of the text.[6] This edition was later corrected and republished with lithographic plates of the pages of the text (although these images are unreadable in places).[7] In the early 1980s images of the text were produced for only the second time, these were of much higher quality than the lithographs.[8] Unfortunately at some point subsequent to that date, the codex went missing from the Coptic Museum in Cairo where it was housed, and it has not been possible to elicit a response from the curators of the collection concerning the whereabouts of the text.[9]

2. *The Contents of the Text*

While there is no damage to the beginning of the first page of the text, and there is sufficient space at the end of the extant portion of text to decorate the manuscript with three Coptic crosses and other ornamental features, the text both begins and ends mid-sentence. What is to be made of this phenomenon? The most likely explanation is that the scribe was copying this text from an

5. See the discussion in J. A. Robinson and M. R. James, *The Gospel according to Peter, and the Revelation of Peter: Two Lectures on the Newly Recovered Fragments together with the Greek Texts* (London: C. J. Clay and Sons, 1892), esp. 20.

6. Bouriant, 'Fragments du texte grec du livre d'Énoch et de quelques écrits attribués à saint Pierre', 137–142.

7. A. Lods, 'L'Évangile et l'Apocalypse de Pierre avec le texte grec du livre d'Hénoch. Text publié en facsimilé, par l'héliogravure d'après les photographies du manuscript de Gizéh' dans *Mémoires publié par les membres de la Mission archéologique française au Caire* (t. IX, fasc. 3; Paris 1893) 217–231, 322–335. The page numbers are often cited as 217–235. This is fully understandable because page 322 follows page 231 without any intervening or lost material. The change to numbers in the 300 range is presumably due to an error in typesetting. These lithographic images are also available in O. von Gebhardt, *Das Evangelium und die Apokalypse des Petrus. Die neuentdeckten Bruchstücke nach einer Photographie der Handschrift zu Gizéh in Lichtdruck herausgegeben* (Leipzig, 1890).

8. The new high quality set of photographs are available online at http://ipap.csad.ox.ac.uk/GP/GP.html (last accessed on 25 March 2008). In personal correspondence with the photographer, Adam Bülow-Jacobsen, he stated that his recollection of the date of photographing the codex is no longer certain. When pressed on the issue he stated, 'As for the date, I honestly don't know. I worked in Cairo most years between 78 and 87. There is a possibility that they were taken for Cornelia Römer for whom I did a number of things when we were both in the museum in 1981' (10 March 2006).

9. Tobias Nicklas and Thomas Kraus have informed me that the text can no longer be located. I have emailed the Coptic Museum in Cairo on two occasions seeking information about the codex and have sent a written letter to the Director of the Museum during the course of my own research over the past 2 years. I have not been successful in gaining any response to my enquiries.

exemplar that was itself mutilated.[10] Alternatively, the poor quality of penmanship may even suggest that the text was copied as a writing exercise with the starting point chosen at random. For convenience, the text has been divided by modern editors into a series of chapters and verses. However, different systems were developed by scholars, which lead to some confusion when comparing references especially in early work on the text. Swete divided the text into 12 chapters,[11] Robinson broke it into 14 chapters,[12] while Harnack adopted a system of 60 shorter subdivisions which are similar to the versification in the Bible.[13] Swete's numbering system has fallen by the wayside. The standard referencing system now consists of citing Robinson's chapter reference along with Harnack's verse number, that is, *Gos. Pet.* 8.33. In reality the chapter numbers are superfluous, since the verse numbers do not recommence at the beginning of each chapter, so a verse number alone would designate a unique reference. In order to alleviate this anomaly Arthur Dewey has recently attempted to correct this by recommencing the verse numbers at the start of each chapter. Thus *Gos. Pet.* 8.33, the last verse in Chapter 8, is designated by Dewey as *Gos. Pet.* 8.6.[14] While his reasons for doing this is to make the numbering system more consistent with biblical referencing, in truth the introduction of another system serves only to further confuse the referencing of material in the text. Consequently, his scheme has not been widely adopted.

The text opens with a scene not described in the canonical gospels, although it does appear to presuppose an incident in the Matthean account, that of Pilate washing his hands (Mt. 27.24).[15] The opening sentence depicts the refusal of the Jews, Herod Antipas and his judges to wash their hands, which results in Pilate departing – presumably in protest or disgust (*Gos. Pet.* 1.1). From this point Herod becomes the principle authority in the trial. He determines the fate of Jesus and hands him over to the Jews who carry out a mob killing. There is a brief interlude, when Joseph (presumably of Arimathea – although only named Joseph) requests the body of Jesus from Pilate prior to the crucifixion. This Joseph is described as 'the friend of Pilate and of the Lord' (*Gos. Pet.* 2.3). The Jewish mob drag Jesus to the place of execution,but stop *en route* to sit him on the judgement seat, and taunt him with mock deference by saying

10. Swete hints at this as being the most likely explanation when he comments, 'It is worthy of notice that while each of the Petrine fragments is followed by a blank, as if the writer had stopped because he had reached the end of his copy, there is no such blank between the fragments of Enoch or at the end of the Codex.' Swete, *The Akhmîm Fragment of the Apocryphal Gospel of St Peter*, xlvi.

11. Swete, *The Akhmîm Fragment of the Apocryphal Gospel of St Peter*, 25–28.

12. Robinson and James, *The Gospel according to Peter, and the Revelation of Peter*, 83–88.

13. Harnack, *Bruchstücke des Evangeliums und der Apokalypse des Petrus*, 8–12.

14. See A. J. Dewey, 'The Passion Narrative of the Gospel of Peter', *Forum*, New Series 1.1 (1998) 53–69, esp. 54–57.

15. Robinson and James, *The Gospel according to Peter, and the Revelation of Peter*, 16.

'judge righteously, King of Israel' (*Gos. Pet.* 3.7).[16] Perhaps the most striking deviation from the canonical accounts of the passion is the form of the only words that Jesus utters in the entire fragment of this text. Both Matthew and Mark record a cry of dereliction from the cross, 'My God, my God why have you forsaken me' (Mt. 27.46//Mk 15.34). By contrast, Luke transforms this desperate cry into a pious utterance 'Father into your hands I commit my spirit' (Lk. 23.46). The *Gospel of Peter* records a further alternative, 'My power, the power, you have forsaken me' (*Gos. Pet.* 5.19). Many early writers commenting on this passage saw it as a clear indication of the Docetism that Serapion attributed to this text.[17] In a number of docetic writings the divine Christ leaves the human Jesus to suffer on the cross, and in some accounts this divine logos looks down on the crucifixion scene at those who think they are putting the Christ to death (cf. *Acts of John* 101–102). There are a number of problems with this interpretation. First, if this is the moment of departure of the Divine Christ, then he has not evaded suffering; in fact he has suffered most horribly and only gains relief at the same instant as does the human Jesus through death. Secondly, when the corpse is taken off the cross and laid on the ground, the very earth recognizes the sacredness of the body by quaking at its touch. Rather than understand this formulation as part of a docetic Christology, it appears that, like the author of Luke's Gospel, the author of the *Gospel of Peter* had trouble with the notion of Jesus uttering a cry of God-forsakenness and changed his words to avoid this theological conundrum.

More than half of the fragment focuses on post-crucifixion events. The story of the guard at the tomb, known only from Matthew among the canonical accounts (Mt. 27.62–66; 28.4, 11–15), receives much greater attention in the *Gospel of Peter*. The request is made to Pilate for soldiers, in anticipation that the disciples might attempt to steal the body (*Gos. Pet.* 8.30). By contrast, in Matthew, the story of the disciples stealing the body is only hatched after the corpse has gone missing. Additional novelistic details are added to the narrative which both fill gaps and add colour to the story. Readers are informed that the name of the centurion in charge of the guard detail is Petronius, that seven seals were attached to the tomb, that a tent was pitched on site and that the soldiers kept watch in pairs while the rest of the detachment slept in the tent (*Gos. Pet.* 8.33–9.35). It is the soldiers and those Jews present at the burial

16. In Jn 18.13 the Greek text is actually ambiguous as to whether it is Pilate or Jesus who sits on the judgement seat, ὁ οὖν Πιλᾶτος ἀκούσας τῶν λόγων τούτων ἤγαγεν ἔξω τόν Ἰησοῦν καὶ ἐκάθισεν ἐπὶ βήματος εἰς τόπον λεγόμενον λιθόστρωτον, Ἑβραϊστὶ δὲ Γαββαθα (Jn 19.13).

17. Cf. Robinson and James, *The Gospel according to Peter, and the Revelation of Peter*, 21; Describing the author of this text Rendel Harris declares, 'one thing is clear: he is a Docetist, and the Power which has left the Lord is the Christ which had descended upon Him at some earlier time, probably at Baptism.' J. Rendel Harris, *A Popular Account of the Newly Recovered Gospel of St Peter* (London: Hodder and Stoughton) 35.

place on the first Easter morning who observe two men descend from heaven who, after the stone rolls away of its own accord, enter the tomb and emerge supporting a third man.[18] Upon leaving the tomb a change has occurred to the bodily forms of all three. The heads of the two men reach up to the heavens, but the head of the third man reaches up far beyond the heavens. Such polymorphic transformations are not uncommon in early Christian texts which reflect Christologically on the post-resurrection significance of Jesus. Among the canonical gospels Jesus' identity is hidden from those with whom he converses on the Emmaus Road (Lk. 24.16), in the fourth gospel the risen Jesus is able to materialize in a locked room (Jn 20.19) and in the transfiguration accounts (which may function proleptically as a vision of resurrection glory) both Jesus' appearance and apparel are transformed (Mt. 17.1–8//Mk 9.2–8//Lk. 9.28–36). Such polymorphisms are even more developed in extra-canonical traditions. In the *Acts of Peter* in a post-resurrection appearance the onlookers report having seen Jesus in a number of different forms: some see an old man, others a young man and still others report seeing Jesus in the form of a boy.[19] The *Acts of John* narrates an occasion when Jesus, standing on the shore, appears to two of his disciples, the brothers James and John, in a variety of forms. James first sees Jesus as a child, Johns sees a man 'who is handsome, fair and cheerful looking'. Then Jesus appears to the pair again. To John he is 'rather bald-headed but with a thick flowing beard', whereas James sees 'a young man whose beard was just beginning' (*Acts John* 88–89). The version of the transfiguration in the *Acts of John* also portrays a Jesus changed in body size, but here his form is not enlarged, but diminished. On approaching Jesus during the mystical experience on the mountain, John states, 'he appeared as a small man' (*Acts John* 91). The recently discovered *Gospel of Judas* contains the enigmatic line 'often he did not appear to his disciples as himself, but he was found among then as a child'.[20] While bodily enlargement is not extremely common

18. In Matthew's account a single angel descends from heaven and physically pushes the stone away, but does not enter into the tomb. Instead he sits on top of the stone (Mt. 28.2).

19. And as we lay there, only those widows stood up which were blind; and the bright light which appeared unto us entered into their eyes and made them to see. Unto whom Peter said: Tell us what ye saw. And they said: We saw an old man of such comeliness as we are not able to declare to thee; but others said: We saw a young man; and others: We saw a boy touching our eyes delicately, and so were our eyes opened. Peter therefore magnified the Lord, saying: Thou only art the Lord God, and of what lips have we need to give thee due praise? and how can we give thee thanks according to thy mercy? Therefore, brethren, as I told you but a little while since, God that is constant is greater than our thoughts, even as we have learned of these aged widows, how that they beheld the Lord in various forms. (*Acts Pet.* 21)

20. Page 34 lines 18–20. A proper referencing system has not yet been developed, but the Coptic text can be accessed at www.nationalgeographic.com/lostgospel/document_nf.html (last accessed on 25 March 2008).

(but cf. *The Gospel of the Twelve Apostles*, the section relating the 'Revelation of Simeon Kepha'), depictions of Jesus' altered bodily form are to be found in various texts. Thus, the enlarged figures who emerge from the tomb need to be understood against the wider background of the phenomenon of early Christian reflection on the Christological significance of the resurrected Christ that depicted his polymorphic characteristic.

Perhaps the most popularizing element in this account occurs when a voice from heaven addresses the party of three men asking if they 'have preached to those who sleep?' (*Gos. Pet.* 10.41). While the audience may expect an answer from one of the three figures, it is the cross that responds with an emphatic 'Yes' (*Gos. Pet.* 10.42). Here, admittedly in embryonic form, there appears to be the initial stages of the 'harrowing of hell' tradition, along with reflection on the central role of the cross as part of the narrative depicting the liberation of the faithful souls of the Old Testament from the bonds of Hades.[21]

The final sections of the text present a number of different post-resurrection scenes. First, after the guard reports to Pilate the events at the tomb, the Roman Prefect is harangued by the Jews to suppress the facts of the resurrection (*Gos. Pet.* 11.47–49). Next follows a scene describing the visit of Mary Magdalene and other female friends to the tomb, unaware of what has already happened. This part of the narrative draws on Mark's Gospel for its basic outline, and there are a number of striking verbal correspondences with Mark's account that make direct literary dependence between these two texts highly likely. Finally the text reports the disciples quitting Jerusalem on the last day of the festival of the unleavened bread and returning to the fishing industry (*Gos. Pet.* 14.58–60). It appears that the text is about to commence recounting a post-resurrection appearance similar to that contained in Jn 21, but the text breaks off before it is possible to be certain.

3. *Theological Concerns of the Text*

From the outset it should be noted that this text is not theologically sophisticated, it is a popularizing version of the crucifixion and resurrection, which blackens the role of the Jews and elevates the miraculous elements contained in the tradition. Yet there are some latent theological perspectives that are worth noting. First, the author displays a pious attitude towards Jesus by consistently referring to him as the Lord, while other titles are placed on the lips of various characters, when the narrator refers to Jesus he uses the title ὁ κύριος exclusively. Of the 13 times this title is used, on 11 occasions it is written using the widespread Christian abbreviation practice known as *nomina sacra*.[22]

21. See the *Gospel of Nicodemus*, esp. Latin recension B, *Gos. Nic.* 10(26) 1.

22. L. W. Hurtado, 'The Origin of the *Nomina Sacra*: A Proposal', *JBL* 117(1998) 655–673; C.H. Roberts, '*Nomina Sacra*: Origins and Significance', ch. 2 of his *Manuscript, Society and Belief in Early Christian Egypt* (London: Oxford University Press, 1979) 26–48.

In the Ethiopian Orthodox Church Pontius Pilate is venerated as a saint. While the *Gospel of Peter* does not go quite so far, it is easy to see it as part of that same trajectory which absolves Pilate, while simultaneously attributing greater guilt to the Jews for both the crucifixion of Jesus and the suppression of the truth concerning the resurrection. Such attitudes can be seen as already evolving in the later canonical accounts with Matthew presenting the Jews as circulating the rumour that the disciples stole Jesus' body and invented the story of the resurrection (Mt. 28.13–15). Similarly, in John, the Jews are paradigmatically the opponents of both Jesus and the Johannine Christians for whom the gospel is written. In the *Gospel of Peter* Herod Antipas marshals the Jewish mob, which brutalizes Jesus and then carries out the crucifixion. The anti-Jewish tendency contained in the *Gospel of Peter* reflects part of a growing sentiment in early and medieval Christianity.

4. *Date and Relationship to the Canonical Gospels*

The questions of date and relationship to the canonical gospels are not unrelated.[23] Throughout most of the history of scholarship on this writing it has been suggested, based on the identification with Serapion's *Gospel of Peter*, that this is a second-century text. Some have also argued that the writings of Justin Martyr are dependant on the *Gospel of Peter*, and consequently date the composition to the second quarter of the second century. Others who deny such a literary relationship are thus inclined to date it later in the second century. Recently, this second century dating has been called into question, primarily by John Dominic Crossan. He has suggested that the majority of the surviving text (on his theory there are some later redactional additions) preserves a source named the Cross Gospel, which actually predates the canonical accounts, and was used by them as a source for their Passion accounts. Although, it is argued, this source is preserved in its more pristine form in the *Gospel of Peter* than it is in the heavily reworked canonical passion narratives.[24] Crossan recognized that a number of sections of the text showed clear signs of dependence on the canonical gospels, so he bracketed these off from his reconstructed early source as later accretions. In particular, the large block of text dealing with the visit of the women to the tomb (*Gos. Pet.* 12.50–13.57) was excluded from the hypothetical Cross Gospel, because of the clear dependence, even in Crossan's mind, on Mk 16.1–8. Others who have followed this thesis have perhaps not maintained the same level of sophistication in the articulation of their theories. Perhaps one of the more notable cases of modifying Crossan's thesis occurs in

23. For an extended discussion on this entire issue see P. Foster, *A Commentary on the so-called Gospel of Peter* (Oxford: Oxford University Press, forthcoming), esp. the section titled 'Literary Relationships with the So-Called Gospel of Peter'.

24. Crossan's more extensive treatment of the topic appeared in *The Cross That Spoke: The Origins of the Passion Narrative* (1988), see esp. 16–30.

the *Anchor Bible Dictionary* entry on the *Gospel of Peter*. Paul Mirecki makes even more radical claims than those advanced by Crossan. He states, 'The *Gospel of Peter* (= *Gos. Pet.*) was a narrative gospel of the synoptic type which circulated in the mid-first century under the authority of the name Peter. An earlier form of the gospel probably served as one of the major sources for the canonical gospels.'[25] Thus, for Mirecki, the final version of the *Gospel of Peter* appears to have been in circulation by the middle of the first century, presumably prior to the composition of any of the canonical accounts. Yet, there was also an earlier literary stage which the evangelists drew upon in composing their own narratives. It is uncertain when this primitive form was composed, but according to Mirecki's outline this must have been earlier than 50 CE. The major departure from Crossan's thesis is in suggesting that the final form of the *Gospel of Peter* was completed prior to the composition of the canonical gospels. This stands in opposition to one of Crossan's most direct statements: 'I agree, of course, that our present Gospel of Peter is dependent on the canonical gospels. That has always been my position.'[26]

Notwithstanding the attempt of Crossan to exclude material which is obviously dependent upon the canonical gospels from this hypothetical source, even the remaining reconstructed kernel of the Cross Gospel appears to represent a theological development of canonical traditions. Considering just one example – that of the penitent thief contained in the *Gospel of Peter* 4.13–14, it appears impossible to maintain that the material in the putative Cross Gospel source is prior to the versions of that story contained in the three synoptic accounts. In the first two canonical accounts the two men crucified alongside Jesus follow the example of those standing round the cross, by mocking and abusing Jesus (Mt. 27.44//Mk 15.32b). By contrast, according to Luke, while one of the thieves casts insults (Lk. 23.39), the other rebukes his companion and defends Jesus as one who did no wrong. The account in the *Gospel of Peter* is different again. It deletes any reference to either thief rebuking Jesus; instead the penitent thief alone speaks and castigates the Jews for their actions. Although Crossan and other supporters of the Cross Gospel source place the version of this story that occurs in the *Gospel of Peter* in the pre-canonical layer or original stratum which pre-dates the synoptic accounts, thus making it a source for the synoptic gospels,[27] this seems untenable. This is because it appears impossible to formulate a plausible theological trajectory which originates with an account of a single thief defending Jesus' status as 'saviour of men' in the *Gospel of Peter*, but then accounts for a later redactor introducing a mocking thief into the scene with the penitent thief uttering the watered down

25. Mireki, 'Peter, Gospel of', *ABD* V, 278.

26. Crossan, 'The Gospel of Peter and the Canonical Gospels: Independence, Dependence, or Both?', 31.

27. Crossan, *The Cross That Spoke*, 25.

confession that 'this man has done no wrong' (Lk. 23.41). Finally, according to the scheme required by Crossan's model, either independent of Luke, or as a modification of the Lukan alteration, Matthew and Mark deleted the penitent thief from the scene, thus producing an account with two recalcitrant and reviling thieves. Rather, the *Gospel of Peter* continues a process that, as it appears, from his replication of the narrative framework at the beginning of *Gos. Pet.* 4.13, he knew directly from Luke. He deletes the embarrassing reference to a mocking thief and has the penitent thief present heightened Christological claims for Jesus while simultaneously increasing the complicity of the Jewish crowd in carrying out the unjust crucifixion of 'the saviour'. Hence theories that attempt to press the text of the *Gospel of Peter*, or a source embedded within it, back into the first century are not sustainable. The text is best understood as a reflection on canonical traditions, and it also demonstrates theological trajectories that are part of later Christianity.

Attempts have been made to identify other early fragments of text as portions of the *Gospel of Peter*. These items include two scraps of text from Oxyrhynchus,[28] the Fayyum Fragment,[29] an ostracon containing an image of Peter with the legend 'Peter, the holy one, the evangelist',[30] and Papyrus Egerton 2.[31] Only the first of the Oxyrhynchus fragments has any overlap with the extant portion of the text discovered in the monk's grave at Akhmîm. Yet, even this first text has only limited overlap with *Gos. Pet.* 2.3.5a. As part of a recent article it was observed that 'the identification [is] based on 44 shared letters out of a text of 238 letters or an 18.49% (to 4 sig. figs) correspondence between texts.'[32] Such a low level of correspondence does not inspire great confidence that any other textual witness to the text discovered at Akhmîm has yet been discovered. Thus we are left with a single witness to this text, the manuscript discovered in the monk's burial place, which is dated some time between the seventh and ninth centuries. While this may, more likely than not, be the same text as the *So-Called Gospel of Peter* mentioned by Serapion, certainty is not possible. After all, at least three different texts bear the name *Apocalypse of Peter* and in the text titled *The Acts of Peter and the Twelve* (NHC VI.1), Peter also speaks in the first person voice.[33]

28. These are catalogued as P.Oxy. 2949 and P.Oxy. 4009.

29. This fragment of text is also designated as P. Vindob.G 2325.

30. Catalogued in J. van Haelst, *Catalogue des Papyrus Littéraires Juifs et Chrétiens* (Université de Paris IV. Paris-Sorbonne. Série 'Papyrologie', 1: Paris 1976) as item 741. Hence, it is referred to in the literature as van Haelst Nr. 741.

31. Usually referenced as P.Egerton 2.

32. P. Foster, 'Are There Any Early Fragments of the So-Called *Gospel of Peter*?', *NTS* 52 (2006) 1–28.

33. See the translation of D. M. Parrott and R. McL. Wilson, 'The Acts of Peter and the Twelve Apostles (VI, *1*)' in J. M. Robinson, *The Nag Hammadi Library in English* (4th rev. edn, Leiden: Brill, 1996) 287–294, 289.

5. *Conclusions*

The text identified as the *Gospel of Peter* represents a fascinating snapshot of the way gospel traditions were handled in at least one corner of the ancient world by some early Christians. This story of the crucifixion and passion is embellished with more spectacular miracles and vivid, if not lurid descriptions. The Jews are made more blameworthy for the crucifixion and Pilate is almost totally exonerated. Despite alleged docetic tendencies the fragment that is preserved does not have any features that must obviously be classified in that manner. Although certainty about dating is not possible, the most likely suggestion is that the writing discovered at Akhmîm represents a text originally composed in the second half of late second century (although if it is not the same text as that known by Serapion it could be later).[34] The text does not present a radically unorthodox form of Christianity,[35] rather it seeks to make canonical traditions more lively and engaging. This text meant enough to one Egyptian monk for his friends to inter it with him as a precious keepsake. For modern scholarship it has also been a precious text, illustrating the vibrancy and creativity of early Christian communities.

Bibliography

U. Bouriant, 'Fragments du texte grec du livre d'Énoch et de quelques écrits attribués à saint Pierre', dans *Mémoires publié par les membres de la Mission archéologique française au Caire* (t. IX, fasc. 1; Paris 1892) 93–147.

J. D. Crossan, *The Cross That Spoke* (San Francisco: Harper and Row, 1988).

J. D. Crossan, 'The Gospel of Peter and the Canonical Gospels: Independence, Dependence, or Both?', *Forum*, New Series 1, 1 (1998) 7–51.

B. D. Ehrman, *Lost Christianities: The Battles for Scripture and the Faiths We Never Knew* (Oxford: Oxford University Press, 2003) 13–28.

P. Foster, 'Are There Any Early Fragments of the So-Called *Gospel of Peter*?' *NTS* 52 (2006) 1–28.

P. Foster, 'The Discovery and Initial Reaction to the So-Called Gospel of Peter', in T. J. Kraus and T. Nicklas (eds), *Das Evangelium nach Petrus Text, Kontext, Intertexte* (Berlin: De Gruyter, 2007) 9–30.

P. Foster, 'The Disputed Fragments of the So-Called *Gospel of Peter* – Once Again', *NovT* 49 (2007) 402–406.

P. Foster, *A Commentary on Gospel of Peter* (forthcoming).

A. von Harnack, *Bruchstücke des Evangeliums und der Apokalypse des Petrus*, (Leipzig: J. C. Hinrichs'sche Buchhandlung, 1893).

T. Kraus and T. Nicklas, *Das Petrusevangelium und die Petrusapokalypse: Die griechischen Fragment mit deutsche und englisher Übersetzung* (Berlin: Walter de Gruyter, 2004).

34. Foster, 'Are There Any Early Fragments of the So-Called *Gospel of Peter*?', 27–28.

35. See the discussion in B. D. Ehrman, *Lost Christianities: The Battles for Scripture and the Faiths We Never Knew* (Oxford: Oxford University Press, 2003) 13–28.

A. Lods, 'L'Évangile et l'Apocalypse de Pierre avec le texte grec du livre d'Hénoch. Text publié en facsimilé, par l'héliogravure d'après les photographies du manuscript de Gizéh' dans *Mémoires publié par les membres de la Mission archéologique française au Caire* (t. IX, fasc. 3; Paris 1893) 217–231, 322–335.

P. Mireki, 'Peter, Gospel of', *ABD* 5 (New York: Doubleday, 1992) 278–281.

J. A. Robinson and M. R. James, *The Gospel according to Peter, and the Revelation of Peter: Two Lectures on the Newly Recovered Fragments together with the Greek Texts* (London: C. J. Clay and Sons, 1892).

H. B. Swete, *The Akhmîm Fragment of the Apocryphal Gospel of St Peter* (London: Macmillan and Co., 1893).

L. Vaganay, *L'Évangile de Pierre* (2nd edn; Paris: Librairie Lecoffre, J. Gabalda et Fils, 1930).

Chapter 4

THE *GOSPEL OF MARY*

Christopher M. Tuckett

The *Gospel of Mary* is a text which has aroused considerable interest in recent years in both scholarly and non-scholarly circles.[1] As with other non-canonical gospels, it shares in the revival of interest in these texts in the modern era. It takes its name from the figure of 'Mary', who is almost certainly intended to be Mary Magdalene;[2] and the figure of Mary Magdalene has been the focus of a lot of attention in recent years.[3] In particular, the *Gospel of Mary* has been used as part of the evidence that Mary Magdalene exercised a significant leadership role in the early church, and/or more general claims about the leadership roles of women in early Christianity.

1. *Manuscripts and Attestation*

The *Gospel of Mary* is a text which only came to light in the modern era from manuscript finds. Perhaps surprisingly, it is not attested anywhere outside the manuscripts containing the text: it is not cited or mentioned by any of the Church Fathers, and it is not listed in any of the discussions or lists of canonical books (e.g. the Muratorian Canon, or the Gelasian Decree).

1. Recent scholarly monographs include Karen L. King, *The Gospel of Mary of Magdala. Jesus and the First Woman Apostle* (Santa Rosa: Polebridge Press, 2003), and Esther A. De Boer, *The Gospel of Mary. Beyond a Gnostic and a Biblical Mary Magdalene* (London and New York: T&T Clark International, 2004), as well as many other sections of other studies. See also my *The Gospel of Mary* (Oxford: Oxford University Press, 2007) for more detailed discussion and with fuller references than are possible here. An English translation of the text is given in all the studies above, also in J. M. Robinson (ed.), *The Nag Hammadi Library in English* (Leiden: Brill, 1977) 471–474.

2. The overwhelming majority opinion is that the 'Mary' of the text here is Mary Magdalene.

3. In more popular circles, cf. the interest is aroused by Dan Brown's novel *The Da Vinci Code*. In more scholarly circles, see A. Marjanen, *The Woman Jesus Loved. Mary Magdalene in the Nag Hammadi and Related Documents* (Leiden: Brill, 1996); J. Schaberg, *The Resurrection of Mary Magdalene* (London and New York: Continuum, 2002); A. G. Brock, *Mary Magdalene, the First Apostle* (Cambridge, MA: Harvard University Press, 2003) and others.

It survives today in three manuscripts, all of them fragmentary (to a greater or lesser degree). The most extensive is the version which appears in the Berlin Codex BG 8502. This manuscript, written in Coptic and probably to be dated to the early fifth century, has been known about since the 1890s, although due to a variety of circumstances, its full text was not published until 1960.[4] The text of the *Gospel of Mary* which appears here is fragmentary. The whole text appears to have occupied pages 1–19 of the codex, but pages 1–6, 11–14 are now missing. We thus have pages 7–10, 15–19, that is, about half of the original text.[5]

The other two manuscripts comprise only scraps. However, both are in Greek (normally assumed to be the original language of the gospel) and both are (relatively) very early, namely, early third century. Rylands Papyrus 453 was published in 1938: it contains two sides of a small page with what appear to be the last two pages of the *Gospel of Mary*.[6] Oxyrhynchus Papyrus 3525, published in 1983, is a scrap of writing on one side of papyrus only. It contains part of pages 9–10 of the gospel.[7]

The existence of the Greek fragments has an important bearing on the possible date of composition of the gospel: the fact that both manuscripts are to be dated to the early third century, and that both are probably copied from earlier manuscripts (see below), indicates that the gospel must be dated before the end of the second century. The gospel is thus a relatively early text.

The two Greek fragments overlap completely with the BG text. This is useful in that it enables one to compare the (translated) BG version at some points with a version of the text in the (assumed) 'original' language. But it also means that the Greek fragments provide no more of the substantive text beyond what is contained in the BG text.

The texts do not agree at a number of points. Some of the differences are trivial, some not so trivial. Also some copying errors evident in both the Greek and Coptic versions imply that neither Greek version is the direct *Vorlage* of the BG text, which in turn probably had a Coptic manuscript from which it was

4. The *editio princeps* is W. C. Till, *Die gnostischen Schriften des koptischen Papyrus Berolinensis 8502* (Berlin: Akademie, 1960; second edition 1972). The codex contains three other works, two of which (the *Apocryphon of John* and the *Sophia of Jesus Christ*) are also among the texts of the Nag Hammadi library: hence the *Gospel of Mary* is often considered along with the Nag Hammadi texts, though its text is not actually found in the Nag Hammadi library itself.

5. This does assume that the text of the gospel occupied all the (now) missing pages of the codex. It is of course theoretically possible that the early pages of the codex included another complete, but short, text and the *Gospel of Mary* was rather shorter. There is no way of knowing for certain (unless the missing pages of the codex reappear!)

6. *Editio princeps* in C. H. Roberts, '463. The Gospel of Mary', *Catalogue of the Greek Papyri in the John Rylands Library* III (Manchester: University Press, 1938) 18–23.

7. *Editio princeps* in P. J. Parsons, '3525. Gospel of Mary', *The Oxyrhynchus Papyri* 50 (London: Egypt Exploration Society, 1983) 12–14. In referring to 'page numbers' of the gospel, the standard convention is to use the page (and line) numbers of the text in the BG version. Hence '9.12' refers to the text found on page 9, line 12, of the BG text of the gospel.

copied; and each of the Greek versions has probably been copied from earlier (Greek) manuscripts. Hence the text was copied quite often as well as being translated into at least one other language (Coptic, with in turn more than one copy being made of the text in that language). The text must then have circulated fairly widely and been popular in parts of the early church.

2. *Contents*

The contents of the text can be divided fairly neatly into four separate parts.

(1) 7.1–9.4. What is evidently the conclusion of a block of teaching given by Jesus (almost always referred to here as 'the Saviour') in response to questions by the disciples occurs in 7.1–8.9. The extant text only provides the conclusion of this, so the full contents are not known, but the teaching appears to focus on the nature of matter, its ultimate dissolution and hence its unimportance. This is then followed by a series of instructions (8.12–9.4) by Jesus sending the disciples out to preach the gospel they have heard from him.

(2) 9.5–10.10. The disciples are troubled and anxious about the teaching they have heard; but Mary appears on the scene to comfort them and encourage them. Peter then says that the Saviour loves Mary more than all other women (10.2–3) and asks her to tell them some of the things that she alone knows.

(3) 10.11–17.7. Mary gives an account of a vision which she has had where, she claims, she has 'seen the Lord' (10.10–13: probably an echo of the words of Mary Magdalene in Jn 20.18). Much of this is now lost (pp. 11–14 of the BG text) but it seems to be taken up with an account of the ascent of a soul (probably the Saviour's soul after his physical death): certainly when the extant text resumes on page 15, the account is in the middle of an extended account of this journey which then continues on until the end of this section on page 17. In this journey, the soul encounters a series of hostile powers who seek to question it and prevent it from passing; but the soul answers all their questions successfully and finally reaches its destiny of repose in 'silence' (17.7).

(4) 17.7–end. Mary's account of her vision provokes a negative response from some of the hearers: Andrew complains that what Mary has said cannot be from the Saviour as it differs from his thought (17.13–15); and Peter complains that the Saviour would never have revealed such things to a woman secretly (17.19). After a brief response by Mary, Levi appears on the scene to defend her: he calls Peter 'hot tempered' (18.6) and claims that the Saviour loved Mary more than all others (presumably men as well as women). He then effectively repeats some of the commands given earlier by the Saviour (about 'putting on the perfect humanity', and a requirement not to lay down any [?new] 'laws'). The final sentence of the

gospel is tantalizingly unclear with the two manuscripts extant at this point disagreeing: according to the Coptic text, 'they' (plural) then go out and preach the gospel (presumably Levi and the others are in mind); in the version in the Rylands fragment 'he' (singular) goes out to preach the gospel (presumably implying Levi alone and excluding Peter, Andrew and whoever else may have sided with them).

The evident division of the text into different sections, together with some differences and tensions between the separate parts, has led some to argue that the present text is composite and originally consisted of two separate texts which have been combined only secondarily. Thus Peter's apparently positive reaction to Mary earlier in the gospel is felt by some to contrast forcibly with his negative reaction at the end. Also the first section of the gospel, where Jesus himself teaches the disciples, seems separable from the account of Mary's vision where Mary is the narrator and the Saviour (or his soul) is the object of the discussion, not the teacher himself.

However, theories about the composite nature of the text may go beyond the available evidence. We have no firm manuscript evidence for the existence of prior versions of parts of the text existing separately. Further, any alleged tensions between different parts of the text may be exaggerated. For example, Peter's different reactions may be due to what some have called a 'plot development' and one should perhaps seek to take account of both reactions of Peter simultaneously. I will therefore assume here that the text as we have it (in the BG text at least) is a unity. Undoubtedly, the present text utilizes a number of earlier traditions, and some of these may have constituted pre-formed units at some stage in the earlier tradition. But perhaps we should take the text in its present (i.e. BG) form to try to seek to make sense of it as it stands before rushing too quickly to theories about earlier stages in the history of the text.

3. *Genre*

Determining the genre of the so-called *Gospel of Mary* is not straightforward. Clearly, at one level the text claims for itself the 'title' 'Gospel according to (*kata*) Mary': this is the wording of the colophon at the end of the text in the BG version (19.3–5). It would seem that the slightly unusual wording, with the word *kata* ('according to'), is claiming parity with the canonical gospels and their traditional titles as being 'the Gospel according to (*kata*) . . .'

Certainly too the *Gospel of Mary* appears to know the four canonical gospels.[8] Thus the commissioning charge of Jesus to the disciples at the end of

8. It is of course possible that the *Gospel of Mary* knows (only) the traditions contained in the canonical gospels, rather than the gospels themselves. However, I would argue that it knows these traditions as mediated through the finished gospels: for more detailed discussion, see my *Gospel of Mary*, 55–74.

the first part of the gospel (8.14–22) forms a pastiche of sayings (at times slightly altered) from the canonical gospels. Here Jesus says 'Peace be with you (cf. John 20.19, 21, 26). My peace receive for yourselves (cf. John 14.27). Beware that no one leads you astray (cf. Mark 13.5 and pars.), saying "See here" or "See there" (cf. Mark 13.21 and pars), for the Son of Man is within you (cf. Luke 17.21). Follow him (cf. Mark 8.34 and pars.). Those who seek him still find him (cf. Mt. 7.7 and par.). Go then and preach the gospel of the kingdom (cf. Matt 24.14 and pars.).' The similarity in the form of the title at the end of the gospel thus probably represents a conscious imitation of the titles of the (later to become) canonical gospels.

The problems surrounding the use of the Greek word *euaggelion* ('gospel') are well known, especially in its usage referring to a literary document, or book, rather than to the Christian proclamation. Nevertheless, it is clear that the word was used by Christians relatively early (at least by the early-mid second century) to refer to literary documents. In the case of the 'gospels' which later became canonical, these were accounts of the life and teaching of Jesus prior to his death with more or less extended accounts of his passion and death, as well as (relatively) brief accounts of his appearances to others after his death, with relatively little new teaching given here.

Although the *Gospel of Mary* claims the same title of 'gospel' for itself, it is clear that it is a rather different kind of document from the canonical gospels. The setting is almost certainly primarily a post-resurrection one so that, where Jesus speaks, it is as the Risen One. There is no account apparently of his passion, or indeed his pre-Easter ministry. Further, much of the teaching is given in the form of a dialogue with the disciples: they ask questions and Jesus develops his teaching by responding to these questions.

In all these respects, the *Gospel of Mary* displays close similarities with a number of other early Christian texts which take the form of the risen Jesus presenting further teaching to his disciples, often in the form of a dialogue between Jesus and his followers. These include other texts (many from Nag Hammadi) such as the *Apocryphon of John*, the *First Apocalypse of James*, the *Hypostasis of the Archons*, *Pistis Sophia*, the *Letter of Peter to Philip*, and so on. Many of these other texts are often referred to as 'Gnostic' texts, as indeed is the *Gospel of Mary* (see below). It seems to have been a characteristic feature of many so-called Gnostic texts to exploit the relative 'gap' left by the accounts in the canonical gospels and have the risen Jesus give considerably more teaching in a post-resurrection context. Thus Gnostic texts characteristically present Jesus in a post-resurrection scene (typically on a mountain, perhaps in dependence on Mt. 28.16) in dialogue with his disciples and presenting them with further teaching which by implication is for them alone and unavailable to the general public.

The name given to this type of writing has varied among different scholars: for example, the terms 'revelation dialogue', or 'dialogue gospel', have been suggested.[9] Whether such a 'gospel' is inherently 'Gnostic' is questionable; and, for example, a text such as the *Epistula Apostolorum* seems to have adopted this genre precisely in order to develop a *non*-Gnostic text. The issue of whether the *Gospel of Mary* is 'Gnostic' will be discussed shortly. Nevertheless, it is clear that the genre of the *Gospel of Mary* is different from that of the canonical gospels (despite claiming the same word 'gospel' to refer to itself) while showing clear generic affinities with these other texts from early Christianity.

We may though also note here that, as well as these similarities with other 'Gnostic' texts, the *Gospel of Mary* also shows some differences from these texts. Thus here Jesus' teaching in the form of a dialogue is followed by an extensive monologue from Mary herself, giving her account of the vision she has had. Also both Jesus' dialogue and Mary's vision account are both followed by sequels of some substance: Jesus' teaching is followed by the doubts of the disciples and Mary's efforts to comfort them; Mary's teaching is followed by the debate involving Peter, Andrew and Levi. It is not easy to find parallels to these features in the other so-called revelation discourses or dialogue gospels. To say that a text is *sui generis* is clearly a hazardous one in any discussion of the genre of a particular text. But equally one cannot deny that individual texts have their own individual and characteristic features, despite their generic similarities. Maybe then the most one can say is that the *Gospel of Mary* shows the closest generic similarities with 'revelation discourses' or 'dialogue gospels' from Nag Hammadi and elsewhere, even though it also displays some distinctive features of its own.

4. *Theological Perspectives and Background*

Two issues may be discussed here: first, whether the *Gospel of Mary* is a 'Gnostic' text, and second what is implied here about the leadership roles of Mary and/or other women.

The question of whether the *Gospel of Mary* is a 'Gnostic' text has been disputed in recent years. Earlier scholarship assumed without any question that the text was 'Gnostic' in some sense. More recently, however, there have been serious doubts raised about the category of 'Gnosticism' itself, and whether it is meaningful enough to enable anything to be described as 'Gnostic'.[10] In turn this has led at least one scholar to claim that the *Gospel of Mary* is not Gnostic.[11] Others too, while accepting that the term 'Gnostic' might have some

9. For the first, cf. P. Perkins, *The Gnostic Dialogue* (New York: Paulist Press, 1980); for the second, cf. H. Koester, *Ancient Christian Gospels* (London: SCM, 1990) 173–200; J. Hartenstein, *Die zweite Lehre* (Berlin: Akademie, 1998) 1–32.

10. See, for example, M. A. Williams, *Rethinking 'Gnosticism'. An Argument for Dismantling a Dubious Category* (Princeton: Princeton University Press, 1996); K. L. King, *What Is Gnosticism?* (Cambridge, MA and London: Harvard University Press, 2003).

11. See King, *Gospel of Mary*, 155–156.

meaning, nevertheless claim that the *Gospel of Mary* does not fit into this category. Thus Esther de Boer argues that the text is to be interpreted primarily in terms of a Stoic background of thought;[12] and Antti Marjanen claims that, if one defines 'Gnostic' clearly as a system of thought that includes the idea of an evil or ignorant Demiurge, who is not identical with the supreme God, then the *Gospel of Mary* does not contain such an idea explicitly and hence is not to be regarded as 'Gnostic'.[13]

Much then depends on how one defines 'Gnostic' or 'Gnosticism'. While some would insist on a very tight definition, demanding a clear unambiguous reference to an evil/ignorant creator figure (cf. above), others would be willing to accept a broader definition. Thus, for example, Markschies argues that 'Gnosticism' includes an idea of an evil or ignorant Creator god, but also has associated ideas of the soul as imprisoned in the world, seeking to escape on the basis of knowledge, together with ideas of the enlightened soul containing within itself a spark of the divine.[14] Further, we must remember that the portion of the text of the *Gospel of Mary* which we possess is fragmentary: hence it is potentially somewhat dangerous to base claims on what the text does *not* say when there is probably 50 per cent of the text missing from the parts we have.

Bearing all these factors in mind, it seems hard to deny that the *Gospel of Mary* is 'Gnostic' in at least some sense (*if* one allows that the term has some meaningful significance at all). It is true that there is no explicit reference, at least in the extant parts of the text, to an evil/ignorant Demiurge figure. On the other hand, there are some hints and allusions which suggest that one is in the same thought world. For example, the names of the powers which the soul encounters in its ascent in the account of Mary's vision can be shown to be closely linked to the names of some of the powers linked with the Demiurge figure Ialdabaoth in the *Apocryphon of John* and elsewhere.[15] Further, the teaching of the Saviour that 'the Son of Man is within you' (8.18–19), which is probably also echoed in Levi's exhortation to 'put on the perfect humanity' (18.16),[16] almost certainly reflects ideas of a spark of the divine dwelling in each human being, and in turn this may be part of the broader aspects of 'Gnosticism' as highlighted above. So too the basic soteriological model here is evidently one of shedding the body and bidding farewell to the earthly life and the shackles it represents in order to ascend to the spiritual sphere above.

12. De Boer, *Gospel of Mary*.

13. A. Marjanen, 'The Mother of Jesus or the Magdalene? The Identity of Mary in the So-Called Gnostic Christian Texts', in F. Stanley Jones (ed.), *Which Mary? The Marys of Early Christian Tradition* (Atlanta: SBL, 2002) 31–42, on 32 (changing his mind from his earlier study of the gospel).

14. See C. Markschies, *Gnosis: An Introduction* (London: T&T Clark, 2003), esp. 16–17.

15. See Till, *BG 8502*, 45. More detailed discussion in my forthcoming study in my *Gospel of Mary*, 175–180.

16. The wording here seems to echo clearly the language of parts of the Pauline corpus (cf. Eph. 4.13, 24; Col. 1.28), suggesting that the author of the *Gospel of Mary* knows the Pauline letters as well as the canonical gospels.

Again, this is all of a piece with 'Gnostic' soteriology and part of the broader framework of thought within which the myths about the evil/ignorant Demiurge figure are at home.

It thus seems highly likely that the *Gospel of Mary* is to be located within the broader spectrum of thought and/or texts usually described as 'Gnostic'.

The second main area of interest which the text has aroused concerns the role played by Mary, and the implications which this might have for ideas about the role of women, and/or women's leadership in the early church. In particular, attention has often been focused on the final section of the text, where Peter and Mary appear to be engaged in some kind of dispute or argument; and within this section, Peter's apparently dismissive comment that Mary is not to be believed, and that the Saviour 'did not speak *with a woman* without our knowing, and not openly, did he?' (17.18–20) is often taken as highly prejudicial against women as women. This is sometimes taken as reflecting a possible power struggle in the early church, perhaps between Peter and Mary themselves (cf. Brock), perhaps with Peter and Mary as the representatives of men and women as potential leaders. Conversely, the negative portrayal of Peter here is seen as a reflection of a negative view of men more generally and the power or authority they seek to wield as men (cf. Schaberg); perhaps too the figure of Mary is presented as the ideal figure who, as such, represents the archetypal character of the true preacher of the gospel (cf. King).

It may be however that some of these interpretations are in danger of overplaying the evidence. First, we should recall that this final section is only one, relatively small, part of a longer whole: and the rest of the gospel gives little indication of an intense rivalry between Mary and Peter. It is true that earlier in the gospel, Mary appears on the scene to comfort the male disciples, but there is no hint there of any rivalry. Thus to make one small part of Peter's complaint against Mary into the key for the interpretation of the whole of the text of the gospel may be in danger of exaggerating its importance.

Second, we should note that this final section involves four characters: in addition to Mary and Peter, there is also Andrew and Levi. On the side of Peter, Andrew too voices doubts about Mary. But here there is no hint that Mary's gender is an issue: he simply says that he cannot believe what Mary has said because it is different from the teaching known from elsewhere (18.15). The issue is then the content of Mary's teaching, not the gender of Mary herself. On the side of Mary, we should also note that most of her defence, and the counter to Peter, is voiced by the figure of Levi, not by Mary. If there is any 'leading role' to be played, such a role seems to be taken by the male Levi rather than the female Mary.[17] Further, it is Levi rather than Mary who here is made to repeat the Saviour's earlier teaching about the 'new man'/'Son of Man' and about laying down new laws.

By contrast Mary plays a somewhat passive role in this final scene. She is not completely silent (in 18.1–6 she makes an initial response to Peter); and indeed her immediate response to Peter's outburst is to 'weep' (18.1), thus showing the same reaction as the (male) disciples did earlier to Jesus' own teaching (9.6) and where such action is usually taken to be regarded negatively by the writer. Mary is thus not necessarily presented in the text as an ideal figure, or even as the prototype of a leader figure in any community (whether in her own right as an individual or as the representative of other women). Rather, her prime role appears to be as the recipient, and the mediator, of the teaching itself as she hands on her experience of the vision she has received.

Further, just as important as any gender issue in the debate between Peter and Mary is the fact that Mary's teaching seems to be something that is *new* for 'Peter'. It is this that is the focus of Andrew's complaint: what Mary has said is unlike anything else he has heard before. For Peter too, what is implied in his complaint is that Mary's teaching has been given to her in secret, rather than to all the others as well: hence by implication it is something he did not know about before. This element is certainly present in Peter's words, and may be just as, if not more, important than the fact that the revelation has been given to a woman rather than to a man. Nor is it (just) about who is/are the authorized preacher(s) of the gospel: it is quite as much about which gospel message is to be preached and what content should be put into this message.

Rather than any gender issue, what may be much more significant here is the issue of whether teaching from Jesus is given secretly, to a few only, or has been given openly to all, and what the content of that teaching is. What is at stake is therefore different perceptions of the *content* of the 'gospel' and how it has been received. All this correlates closely with what we know from elsewhere about debates between 'orthodox' and 'Gnostic' Christians. We know that some Gnostic groups claimed to have received *secret* revelations in (ongoing) visions, and one of the main complaints by the 'orthodox' against them was to challenge this, insisting on the *public* nature of the teaching of Jesus which was given to all.[18]

Insofar as 'Peter' and 'Mary' stand for other groups, they probably represent 'orthodox' and 'Gnostic' Christians; and what is at stake is the *content* of what is being taught and also claims about the *manner* in which this teaching has been received.[19]

17. There is also the textual variant at the end, noted earlier, concerning who goes out to preach at the end of the narrative: Levi alone or a wider group. Even if it is the latter, such a group would include Peter but would not necessarily include Mary who was not in fact present at the earlier commissioning scene when Jesus sends the (male) disciples out. Either way, it would seem, Mary does not go out to preach at all. Thus Mary does not occupy a particularly privileged position as a/the preacher of the gospel. If anyone does, it is Levi.

18. See E. Pagels, 'Visions, Appearance, and Apostolic Authority: Gnostic and Orthodox Traditions', in B. Aland (ed.), *Gnosis. Festschrift für Hans Jonas* (Göttingen: Vandenhoek & Ruprecht, 1978) 415–430.

19. Cf. Marjanen, *The Woman Jesus Loved*, 121; Hartenstein, *Die zweite Lehre*, 135; E. Pagels, *The Gnostic Gospels* (London: Penguin, 1990) 43–44.

It may however be interesting to note that this debate seems to be at a relatively early stage of any developing 'conflict'. The debate (or 'dispute') is in some respects remarkably unpolemical and unhostile. Any 'polemic' is relatively mild.[20] It is true that Peter is called by Levi 'hot tempered' (18.8), but this may be as much as way of excusing Peter as it is of blaming him: his reaction here is implied as not being in line with what he would do and say if he were less excited. Mary in fact calls Peter her 'brother' when responding to his complaints (18.2). And any difference of opinion between the protagonists here is conducted on the basis of a range of common assumptions they share (about the status of Jesus etc.). There are allusions elsewhere in the text to threats from outside the community (cf. 9.10–12: the disciples are fearful that, like Jesus, they will not be 'spared': clearly there is a threat of some kind of external persecution). Among the protagonists in the story here, there is at most a certain disagreement and debate. But the very existence of a debate may suggest that any competing groups are still in dialogue with each other. Strict boundary lines may not yet have been drawn and any 'us v. them' mentality seems to be at a fairly early stage of development. All this may then suggest a relatively early date of the gospel, perhaps one in the earlier part of the second century rather than the latter part.[21]

5. *Conclusion*

The *Gospel of Mary* almost certainly gives us little information about the historical Jesus or the historical Mary. It is not a first-century text. It may however be a relatively early second-century production. The existence of the Greek fragments from the early third century mean that the gospel must have been written by the end of the second century, and the nature of the debates it reflects may indicate a date earlier rather than later in that century. As such it is a fascinating document, giving us a rare glimpse into that period of early Christian history which is shrouded in so much darkness and uncertainty.

Bibliography

A. G. Brock, *Mary Magdalene, the First Apostle: The Struggle for Authority* (Cambridge, MA: Harvard University Press, 2003).

E. A. De Boer, *The Gospel of Mary: Beyond a Gnostic and a Biblical Mary Magdalene*, JSNTSS 260 (London and New York: T&T Clark International, 2004) 1–100.

20. Cf. Hartenstein, *Die zweite Lehre*, 133–134, 150.

21. Although one should be wary of assuming too uniform a development across all Christian groups, the situation here does seem to be less hostile than that reflected in, say, the writings of Irenaeus c. 180 CE when there seem to be much sharper dividing lines between the 'orthodox' and 'Gnostics'.

J. Hartenstein, *Die zweite Lehre: Erscheinungen des Auferstandenen als Rahmenerzählung frühchristlicher Dialoge*, TU 146 (Berlin: Akademie, 1998) 127–160.

Karen L. King, *The Gospel of Mary of Magdala: Jesus and the First Woman Apostle* (Santa Rosa: Polebridge Press, 2003).

A. Marjanen, *The Woman Jesus Loved: Mary Magdalene in the Nag Hammadi and Related Documents*, NHMS 40 (Leiden: Brill, 1996) 94–121.

A. Pasquier, *L'Évangile selon Marie*, Bibliothèque copte de Nag Hammadi. Section 'Textes' 10 (Québec: Les Presses de l'Université Laval, 1983).

J. Schaberg, *The Resurrection of Mary Magdalene: Legends, Apocrypha and the Christian Testament* (London and New York: Continuum, 2002) 168–185.

W. C. Till, *Die gnostischen Schriften des koptischen Papyrus Berolinensis 8502*, TU 60 (Berlin: Akademie, 1960; second edition 1972) 24–32, 64–79.

C. M. Tuckett, *The Gospel of Mary* (Oxford: Oxford University Press, 2007).

R. McL. Wilson and G. W. MacRae, 'The Gospel according to Mary BG, I: 7, 1–19, 5', in D. M. Parrott (ed.), *Nag Hammadi Codices V, 2–5 and VI with Papyrus Berolinensis 8502, 1 and 4*, NHS 11 (Leiden: Brill, 1979) 453–471.

Chapter 5

JEWISH-CHRISTIAN GOSPELS

Andrew Gregory

This chapter offers a brief introduction to the quotations in certain Church Fathers that are usually identified as Jewish-Christian gospel tradition, and discusses the number of gospels to which they should be attributed. Next, it addresses the question of how these texts might be witnesses to Jesus, and the relationship of their content to that of the canonical gospels. It also includes a discussion of a selection of these extracts, and offers some comments on what may be concluded about the two or three gospels from which they might come.

1. *Introductory Questions*

1.1 *What Do We Mean by 'Jewish-Christian Gospels'?*

Modern scholars use the term 'Jewish-Christian gospels' to refer to a number of texts that may be partially reconstructed on the basis of what appear to be citations from, or references to, particular gospel traditions in the writings of certain Church Fathers. There is no independent manuscript tradition for any of these texts, so they are available to us only as they are preserved by these other writers. This means that it is important to try to establish why these Church Fathers drew on these texts in order to find some sort of context in which their citations or references may be placed. It also means that we must be very cautious about moving from an analysis of individual fragments to any attempt to offer an analysis of the texts from which those fragments appear to have come.

Broadly speaking, these excerpts contain material that is concerned with things that Jesus did or said. Thus (assuming that these fragments may be considered representative of the texts from which they are excerpted) there is no compelling reason why these writings should not be considered generically similar to the canonical gospels. Therefore both in content and in form these texts are closer to the canonical gospels than they are to some other non-canonical texts that refer to themselves, or have been referred to by others, as gospels.

Perhaps less straightforward than their description as gospels is their description as Jewish-Christian. Many recent studies of Jewish-Christianity agree that the term is best used for those early communities who both acknowledged Jesus as a Messianic figure and also obeyed the Law of Moses, thus living in a manner similar in most respects to that of Law-observant Jews who did not acknowledge Jesus as a Messianic figure.[1] Various texts have been attributed to such Jewish-Christian groups, including those identified as Nazoraeans and as Ebionites, but it is unclear to what extent this definition of Jewish-Christianity is helpful when it comes to interpreting Jewish-Christian gospel tradition. These excerpts may well come from texts that presuppose a Jewish-Christian outlook, but it is difficult to show from the surviving excerpts that this was the case. Further, the fact that modern scholars (unlike the Fathers) attribute the excerpts to at least two distinct gospels, and are sceptical of much of the ancient testimony about them, raises questions as to why these two or three postulated gospels are still associated so closely with one another.

1.2 *What Might They Tell Us about Jesus?*

Two reasons may be noted why these texts might be considered potential sources of information about Jesus that is independent of, or earlier than, the canonical gospels. The first is that some of our ancient sources suggest that Jewish-Christian gospel tradition may derive from an original Hebrew gospel of which the canonical Greek text of Matthew is a later translation. However, the reasons for believing that Matthew was composed in Greek are so compelling that the quest for a Hebrew original is best regarded as a dead end, no matter how romantic its pursuit might seem.[2]

The second reason is the supposition that gospels described as Jewish-Christian might be thought likely to have been transmitted in an unbroken chain of transmission that may be traced back to the earliest Jewish followers of Jesus. If so, they could provide access to a Palestinian Jesus undistorted by non-Palestinian influences. However, this hypothesis is also difficult to sustain. Certainly the earliest followers of Jesus were Law-observant Jews, but it is by no means clear how much continuity may be traced between the early Jerusalem church and later Jewish-Christian circles. The church historian Eusebius, writing in the fourth century, claims that Jerusalem-based followers of Jesus fled Jerusalem before it was destroyed and then regrouped in Pella (*Ecclesiastical History* 3.5.3). This would support arguments for continuity, but Eusebius' evidence is problematic and contested. If the Roman destruction of Jerusalem and its Temple in 70 CE lead to as great a rupture between pre- and post-70 Jewish-Christianity as it did between pre- and post-70 Judaism, there would be

1. For further discussion and bibliography on this point, see A. Gregory, 'Hindrance or Help? The Category "Jewish-Christian Gospels"', *JSNT* 28.4 (2006) 387–413, see 390.

2. On the likely medieval origin and patristic antecedents of a later Hebrew version of Matthew, see W. Horbury, 'The Hebrew Text of Matthew in Shem Tob Ibn Shaprut's Eben Bohan', in W. D. Davies and D. C. Allison, *A Critical and Exegetical Commentary on the Gospel according to Saint Matthew*, Volume III (Edinburgh: T&T Clark, 1997) 729–738.

no reason to suppose that later Jewish-Christians are any more likely to have had privileged access to early traditions about Jesus than did any other part of the early Christian movement. This does not mean that Jewish-Christian gospels may not contain early traditions independent of the canonical gospels, but it does mean that there is no *a priori* reason to suppose that they did. Therefore, the question of their value as historical sources depends on considerations such as their date rather than the theological outlook of those by whom they were used or with whom they were particularly associated.

Further, the question of the historical value and theological outlook of these excerpts can be answered only by reference to individual gospels rather than to Jewish-Christian gospel tradition as a whole. This means turning next to the most complex problem in the study of this material: from how many gospels do these excerpts come?

1.3 *How Many Jewish-Christian Gospels Were There?*

Modern scholars agree that either two or three gospels associated with Jewish Christians may be identified as the sources of a number of fragments preserved in the writings of some Church Fathers. These texts are usually referred to as the *Gospel according to the Hebrews* (or, sometimes, the *Gospel of the Hebrews*), the *Gospel of the Ebionites* and the *Gospel of the Nazoraeans*. Only the first of these titles appears in our ancient sources; the other titles are convenient ways in which to refer to material that ancient sources identified with particular Jewish-Christian groups. A clear majority of primarily German and English speaking scholarship supports the hypothesis that three such gospels should be postulated, but others argue that we should postulate only two such texts – the *Gospel according to the Hebrews* (which, on this hypothesis, includes excerpts otherwise assigned to the *Gospel of the Nazoraeans*) and the *Gospel of the Ebionites*. Therefore it seems premature to speak of any consensus as to whether two or three gospels should be postulated,[3] although there is agreement that there was more than one. Simon Claude Mimouni may speak on behalf of a minority opinion when he advocates the hypothesis of two rather than three gospels, but he is correct when he observes that no unanimity has been reached as to which of these competing hypotheses is correct.[4]

This modern belief that there were at least two different Jewish-Christian gospels is in contrast to the patristic understanding, for the Fathers appear to have assumed that only one such gospel existed, albeit perhaps in different forms. This remained the traditional understanding until the nineteenth century,

3. Here I differ from A. F. J. Klijn, *Jewish-Christian Gospel Tradition* (VCSupp XVII; Leiden: Brill, 1992) 41, where he writes that 'The presence of three Jewish Christian Gospels is an established fact.'

4. S. -C. Mimouni, *Le judéo-christianisme ancien: essays historiques* (Patrimoines; Paris: Éditions du Cerf, 1998) 209.

sometimes with the qualification that the diverse nature of the fragments indicated that the gospel took very different shapes in different times and places.[5] This understanding is not unproblematic, but is by no means ridiculous, for it is possible to collect together most of the excerpts that the Fathers preserved and to read them as if they might all originate from one source.[6] If we do this, the major difficulty centres on those excerpts that deal with Jesus' baptism. There are three in total, which has led some scholars to suggest that there must therefore have been three gospels.[7] Yet of these three excerpts, only two offer a narrative of the baptism. The third is a conversation that refers to the baptism, but does not describe how it took place. Thus it could stand in the same text as either of the narrative accounts. If so, these three perspectives on Jesus' baptism need require not three gospels but two.

The earliest witness to the existence of a Jewish-Christian gospel is Irenaeus, who was Bishop of Lyons in the late second century. He writes of Ebionites using a gospel, which he identifies as a version of Matthew (*Against the Heresies* 1.26.2; 3.11.7), but suggests elsewhere that they deny the virginal conception of Jesus (*Against the Heresies*, 3.21.3; 5.1.3). Therefore, if Irenaeus tells us anything about the content of this gospel, it may be only that it differs from canonical Matthew in respect of the birth of Jesus.

Our earliest direct evidence for a Jewish-Christian gospel comes from Clement of Alexandria, who lived in the latter part of the second century and the beginning of the third. Clement quotes one saying that he explicitly attributes to the *Gospel according to the Hebrews*, as well as a similar but unattributed saying that is closely paralleled in the *Gospel of Thomas*. Thus he may refer to one or two sayings in the *Gospel according to the Hebrews*, which may overlap with the *Gospel of Thomas*. Clement is the first of three Alexandrian scholars who quote from or refer to this text. The others are Origen (c. 185–c. 251) and Didymus the Blind (313–398). Thus it appears that the *Gospel according to the Hebrews* was known in Alexandria by the end of the second century and that it continued in use there until at least the middle of the fourth century.

There is also some evidence for knowledge of this text outside Alexandria. Jerome (c. 347–c. 419/20), who studied under Didymus and relied heavily on the writings of Origen, appears to have known the text, at least in part. It is possible that he obtained a copy when he was in Alexandria. Eusebius, writing

5. For bibliography and brief discussion, see P. Luomanen, 'Where Did Another Rich Man Come from? The Jewish-Christian Profile of the Story about a Rich Man in the "Gospel of the Hebrews" (Origen, *Comm. Matt.* 15.14) *VC* 57 (2003) 243–275, on 245 n.10.

6. See E. B. Nicholson, *The Gospel according to the Hebrews* (London: C. Kegan Paul & Co, 1879); reprinted by Kessinger Publishing (Whitefish, MT), 2007 for a presentation of these fragments as excerpts from one gospel. Nor is this view altogether without support in contemporary scholarship. See W. L. Petersen, *Tatian's Diatessaron: Its Creation, Dissemination, Significance, & History in Scholarship* (VCSupp XXV; Leiden: Brill, 1994) 29–31, 39–41.

7. For example, H. -J. Klauck, *Apocryphal Gospels: An Introduction* (trans. Brian McNeil; London: T&T Clark International, 2003) 37.

in the fourth century, places the *Gospel according to the Hebrews* among the books whose status as Scripture was disputed, not among those considered heretical (*Ecclesiastical History* 3.25.3), but it is difficult to know if he had seen the text for himself. He also suggests that it was known to Papias (*Ecclesiastical History* 3.39.17) and Hegesippus (*Ecclesiastical History* 4.22.8), each of whom was active in Asia Minor in the second century.

There is widespread agreement that the evidence from Clement, Origen and Didymus provides the core material for our knowledge of this gospel, but there is continuing debate about how Eusebius' testimony should be related to that of the Alexandrian witnesses. This is one of the major problems in seeking to determine how much evidence survives of the text of this gospel. The other is the question of what we are to make of the testimony of Jerome. Does all the Jewish-Christian gospel tradition on which he draws come from the *Gospel according to the Hebrews*, or did Jerome have access also to a second gospel, the *Gospel of the Nazoraeans*?

Jerome's testimony, which is drawn from writings spanning a period of more than 20 years, is both complex and confusing. If taken at face value, it seems to suggest that he knew only one Jewish-Christian gospel (to which he refers as the *Gospel according to the Hebrews*), although perhaps in more than one version. Yet Jerome makes many statements that make it difficult to take him at his word, so a significant number of scholars have argued that some of the gospel tradition that he introduces should be attributed to a source other than the *Gospel according to the Hebrews*. This decision depends variously on an assessment of Jerome, and on the belief that the gospel tradition to which he first introduces us is of another character altogether from that found in our Alexandrian witnesses to this gospel and is therefore likely to be from another text. Jerome's own evidence may certainly be read either way, but the latter argument is much less secure than the former. By no means is it clear why the synoptic-like material often assigned to the *Gospel of the Nazoraeans* could not have been contained in the same text as the admittedly quite different material found in the core Alexandrian witnesses to the *Gospel according to the Hebrews*. As Petri Luomanen has argued, the fact that the *Gospel of Thomas* contains some material that is like the synoptic tradition as well as other material that is quite different demonstrates that a gospel can include different types of content.[8] Thus the question of whether or not there was ever a *Gospel of the Nazoraeans* should be considered as remaining very much open.

Given the complexities of the evidence for the *Gospel according to the Hebrews*, and for a possible *Gospel of the Nazoraeans*, the relative simplicity of Epiphanius' late fourth-century direct testimony to the *Gospel of the Ebionites*

8. P. Luomanen, 'Let Him Who Seeks, Continue Seeking': The Relationship between the Jewish-Christian Gospels and the Gospel of Thomas', in J. Ma. Asgeirsson, A. D. DeConick and R. Uro (eds), *Thomasine Traditions in Antiquity: The Social and Cultural World of the Gospel of Thomas* (NHMS 59; Leiden: Brill, 2006) 119–153, esp. 124–125.

comes as something of a relief. Epiphanius himself tries to associate the text from which he quotes as a version of a text used also by the Nazoraeans, but modern scholars agreed that his quotations come from a text quite unconnected with the excerpts which Jerome associates with that group. We do not know what relationship, if any, there is between this text and the text that Irenaeus had associated with the Ebionites two centuries before.

Therefore what emerges from this discussion of the number of Jewish-Christian gospels is as follows. Two at least may be identified. One is the *Gospel of the Ebionites*, preserved only by Epiphanius, but perhaps known to Irenaeus. The other is the *Gospel according to the Hebrews*. Further Jewish-Christian gospel tradition may also be noted, but there is continuing debate whether it comes from a third text, a *Gospel of the Nazoraeans*, or should be explained in another way, not necessarily as part of the *Gospel according to the Hebrews*. As Hans-Josef Klauck observes, it is better to 'assume the existence of a broader stream of transmission, with oral traditions and a larger number of literary sources than merely two or three texts (or than a variety of redactions of those two or three texts)'.[9] I fully agree, but for the sake of convenience I shall arrange the rest of this chapter in such a way that takes account of the attribution of Jewish-Christian gospel tradition to three different gospels.

2. *The Gospel According to the Hebrews*

Since our earliest direct evidence for a Jewish-Christian gospel is for the *Gospel according to the Hebrews*, and since this is the only title for a Jewish-Christian gospel that is used in our ancient sources, it makes sense to start with it. We have very little direct evidence for its text, so it is possible to provide in full the excerpts that we find in Clement and in Origen.

Clement's one attributed citation is brief: 'He who marvels shall be king and he who is king shall rest' (*Stromata* 2.45.5). This may be compared to another saying that he cites without giving its source, and which has a partial parallel in the *Gospel according to Thomas*: 'He who seeks will not stop until he finds; having found he will marvel, and having marvelled he will be king, and having been king he will rest' (*Stromata* 5.96.3). Readers familiar with the synoptic tradition may find echoes of it in this saying (e.g. Mt. 7.7//Lk. 11.9 and Mt. 11.28). This language of seeking, finding and resting suggests affinities with Jewish Wisdom literature, but the part of the saying to which Clement draws attention is its reference to wonder. Clement has just quoted from Plato's *Theaetetus* and from the *Traditions of Matthias* (which survives only in quotations in Clement) to support his point that wonder is the first step towards attaining the knowledge that comes from beyond, so it is to further establish this point that Clement introduces this excerpt.

9. Klauck, *Apocryphal Gospels*, 37.

Origen's quotation (which appears in two slightly different forms, one with and one without the reference to hair) is as follows: 'Just now my mother, the Holy Spirit, took me by one of my hairs and carried me off onto the great mountain, the Thabor, etc' (*Commentary on John* 2.12; cf. *Homilies on Jeremiah* 15.4). This same saying is also quoted three times by Jerome, but we do not know if he had access to it other than through its use in Origen. The saying is striking. Its depiction of the Holy Spirit as Jesus' mother is usually taken to reflect a Semitic influence, for it is only in Semitic languages (rather than in Greek or Latin) that the word for spirit is feminine. This may also fit with the way in which Divine Wisdom is personified both as a woman and as a mother (e.g. Prov. 8.32, Sir. 4.11, Lk. 7.35). The idea of a prophet being lifted by his hair and transported is found in Jewish Scripture (Ezek. 8.6 and Dan. 14.36) and there is an interesting Diatessaronic reading of Lk. 4.29–30 in which Jesus is hurled off the cliff but is miraculously unhurt, perhaps because he flew to safety.[10] Early Christian tradition associates Mount Thabor both with Jesus' temptation and with his transfiguration, so this excerpt might refer to either event. If so, it could fit easily alongside the sort of material that we find in the synoptic tradition and in the fourth canonical gospel.[11]

The final Alexandrian reference to the *Gospel according to the Hebrews* is found in Didymus' *Commentary on the Psalms*. There he notes that it may be seen in the *Gospel according to the Hebrews* that Matthias, who replaced Judas, is the same person as the Levi mentioned in the gospels. This reference is good direct evidence in favour of the view that this gospel could well have contained material that was similar to that found in the synoptic tradition, and that therefore it may have contained other such material found in Jerome that has been assigned to the *Gospel of the Nazoraeans*.

3. *The* Gospel of the Nazoraeans

The gospel tradition that is sometimes attributed to the *Gospel of the Nazoraeans* may be dealt with more briefly. Epiphanius refers to a gospel that the Nazoraeans used, as does Jerome. But most of our direct evidence for its content comes from excerpts found in Jerome, many of them in his *Commentary on Matthew*. Jerome appears to cite a number of passages of Jewish-Christian gospel tradition that are not known from other witnesses to the *Gospel according to the Hebrews*, and he tells us that he translated them himself from Hebrew or Aramaic into Greek. Questions may be asked about this claim, for among those excerpts that Jerome claims to have translated or some that earlier

10. See Tj. Baarda, '"The Flying Jesus", Luke 4:29–30 in the Syriac Diatessaron', *VC* 40 (1986) 313–341.

11. Another text that may be attributed to this gospel, the story of another rich man, is found in the Latin translation of Origen's *Commentary on Matthew*, but not in the Greek original.

witnesses already preserved in Greek. Jerome is notoriously unreliable in some of the claims that he makes, but scholars who believe that Jerome had access to two gospels tend to divide his excerpts between the *Gospel according to the Hebrews* and this other Semitic source to which he refers.

Excerpts that have been attributed to a postulated *Gospel of the Nazoraeans* include the story of a mason with a withered hand who appeals to Jesus for help (*Commentary on Matthew* 12.13), and a reference to the temple lintel being broken and smashed apart (*Commentary on Matthew* 27.51). Like other excerpts attributed to this gospel, each of these would fit easily in a synoptic-like account. However, not only is this an insufficient reason to differentiate theses excerpts from some of the material attributed to the *Gospel according to the Hebrews*, it can also be used in support of the hypothesis that Jerome's Hebrew or Aramaic gospel is better understood as a translation from the Greek Gospel according to Matthew rather than as a different gospel. If so, it is quite possible that this tradition would show signs of the influence of other synoptic gospels. It could also be the basis of the marginal readings which certain manuscripts of Matthew ascribe to the *Ioudaikon*, which may be translated 'Jewish [gospel]' and is often referred to as the 'Zion Gospel edition' on the basis that it may once have been kept in the basilica on Mount Zion.

4. *The* Gospel of the Ebionites

The sole witness to the text to which modern scholars refer as the *Gospel of the Ebionites* is Epiphanius, who is best known for his attempts to refute heresy and to maintain Nicene orthodoxy. These concerns may be seen in his lengthy work the *Panarion* or 'medicine chest' in which he set out to describe and to attack the work of those whom he branded heretics. It is in Chapter 30 of this book, his account of the Ebionites, that Epiphanius quotes from a gospel that he said was used by this group. He associates Ebion, the putative founder of the Ebionites, with the Nazoreans, but also notes differences between each group. His account appears confusing and confused, not least in what he says about the gospel text used by the Ebionites, to which he refers variously as the Gospel according to Matthew and the *Gospel according to the Hebrews*. He notes the association of this text with a putative original written in Hebrew by Matthew, but also appears to question that this was the case. So confusing are the ways in which he refers to this text that it seems better to base any conclusions about it entirely on what may be gleaned from the evidence of the excerpts themselves. Two things seem clear. Not only are the excerpts written in Greek, but they appear to contain material that depends on at least Matthew and Luke.[12] This use of the synoptic gospels, together with the presence in one excerpt of a

12. See D. A. Bertrand, 'L'Évangile des Ébionites: une harmonie évangélique antérieure au Diatessaron', *NTS* 26 (1980) 548–563; A. Gregory, 'Prior or Posterior? The *Gospel of the Ebionites* and the Gospel of Luke', *NTS* 51.3 (2005) 344–360.

pun that works only in Greek, strongly suggests that Greek was the language in which this text was composed. There is no reason to believe that Epiphanius (or anyone else) had translated these excerpts from Hebrew or Aramaic. Further, the presence of material that comes from Luke strongly suggests that this gospel may be better thought of as a gospel harmony rather than as a version of Matthew.

The use that this gospel makes of both Matthew and Luke means that it can be dated no earlier than a time when these two works were in circulation. This means that it could hardly have been written much before the end of the first century, and probably sometime later than that. It must also have been written before the late fourth century, when Epiphanius composed his *Panarion*, but the internal evidence of the text gives little help in establishing more precise dates within this range. If it is to be identified with the Gospel according to Matthew that Irenaeus said that Ebionites used, this would place its date of composition before the final quarter of the second century. That would certainly be late enough to draw on Matthew and Luke in the way that its author appears to have done, and would place the composition of this text around the time of the composition of other gospel harmonies such as the *Diatessaron*. However, the *Diatessaron* draws on John as well as the synoptic gospels, so it has been suggested that the *Gospel of the Ebionites* should be dated around 150 on the grounds that its author could not have failed to use John had he been writing any later than this.[13] However, this seems to me little more than an argument from silence, and it is particularly problematic because it is applied to a text that survives only in part. So little of the text is extant that it seems unsafe to assume either that its author did not draw on the fourth gospel, or that he could not have had a good reason for choosing not to do so.

Epiphanius preserves a total of seven different excerpts from the *Gospel of the Ebionites*, one of which he cites in a longer and shorter form. Since there is little debate about what may be ascribed to this text, its surviving excerpts may be listed as follows. I have arranged them in what appears to be a reasonable narrative order, assuming that the outline of the text is broadly similar to that of the synoptic gospels:

• the ministry and lineage of John	*Panarion* 30.13.6; 30.14.3
• the ministry and diet of John	*Panarion* 30.13.4–5
• John's baptism of Jesus	*Panarion* 30.13.7–8
• Jesus' call of the Twelve	*Panarion* 30.13.2–3
• a saying of Jesus about his family	*Panarion* 30.14.5
• a saying of Jesus about the abolition of sacrifices	*Panarion* 30.16.5
• a saying of Jesus about the Passover	*Panarion* 30.22.4–5

13. Klijn, *Jewish-Christian Gospel Tradition*, 29; more cautiously, Bertrand, 'L'Évangile des Ébionites', 551.

The fact that Epiphanius twice cites an account of the ministry and lineage of John, but in different forms, is an important reminder of the difficulties involved in determining the text of this gospel. Epiphanius quotes from this gospel in order to support his polemic against those whom he perceives as heretics, not in order to provide the clear and reliable windows on the different parts of the early Christian movement and their gospel traditions that modern readers might wish to have. The form of the two excerpts, and the ways in which they are introduced (in italics), is as follows:

> *The beginning of their gospel states that,* It happened in the days of Herod king of Judea that there came John baptising a baptism of repentance in the Jordan river, who is said to be of the family of Aaron the priest, son of Zachariah and Elisabeth, and all went out to him. (*Pan.* 30.13.6)

> *For, having removed the genealogies according to Matthew, they begin its opening, as I have said before, with the words* It happened, *they say*, in the days of Herod king of Judea when Caiaphas was high priest, there came a man named John baptising a baptism of repentance in the Jordan river, *and so on*. (*Pan.* 30.14.3)

At no point do the two forms of this excerpt actually contradict each other, and it is quite possible that Epiphanius has chosen to include different details in each instance out of the rhetorical desire to provide variety rather than repetition in his own narrative. It may also be the case that he is quoting from memory. Either way, these variations remind us that Epiphanius did not quote his sources in the same way that modern readers expect of modern authors.

Also of interest in this passage is Epiphanius' statement that it was the beginning of their gospel, and that the Ebionites had removed the genealogies found in Matthew. It seems unlikely that there would have been any internal evidence of such excision in any individual manuscript of the *Gospel of the Ebionites*, so presumably this is an inference that Epiphanius draws. He appears to assume that this gospel is a corruption of Matthew (*Pan.* 30.13.2–3), so any discrepancies between them are to be explained by the editorial activity – in this case, the excisions – of the Ebionites. But this passage actually contains a great deal of material that is closer to Luke than to Matthew. It looks, as may be seen from the translation above, that this passage is in fact based on a conflation and abbreviation of Lk. 1.5 and 3.1–3.

However, if the *Gospel of the Ebionites* has made rather confused use of Luke in setting the historical context in which John appears, its author seems to have been less inclined to follow the way in which Luke appears to emphasize not the person of John but the word of God that comes upon him as John begins his public ministry. Luke's presentation of John in this verse is in keeping with an overall Lucan pattern in which he parallels but subordinates John to Jesus. But, in presenting John as a subject who comes onto the public stage in his own right, the *Gospel of the Ebionites* seems closer to the portrayal of John in Matthew, Mark and John.

Also of interest is the statement that 'all went out' to John, which is paralleled in Matthew, Mark and John. This is the only clear parallel between the *Gospel of the Ebionites* and John, and these two texts use a different verb than Matthew and Mark. Nevertheless, the fact that the statement that people went out to John is recorded also in Matthew and Mark means that this verbal parallel cannot be taken as evidence for literary dependence on John.

That three of Epiphanius' seven excerpts concern John and baptism suggests that these were important themes in this text. Yet it is also important to emphasize that the fact that this is true of a significant proportion of the surviving excerpts need not mean that this was so of the rest of the gospel, and that the space that it allocated to John may not have been significantly different from that of (say) Matthew or Luke. Nevertheless, it is of interest to note what this text tells us about John that is not present in canonical accounts. One small detail in the passage that we are discussing is its claim that John was a descendant of Aaron, which perhaps is an inference from Luke's description of Zachariah as a priest. Another is the text's description of John the Baptist and his diet, which may be translated as follows:

> It happened that John was baptising, and there went out to him Pharisees, and they were baptised, and all Jerusalem. And John had a garment of camel's hair and a leather belt about his waist. And his food, *it says*, was wild honey, the taste of which was manna, like a cake in oil, *so that they might change the word of truth into a lie, and might make it say honey cake instead of locusts*. (Pan. 30.13.4–5)

Here again we see how Epiphanius draws our attention to a difference between the Ebionite gospel and its canonical counterparts, and explains it as a further instance of their corruption of the text that they had received. The Greek words for locust and for honey cake are very similar, so this play with words works only in Greek, which strongly suggests that the text was written in that language.

Of interest here is the question why the author of this gospel objected to John eating locusts.[14] Locusts appear to have been accepted as kosher (Lev. 11.22; cf. Deut. 14.19, which seems to have been widely disregarded) and were commonly eaten in the Ancient Near East. Thus there is no reason to see their omission from John's diet as a matter of kashrut. As Epiphanius observes, Jews eat flesh, but with the exceptions of animals considered unclean (*Pan.* 30.22.6–7) – which locusts were not. However their omission does make John's diet vegetarian, so it has often been explained as a consequence of vegetarian beliefs that are attributed to Ebionites for other reasons. These include evidence for vegetarian practice in the Pseudo-Clementines, which

14. For a full discussion of this question, see J. A. Kelhoffer, *The Diet of John the Baptist: 'Locusts and Wild Honey' in Synoptic and Patristic Interpretation* (WUNT 176; Tübingen: Mohr Siebeck, 2005).

Epiphanius takes as evidence of Ebionite practice and belief, and also his explicit statement that the Ebionites abstained from meat (*Pan.* 30.15.3–4). This statement might be taken as an inference based on his reading of those texts, but it may gain independent support from implied personal contact between Epiphanius and contemporaries whom he describes as Ebionites. This seems the natural conclusion to draw from his account of a discussion with Ebionites about their abstention from meat (30.18.7). The possibility that this reflects a rhetorical device rather than an actual encounter cannot be excluded, however.

There may also be evidence for vegetarianism elsewhere in Epiphanius' citations from the *Gospel of the Ebionites*, for it has Jesus deny that he wished to eat meat with his disciples at Passover (*Pan.* 30.22.4, on which see further below). Yet care must be taken in assessing this evidence. The link between those whose practices are reflected in the Pseudo-Clementines and in the *Gospel of the Ebionites* is by no means certain, and Jesus' statement about the Passover may reflect an aversion primarily to sacrifices and to meat associated with sacrifices rather than to meat as such.

If the text's concern is to present John as vegetarian, this could reflect ascetic impulses either of a Christian, 'Jewish-Christian' or pagan variety. There was a strong vegetarian tradition in pagan thought, although the wholesale avoidance of meat was not a common phenomenon in Judaism, nor were those who avoided meat held up for esteem as they were in some pagan philosophical circles. Jewish motivations for abstaining from meat include doing so as a safety measure in a pagan environment or in a time of crisis,[15] or as a particular reaction to the destruction of the temple.[16] It may also have been practiced as an intensification of purity regulations. Fasting and abstinence from meat (and from wine) also appear to have been characteristic forms of Christian asceticism in the second and third centuries.

Another very different explanation for John's diet might be that it represents an aversion to eating locusts. James Kelhoffer has noted that whereas there was ample evidence for eating locusts in the eastern Mediterranean during the Classical Greek and Hellenistic periods, expressions of aversion to this practice are more common in the Roman period. Thus a developing Romanization of diet may offer a reason that reflects no specifically Christian or Jewish reason to remove locusts from John's diet. Patristic authors – among whom the author of the *Gospel of the Ebionites* may be the earliest, depending when this gospel is dated – may be simply reflecting wider cultural norms.[17] If correct,

15. Kelhoffer, *The Diet of John the Baptist*, 185.

16. S. A. Fraade, 'Ascetical Aspects of Ancient Judaism', in A. Green (ed.), *Jewish Spirituality from the Bible through the Middle Ages* (London: RKP, 1986) 253–288, on 271–272.

17. Kelhoffer, *The Diet of John the Baptist*, 60–80.

this explanation suggests that the gospel was written in a context where Roman cultural considerations were important.

Three other excerpts, all sayings attributed to Jesus, may each be noted much more briefly. One is a statement in which Jesus says, 'I came to abolish the sacrifices, and if you will not desist making sacrifices, wrath will not desist from you' (30.16.5). A partial parallel with Mt. 5.17 may be noted, but Epiphanius presents the saying to support his claim that the Ebionites believed that Christ was a creature, an archangel who came and instructed that sacrifices should be abolished. It is introduced in the course of a protracted if not altogether clear account of Ebionite Christology. Similar objections to sacrifice are found also in the *Pseudo-Clementine Recognitions* and are one of a number of parallels between that text and the *Gospel of the Ebionites*.

Another excerpt records Jesus as saying 'I did not earnestly desire to eat meat with you this Passover' (30.22.4) If this is to be read alongside John's non-locust diet, it might be taken to support those who interpret the text as advocating vegetarianism. If, however, it is read alongside Jesus' saying about the abolition of sacrifices it may be seen as concerned primarily with the abolition of the sacrificial cult. We do not need to choose between these two alternatives, for each could complement the other, but it is difficult to draw general conclusions about the tendencies of the text as a whole on the basis of such short extracts.

This may be seen also in reference to a third saying, when Jesus refers to his disciples, 'these who do the will of my father' as 'my brothers and my mother and my sisters'. The saying is clearly parallel in synoptic triple tradition, but Epiphanius presents it as evidence of Ebionite Docetism (the denial that Jesus was really a human being). It is by no means necessary (nor perhaps even obvious) that this excerpt should be read in a docetic way, so once again we find ourselves in a situation in which the text that Epiphanius cites may not support the use to which he wants to put it.

5. *Conclusion*

Perhaps the most striking thing to emerge from this survey is the extent to which Jewish-Christian gospel tradition is broadly congruent and consistent with the canonical gospels, especially the synoptic tradition. There are points on which it adds to that tradition, for example, sayings attributed to Jesus, but there are only a few points where it appears to contradict it. Examples of contradictions include its testimony to the diet of John and its denial that Jesus participated fully in a Passover meal. Each of these is found in the *Gospel of the Ebionites*, which Epiphanius presents as a heretical work, but we may wonder just how different it was from the canonical gospels if these examples are among the most outstanding of its distinctive content. Surely just as important as any differences that it shows from the synoptic tradition is the extent to which it makes use of that material. The *Gospel of the Ebionites* may well reflect unease with certain parts of the synoptic tradition, but it is on that tradition that it draws in presenting its own understanding of Jesus.

Even if we accept Epiphanius' view that the *Gospel of the Ebionites* was in some sense a heretical work, there is no reason to believe that all Jewish-Christian gospel tradition should be treated in this way. Clement, Origen and Didymus each draw on the *Gospel according to the Hebrews* in a matter of fact manner that suggests that it was both widely known and widely acceptable, at least among those for whom they wrote. Eusebius includes it not among books considered heretical, but among those whose status as Scripture was disputed. This further strengthens the impression that this was a text with a wide appeal in the period before the boundaries of the New Testament canon were formally closed. Modern readers whose portraits of Jesus have been shaped by the canonical accounts may well find the suggestion of a flying Jesus bizarre, but it is consistent with prophetic tradition and hardly more problematic than at least some of the miracles contained in canonical texts. Jewish-Christian gospel traditions are not canonical, but they are not far removed from those in the fourfold gospel, and remind us that even texts that became canonical were used in a variety of ways by different early Christian groups. The extent to which the synoptic tradition influenced the development of these other texts, and therefore the important role that it played in the development of other gospels, should not be under-estimated.

Bibliography

H. -J. Klauck, *Apocryphal Gospels: An Introduction* (trans. Brian McNeil; London: T&T Clark International, 2003).

A. F. J. Klijn, *Jewish-Christian Gospel Tradition* (VCSupp XVII; Leiden: Brill, 1992).

D. Lührmann with E. Schlarb, *Fragmente apokryph gewordener Evangelien in griechischer und lateinischer Sprache* (MtS 59; Marburg: N.G. Elwert Verlag).

P. Vielhauer and G. Strecker, 'Jewish-Christian Gospels', in W. Schneemelcher, *New Testament Apocrypha, Volume One: Gospels and Related Writings* (English translation ed. R. McL. Wilson; Cambridge: James Clarke & Co, 1991) 134–178.

Chapter 6

The *Gospel of Philip*

Paul Foster

If there is any truth to the saying 'all publicity is good publicity', then the *Gospel of Philip* is in the fortunate position of being the most cited and well-known non-canonical gospel text. The reason for this is simple, Dan Brown's *Da Vinci Code*. In truth Brown draws only one detail from the *Gospel of Philip* for his novel. After heading to a library, Teabing pulls a book from the shelves titled *The Gnostic Gospels*, he flips open to the middle of the book and memorably states, 'The Gospel of Philip is always a good place to start.' The passage he has indicated is cited in the following form:

> And the companion of the Saviour is Mary Magdalene. Christ loved her more than all the disciples and used to kiss her often on her mouth. The rest of the disciples were offended by it and expressed disapproval. They said to him, 'Why do you love her more than all of us.' (*Gos. Phil.* 63.32–64.4)

He then authoritatively tells his fellow investigator Sophie that 'any Aramaic scholar will tell you, the word *companion*, in those days, literally meant *spouse*.'[1] All publicity might be good publicity, but it is not necessarily accurate. Both the accuracy of this quotation and the meaning derived from it will be discussed further, but first it is appropriate to look at the discovery, origins and contents of the enigmatic gospel text.

The Gospel of Philip is a text with an outlook that is strikingly dissimilar to that of the canonical gospels. It understands salvation not as rescue from sin, but as the reunification of being. This process is possible for those who adhere to the teachings of the group and undergo the ritual of the bridal chamber. Although much of the language of marriage and sexual union is used to describe this process, this appears to be a metaphor for the joining of the male and female parts of a being that have been separated. The text promotes ascetic practices and sexual continence. It gives an insight into the diversity that existed in ancient Christianity.

1. D. Brown, *The Da Vinci Code* (New York: Doubleday, 2003) 245–246.

1. *Discovery of the* Gospel of Philip

The only surviving partial copy of the *Gospel of Philip* was found among the important cache of documents known as the Nag Hammadi library.[2] This collection of texts was discovered in Upper Egypt at the eponymous location of Nag Hammadi in November or December 1945.[3] The find unearthed thirteen codices, or volumes, each containing multiple texts. The *Gospel of Philip* was found as the third text in what has become numbered as Codex II. This contains seven texts, *The Apocryphon of John, The Gospel of Thomas, The Gospel of Philip, The Hypostasis of the Archons, On the Origin of the World, The Exegesis on the Soul* and *The Book of Thomas the Contender*. This arrangement may not be totally arbitrary. The *Apocryphon of John* is a text that is found on three occasions in the Nag Hammadi library, and in each of the three codices in which it is found it stands in first place (codices II, III and IV). It has been suggested that this text may function as a hermeneutical key for understanding the other texts, with its classic formulation of Gnostic myth and ritual.[4] However, the rest of the organization of the codex is harder to determine, with various texts reflecting different forms of Gnostic thought.[5] Like all the texts in the Nag Hammadi corpus (apart from the fragments of Greek writings recovered from the cartonnage of the covers),[6] the *Gospel of Philip* is written in

2. The most convenient single volume edition of these texts is J. M. Robinson (ed.), *The Nag Hammadi Library in English* (rev. edn; Leiden: Brill, 1996). For the standard critical edition with Coptic text see B. Layton (ed.), *Nag Hammadi Codex II, 2–7*, vol. 1 Gospel According to Thomas, Gospel According to Philip, Hypostasis of the Archons, and Indexes (Leiden: Brill, 1989).

3. The dating of the discovery has been a somewhat vexed issue due to various conflicting dates provided by Jean Doresse ranging from 1945–1948. James Robinson seems to have established by firsthand testimony that the discovery occurred at the end of 1945. In part this is fixed through an interview he conducted with the discoverer, Muhammad Ali al-Samman. Although Muhammad Ali was illiterate and could not provide a calendrical date, he knew it happened six months after his father's murder, and shortly before he and his brothers avenged that murder and ate the murderer's raw heart. By consulting the Registry of Deaths held at Nag Hammadi Robinson fixed the date of discovery as November or December 1945. See J. M. Robinson, 'Nag Hammadi: The First Fifty Years', in J. D. Turner and A. McGuire (eds), *The Nag Hammadi Library after Fifty Years: Proceedings of the 1995 Society of Biblical Literature Commemoration* (Leiden: Brill, 1997) 3–6.

4. See A. H. B. Logan, *The Gnostics: Identifying and Early Christian Cult* (London: T&T Clark – a Continuum International imprint, 2006) 6.

5. According to Bentley Layton '[a]t least three distinct ancient currents are represented in the codex: Sethian Gnosticism, a mythopoeic parody or inversion of elements from Judaism, perhaps originally non-Christian in character (*Apocryphon of John, Hypostasis of the Archons*); the school of Valentinus, the most deeply Christian branch of ancient Gnosticism (*Gospel According to Philip*); and yet another kind of Christian spirituality, which mediated upon "twinship" and unity of the self and God and found expression in the figures of Jesus and Judas Thomas the Twin (*Gospel According to Thomas, Book of Thomas*).' B. Layton (ed.), 'Preface' in *Nag Hammadi Codex II, 2–7*, xiii.

6. J. W. B. Barns, G. M. Browne and J. C. Shelton (eds), *Nag Hammadi Codices: Greek and Coptic Papyri from the Cartonnage of the Covers* (Leiden: Brill, 1996).

Coptic. Most scholars believe, however, that the text was originally written in Greek, but it is often suggested that a Syrian provenance for the Greek text is probable, due to 'interest shown in Syriac words (63:21–23, 56:7–9), affinities to Eastern sacramental practice and catecheses, and the espousal of encratite ethics.'[7] This accords well with the well-known flow of ideas between Syrian and Egyptian monastic communities. Although the copy of the *Gospel of Philip* discovered at Nag Hammadi was written around the middle of the fourth century (c. 350 CE), the actual composition of the text was probably much earlier. In his standard critical edition Isenberg proposed dating the composition to the second half of the third century.[8] Scholarly consensus has, however, settled on a slightly earlier dating in the first half of the third century, although some scholars wish to push it even earlier suggesting the second half of the second century.

The title of the text is not unproblematic. In one of his writings on this text, Isenberg states, 'The text is anonymous and may bear Philip's name merely because he is the only apostle referred to by name (73:9–14).'[9] While the text has no *incipit* (a title at the head of the text) it does contain a *subscriptio*, however, unlike other texts such as the immediately preceding *Gospel of Thomas* this is not set off as a separate paragraph with intervening white-space. Rather, it is written as the final line of the text. This has led to the theory that this note concerning authorship was inserted at a later time than the writing of the rest of the text, perhaps as an afterthought.[10]

While the Nag Hammadi manuscript preserves the only copy of the *Gospel of Philip*, a text possessing this title is mentioned by the fourth-century Christian writer Epiphanius. In his work titled the *Panarion* he states:

> They [the Gnostics] quote from another gospel too, which was composed in the name of the holy disciple Philip, the following words:
> 'The Lord revealed to me [Philip] what the soul must say in its ascent to heaven, and how it must answer each of the powers above:
> "I have recognized myself and gathered myself together from all sides and have not sown children to the Archon but have uprooted his roots and have gathered the scattered members and I know who you are; for I belong to those from above."'
> And so it is set free. But if it should prove that the soul has borne a son, it is kept beneath until it is in a position to recover its children and bring them back to itself. (*Panarion* 26.13.2–3.)[11]

7. W. W. Isenberg, 'Gospel According to Philip', in B. Layton (ed.), *Nag Hammadi Codex II, 2–7* (Leiden: Brill, 1989) 134.
8. Isenberg, 'Gospel According to Philip', 134–135.
9. W. W. Isenberg, 'Philip, Gospel of', in D. N. Freedman, *Anchor Bible Dictionary*, vol. 5 (New York: Doubleday, 1992) 312–313.
10. Isenberg, 'Gospel According to Philip', 131.
11. See F. Williams (trans.), *The Panarion of Epiphanius of Salamis* (Leiden: Brill, 1994).

The problem with this citation which Epiphanius alleges is from the *Gospel of Philip* is that although its ideas are not dissimilar from the text discovered at Nag Hammadi it does not match the wording of any portion of that text. There could be a number of reasons for this. The copy of the text from Nag Hammadi is only partially complete, so this could be material from the missing part. Alternatively, the text from Nag Hammadi may have been mislabelled, or Epiphanius might be referring to a second text that bore the title *Gospel of Philip* (there are at least three texts known as the *Apocalypse of Peter*), or maybe Epiphanius has misattributed this saying to the *Gospel of Philip*. With so little evidence it is best not to place too much weight on the testimony of Epiphanius, and instead to treat the text from Nag Hammadi as an entity in its right.

2. *Contents*

It is difficult to produce a helpful table of contents for the *Gospel of Philip*, which might reveal progression in thought and planning on the part of the author or compiler. In fact its arrangement is erratic, with topics and catch-words from previous sections resurfacing at later points.[12] The result is that this at best produces loose links between blocks of somewhat disparate material, rather than sequential argument. Klauck comments on this feature of the arrangement in reference to the opening statements. 'The opening section shows clearly that there exists a thematic connection between the individual paragraphs, despite the loose construction of the text as a whole and the difficulties involved in understanding the contents.'[13] Notwithstanding these obvious problems a table of contents will be given below. It must, however, be recognized that each of the broad headings encapsulates a range of other material (often re-articulating ideas already mentioned) and that it is impossible to fully represent the highly eccentric nature of the contents. It must be understood that the following table of contents is highly compressed, it represents the occurrence of prominent themes, and some of the divisions are arbitrary. In some ways Schenke's catalogue of 127 individual sayings is more helpful, but the drawback is its unwieldy length.[14] In the numbering system in Table 6.1 the first number refers to the page number of the codex and the second to the line number. This is the common referencing system.[15]

12. See the discussion in M. L. Turner, 'On the Coherence of the *Gospel According to Philip*', in J. D. Turner and A. McGuire (eds), *The Nag Hammadi Library after Fifty Years: Proceedings of the 1995 Society of Biblical Literature Commemoration* (Leiden: Brill, 1997) 223–250.

13. H. -J. Klauck, *Apocryphal Gospels: An Introduction* (London: T&T Clark – a Continuum International imprint, 2003) 124.

14. See H. -M. Schenke, 'Das Evangelium nach Philippus', in J. Leipoldt and H. -M. Schenke (eds), *Koptisch-gnostische Schriften aus den Papyrus-Codices von Nag-Hamadi* (Hamburg-Bergstedt: Reich-Evangelischer Verlag, 1960) 38–65.

15. Such a system follows that adopted by Isenberg in his standard edition of the text. Isenberg, 'Gospel According to Philip'.

Table 6.1 Major Themes in the *Gospel of Philip*

Reference	Contents
51.29–52.35	Origin, generation and existence of humans. 'Hebrew' as a reference for an unspiritual being.
53.1–55.23	Christ's soteriological work, dualistic nature of physical world, deceptive names, animal sacrifices unnecessary, deceptive role of archons.
55.24–55.36	Mary's virginal conception not through the feminine Holy Spirit.
55.37–57.28	Concealed valuable objects as a metaphor for soul hidden in the body.
57.30–59.6	Christ's polymorphic appearances, union with Christ.
59.6–60.34	The three Marys, teaching on Holy Spirit, Relationship of Father and Son, comparison with wild and tame animals.
60.34–62.7	Superiority of begotten over created, the Fall, unspiritual are still Hebrews.
62.7–64.31	Different names for Jesus, the name 'Christian, creative elements of fire and breath, Jesus is the Eucharist, Jesus kisses Mary Magdalene, superiority of man over animals, baptismal initiation.
64.31–67.1	Marriage metaphor, discussion of bridal chamber, a neutral view of the flesh, lack of will linked to being a 'sinner'.
67.2–69.1	Elements of water and fire combine to produce a soul, bridal chamber, name 'Christian', baptismal saying, reversal of present states by Christ.
69.1–70.34	Bridal chamber not for animals, three buildings for sacrifice, separation of sexes, reunification in bridal chamber.
70.34–73.8	Jesus begotten before all things, mystery of bridal chamber, Two paradisiacal trees producing animals or men respectively.
73.8–75.2	Philip describes Joseph making Jesus' cross, a second tree in Joseph's garden produces the chrism of resurrection, Jesus gives food that does not lead to corruption, chrism superior to baptism.
75.2–78.12	World not created perfect as was intended, the cup of prayer, origin, generation, union in eternal realm, perfect light, perfecting baptism, knowledge of truth.
78.12–79.33	Metaphor of children resembling the one who fathered them, becoming light, farming metaphor consists of four elements.
80.1–84.14	Becoming perfect like Christ, discipleship, the bridal chamber, destroying the flesh, inner parts hidden.
84.14–86.18	Bridal chamber still hidden, it is the Holy of Holies, reunification, understanding brings true light, dwelling in the eternal realm.
86.19	'The Gospel According to Philip'.

Three things are particularly striking from this summarized list of contents. First, a number of themes such as the bridal chamber recur almost like a refrain throughout this text. Secondly, the topics discussed are highly esoteric and the metaphors employed are often obtuse, with the writer's main point definitely less than obvious. Thirdly, it appears that some of the sayings may be related to the actual cultic practices of the group that read this text. The bridal chamber may have been an actual place where a ceremony of reunification, purification and dedication to a spiritual marriage took place. Similarly, the chrism may have been applied to enable members to enter into the resurrected state.

Some of the more significant themes or metaphors are repeated at various points in the text. Such repetition of themes provides coherence to what may initially appear a disparate collection of material.[16] These repeated themes include the following striking images and metaphors that convey much of the theology of this text.

2.1 *The Bridal Chamber*

As has already been suggested this term appears to reflect a ritual or rite practiced among group members that allowed for the repristination of soul, which had become tainted because of the separation of the sexes. In stark terms the *Gospel of Philip* states 'if the woman had not separated from the man, she would not die with the man' (70.9.11). It has been correctly observed that the woman and the man are not both human beings. As Wilson states, 'the man and the woman . . . represent the Gnostic and his angelic counterpart, with whom he is to be united in the Pleroma.'[17] Thus, the *Gospel of Philip* states that the 'males are they that unite with the souls that inhabit a female form . . . so if the image and the angel are united with one another, neither can any venture to go into the man or the woman' (65.3–4, 24–26). Christ's soteriological function is to repair this 'gender-based' fracturing of the whole being, which was brought about through carnal intercourse. Reunification occurs in the bridal chamber. 'But the woman is reunited to her husband in the bridal chamber. Indeed those who have united in the bridal chamber will no longer be separated' (70.17–22). This pattern of thought may help explain the famous but enigmatic last saying in the *Gospel of Thomas* concerning the need for Mary Magdalene being made male so that she might enter the kingdom of heaven (*Gos. Thom.* 114).[18]

It has been suggested that the *Gospel of Philip* offers two differing sequential patterns of initiation involving the bridal chamber.[19] In the first of these typological descriptions comparison is based the progression into the Holy of

16. See M. L. Turner, *The Gospel According to Philip. The Sources and Coherence of an Early Christian Collection* (Leiden: Brill, 1996).

17. R. McL. Wilson, *The Gospel of Philip* (London: A. R. Mowbray & Co., 1962) 121.

18. Valantasis suggests that '[t]he gendered transformation exactly invokes for women the possibility of attaining the status only open to the other (just as the Hermetic men could take on the gendered functions of women).' See R. Valantasis, *The Gospel of Thomas* (London: Routledge, 1997) 194–195. DeConick sees this related to Fall mythology with Adam, although a male figure, being androgynous because Eve was still hidden inside him. She argues that 'the gender refashioning for women would have stressed encratic behaviour, particularly celibacy and their refusal to bear children.' A. D. DeConick, *The Original Gospel of Thomas in Translation* (London: T&T Clark – a Continuum International imprint, 2006) 297.

19. E. Thomassen, *The Spiritual Seed: The Church of the Valentinians*, NHMS 60 (Leiden: Brill, 2006) 341.

Holies in the Jerusalem Temple. Describing the three buildings or areas of the temple the author states, 'baptism is the holy building; redemption is the Holy of the Holy; the Holy of Holies is the bridal chamber' (69.22–25). Thomassen suggests that the passage also envisages another state more elevated than the bridal chamber. However, the text is lacunose at this point, and it is uncertain whether it is affirming the superiority of the bridal chamber or whether something else exists which is superior to it.[20] The second pattern (see 70.34–71.10) also involves a progression of soteriological rituals, but encompasses some additional stages and different language to describe such rites. The stages involve rebirth, anointing, redemption and the bridal chamber. As the rebirth of Jesus is closely linked with him being 'revealed in the Jordan' (70.34) it appears that rebirth equates to baptism. This is a lower stage of the initiation process than the anointing. This point is made explicitly in the text when the author declares 'the chrism is superior to baptism, for it is from the word chrism that we have been called Christians, certainly not because of the word baptism' (74.12–15). Leaving aside the dubious etymology employed here, it appears that the author is arguing that adherents to the form of Christianity promoted in *The Gospel of Philip* have experienced a higher level of spiritual participation than those who stop at the basic baptismal ritual.

Bridal chamber theology although not systematically explained is the culmination of the sequential initiation process. Redemption may in fact not be a discrete stage, but something that occurs through undergoing the bridal chamber rite. The 'marriage' envisaged is the reunification of the initiate (the male) with his angel (the female). Having undergone this process the reconstituted being must no longer be involved with physical sexual practices. In a broken passage it appears that those who undergo this ritual are seen as being divinized in some sense, and consequently are known as sons of the bridal chamber (76.3–5).

2.2 *When Is a Kiss a Kiss?*

Like so much of the terminology in the *Gospel of Philip* the term 'kiss' appears to be metaphorical. Prior to the report of Jesus kissing Mary Magdalene, the *Gospel of Philip* explains the function of kissing within the group. Before looking at that passage in detail, it is worthwhile recalling that Paul can counsel believers to greet one another with a kiss and even call such an act 'holy', ('Greet one another with a holy kiss', Rom. 16.16, cf. 1 Thess. 5.26). Jewett astutely comments that '[t]he evidence from the Jewish as well as the Greco-Roman environment indicates that "Kisses are for relatives," while other contexts, including the erotic, are secondary.'[21] The *Gospel of Philip* like much other early Christian literature presents a 'fictive kinship' where the Christian

20. Thomassen, *The Spiritual Seed: The Church of the Valentinians*, 341.
21. R. Jewett, *Romans*, Hermeneia (Minneapolis: Fortress, 2006) 973.

family is the real bond of relationship and hence familial signs of affection have a greater reason to be shown in this religious context. In particular, the *Gospel of Philip* presents a kiss not only as a bond of loyalty and relationship between believers, but as part of the process by which the divine essence is transmitted between group members.

> It is from being promised to the heavenly place that man receives nourishment. [. . .] him from the mouth. And had the word gone out from that place, it would be nourished from the mouth and it would become perfect. For it is by a kiss that the perfect conceive and give birth. For this reason we also kiss one another. We receive conception from the grace which is in one another. (58.30–59.6)

Thus it appears that for those people who considered the *Gospel of Philip* a key text the early Pauline tradition of the 'holy kiss' had been further spiritualized. It is probable that at the heart of one of the sacramental rites of the community, kisses were exchanges by group members. These were kisses on the mouth, which were viewed as a spiritual conception. This activity must also be considered in light of what the text says about 'breath'. Objects are said to come into existence through the transmission of breath (63.6–10). Similarly, it is stated that 'the soul of Adam came into being by means of a breath' (70.23–24). In the prelapsarian state, Adam is viewed as the possessor of a soul, but the Fall resulted in the soul being removed, and replaced by a spirit. Those who subscribed to the mythology in the *Gospel of Philip* see their rituals leading to the restoration of such lost souls, and the kiss or the breath seems to be fundamental to that process of recreating the integrated Adamic state, with the female part hidden and undisclosed within the undefiled being.

It is against this background of thought that the kissing of Mary Magdalene must be properly understood. In a number of non-canonical texts she functions as an important figure because of the quality of her discipleship, knowledge or insight – not because of her gender.[22] Although there are gaps in the text at the point at which this saying is recorded, the sense is reasonably clear and the reconstruction fairly certain.

> And the companion of the [Christ is] Mary Magdalene. [The Lord] loved her more than [all] the disciples, and used to kiss her often on her [mouth]. The rest of the [disciples . . .]. They said to him 'Why do you love her more than all of us?' (63.30–64.5)[23]

The answer Jesus gives to this question is enigmatic, but may reveal a critique of the lack of understanding on the part of the disciples by rebuking their lack of perception. Prior to this text there is the line 'As for Wisdom who is

22. Apart from the *Gospel of Philip* see also the *Gospel of Thomas* 114 and the *Gospel of Mary* [*Magdalene*].

23. This reconstruction is common in many editions. See Wilson, *The Gospel of Philip*, 115.

called 'the barren' she is the mother of the angels.' It is uncertain whether this feminine figure Wisdom who fulfils a maternal role is seen as the Magdalene, or if this is an unrelated saying. If the former, then Jesus may be declaring that by his pure kiss he has restored Mary Magdalene's angelic part and thus she is the first to have her being reunified. In this sense she becomes the matriarch of the form of Gnosticism which practices the bridal chamber sacrament of reunification. In opposition to the interpretation of this passage offered by popular authors, it needs to be noted that the notion of Mary Magdalene as the physical sexual partner of Jesus stands in tension with the encratic and sexually ascetic outlook of this text.

2.3 *The Virgin Birth*

Although only occurring as a fleeting reference in the text, the comments on the nature of Mary's (the mother of Jesus) conception are tantalizing.

> Some said, 'Mary conceived by the Holy Spirit.' They are in error. They do not know what they are saying. When did a woman ever conceive by a woman? Mary is the virgin whom no power defiled. She is a great anathema to the Hebrews, who are the apostles and the apostolic men. This virgin whom no power defiled [. . .] the powers defile themselves. And the Lord would not have said 'My Father who is in Heaven', unless he had had another father, but he would have said simply 'My father'. (55.23–36)

Pagels understands the criticism levelled by this text in the following manner. 'Philip castigates those who believe that Jesus' birth was an event that derived its significance from its uniqueness, a miraculous event in which a woman conceives by parthenogenesis.'[24] The central concern, however, does not appear to be the 'uniqueness' of the event, but rather the notion that Jesus was born of two females is problematic for the soteriology of this text which presents the male believer being united with the feminine angel. The two 'females' that the author disputes as being involved in the conception of Christ are Mary the pure virgin (of course) and the Spirit (a feminine noun in Hebrew and Syriac, but a neuter form in Greek and masculine in Coptic) which is equated with the feminine Sophia at other points in the text.

It also needs to be noted that this interpretation seems to be a direct attempt to refute the comment spoken to Mary in Luke's gospel, 'the holy spirit will come upon you, and the power of the Most High will overshadow you' (Lk. 1.35). Thomassen suggests that the apparent surface meaning of this text is not actually the position held by the *Gospel of Philip.*

24. E. Pagels, 'Ritual in the *Gospel of Philip*', in J. D. Turner and A. McGuire (eds), *The Nag Hammadi Library after Fifty Years: Proceedings of the 1995 Society of Biblical Literature Commemoration* (Leiden: Brill, 1997) 285.

> Mary was neither made pregnant by the Holy Spirit, nor was she defiled by any kind of cosmic power. At first sight, the passage seems to deny, then, that either of them played any role in the conception and birth of the Saviour. This is not the case.[25]

It is argued that in the *Gospel of Philip* 73.8–19 the Lord is envisaged as having two fathers, Joseph and his heavenly Father. It is also noted that the text states that Adam came from two virgins (71.16); hence, the saviour must likewise have two virgin mothers, Sophia and Mary. Thomassen concludes 'Jesus Christ, the earthly Saviour, has two sets of parents. The Father of the Entirety and Sophia are the parents of his spiritual being, and the Demiurge-Joseph and Mary produced his material body.'[26] Such a reconstruction of the parentage of Jesus may be unnecessarily complicated. The passage does refute the role of the Spirit in the actual conception, due to its feminine nature. Instead the heavenly father is given a more direct role in this process, although this role is not fully explained. The text maintains the notion of Mary's virginity, and this aligns with the wider thought of the *Gospel of Philip* and its promotion of sexual continence as a means of escaping material defilement.

2.4 *Joseph, and the Making of the Cross*

One striking tradition not contained in the canonical gospels which surfaces in the *Gospel of Philip* is the attribution of the making of the cross to Joseph the carpenter, the earthly father of Jesus. According to the text, not only did Joseph fashion the cross on which Jesus was executed, but he also grew the very tree from which the wood was taken in his own garden.

> Philip the apostle said, 'Joseph the carpenter planted a garden because he needed wood for his trade. It was he who made the cross from the trees which he planted. His own offspring hung on that which he planted. His offspring was Jesus, and the planting was the cross.' But the Tree of Life is in the middle of the Garden. However, it is from the olive tree that we got the chrism, and from the chrism, the resurrection. (73.8–19)

This legend of Joseph's unknowing part in the crucifixion is, according to the text, transmitted by the apostle Philip. Although at first glance this tradition is redolent with irony, there is far deeper salvific significance for those believers who follow the teachings of this text. While emergent mainstream Christianity saw the cross as 'the Tree of Life', for the *Gospel of Philip* this is only a 'low-level' and initial understanding of salvation. The true 'Tree of Life' is the one that produces the oil of chrism with which members of the sect are anointed. This oil, or rather the process of chrismation, produces the spiritualized resurrection realized in the reunion of the two now separated parts of one's being. Again, although 'orthodox' understandings of salvation are not empty, accord-

25. Thomassen, *The Spiritual Seed: The Church of the Valentinians*, 90.
26. Thomassen, *The Spiritual Seed: The Church of the Valentinians*, 92.

ing to the *Gospel of Philip* they are merely the first step towards a fuller spiritual journey. Initiates in the group realize that resurrection is not about the raising of the mortal body, but concerns the transcendence of the reformulated being over the physical passions of the material world. Such a perspective has been seen as aligning with wider Valentinian teachings.

> According to the soteriology of mutual participation characteristic of an important strand of Valentinianism, the Savior shares in the condition of the spirituals he comes to save by assuming a material body . . . In the logic of this soteriology, the Savior lets himself be incarnated in order that the spirituals on their part may be released from the body.[27]

2.5 *Marriage among Those Who Adhere to the Teachings in the* Gospel of Philip

It is not altogether clear whether the *Gospel of Philip* promotes, permits or prohibits sexual intercourse.[28] Part of the reason for this confusion stems from the symbolic nature of the language. Thus it is uncertain whether reference to sexual relationship within the bridal chamber is a metaphor for the union of believers with their angelic counterparts, or if it is a way of acknowledging the reality that some of the adherents will be married and will continue to practice physical aspects of the marriage. What is beyond doubt is that the *Gospel of Philip* views sexual continence or virginity as a more pure state of being. Those who have never participated in sexual acts are seen as being undefiled (55.27–28; 81.34–82.8). As Isenberg notes from the perspective of the *Gospel of Philip*:

> 'Free men and virgins' possess various gifts and privileges. They know the origin and destiny of their existence (64:9–12). They may also be called 'the perfect' who conceive and beget through a kiss (58.26–59.6). The perfect have put on the perfect light (76:25–28, 70:5–9), which will help them elude the heavenly powers (86:7–11).[29]

Such privileges reveal the motivation and reward for following the text's encratic teachings on sexual continence and virginity.

Notwithstanding this, there does appear to be another strand of thinking that regulates the way intercourse may be practiced between a married couple. The text states that it is to take place in the bridal chamber.

27. E. Thomassen, 'How Valentinian Is the *Gospel of Philip*?', in J. D. Turner and A. McGuire (eds), *The Nag Hammadi Library after Fifty Years: Proceedings of the 1995 Society of Biblical Literature Commemoration* (Leiden: Brill, 1997) 269.

28. The larger debate surrounding this issue is discussed in April DeConick's helpful article, 'The Great Mystery of Marriage: Sex and Conception in Ancient Valentinian Traditions', *VC* 57 (2003) 307–342. Her reading of the text supports understanding the community behind the *Gospel of Philip* as promoting sexual relationships as a reflection of their mythological understanding that redemption was the reunification of being in the bridal chamber and that sexual intercourse between Valentinian partners pre-figured and actually triggered the salvific events (see 341–342).

29. Isenberg, 'Gospel According to Philip', 135.

> No one can know when the husband and the wife have intercourse with one another, except the two of them. Indeed, marriage in the world is a mystery for those who have taken a wife. If there is a hidden quality to the marriage of defilement, how much more is the undefiled marriage a true mystery! It is not fleshly, but pure. It belongs not to desire, but to the will. It belongs not to the darkness or the night, but to the day and the light. If a marriage is open to the public, it has become prostitution, and the bride plays the harlot not only when she is impregnated by another man, but even if she slips out of her bedroom and is seen. Let her show herself only to her father and her mother, and to the friend of the bridegroom and the sons of the bridegroom. These are permitted to enter every day into the bridal chamber. But let the others yearn just to listen to her voice and to enjoy her ointment, and let them feed from the crumbs that fall from the table, like the dogs. Bridegrooms and brides belong to the bridal chamber. No one shall be able to see the bridegroom with the bride unless he become such a one. (81.34–82.26)

The problem with this description is that it plays with the imagery surrounding physical marriage – 'the marriage of defilement', and applies it to the spiritual marriage – 'undefiled marriage' – without fully differentiating between when it is speaking about physical or spiritual union. It is little wonder that the fourth-century patristic writer Epiphanius of Salamis understood the 'Gnostics' as practicing actual acts of sexual intercourse during the ritual of the bridal chamber. The language and imagery employed certainly do not save any blushes. However, as Klauck suggests, to see this as reflecting actual acts of physical intercourse in the bridal chamber 'is a distortion of gnostic thinking and praxis.'[30] It is certainly doubtful that the *Gospel of Philip* is advocating the voyeuristic practice of close associates entering into the bridal chamber of a physical marriage. Rather those permitted into the bridal chamber appear to be fellow initiates who are characterized as the 'son of the bridegroom'.

It therefore appears certain that the *Gospel of Philip* advocated sexual continence and saw lifelong virginity as a way to avoid defilement while also allowing the reunification of being. Nonetheless, it also permitted 'the marriage of defilement' (82.4–6), even going so far as to acknowledge that it could have a hidden quality. This hidden quality, however, was at best a mere shadow of the concealed treasure to be enjoyed by those who received an undefiled marriage in the bridal chamber.

2.6 *Resurrection and Baptism*

The Pauline understanding of the resurrection and the perspective on that phenomenon in the *Gospel of Philip* are not readily compatible. Paul sees a future transformation when the last trumpet will sound (1 Cor. 15.52) and then corruptible bodies will be replaced with incorruptible (1 Cor. 15.52–53). In fact

30. Klauck, *Apocryphal Gospels: An Introduction*, 132.

Paul appears to berate the Corinthians for claiming that they are enjoying the fullness of future blessing in their present existence. By contrast, the *Gospel of Philip* sees resurrection as a state that must be entered prior to physical death. Helpfully, resurrection is one of the few key ideas for which the text provides a fairly clear definition. 'Those who say they will die first and then rise are in error. If they do not first receive the resurrection while they live, when they die they will receive nothing' (73.1–8). As is made clear from the discussion of the olive tree in Joseph's garden which provides the oil of chrismation, the resurrection comes about through being anointed with the chrism. In other words, it is consequent on having received the sacraments leading up to the bridal chamber. This passage goes on to disparage the common notion of baptism and Wilson states that 'the whole passage may be a piece of polemic against the beliefs of the "orthodox" Church. Baptism is merely the lowest stage.'[31]

3. *The* Gospel of Philip – *Gnostic, Valentinian or Just a Text?*

The correctness of using the term 'Gnostic' has become highly contested in recent scholarly discussions. Many have seen it as being such an overburdened label that it has been rendered meaningless.[32] Thus Pagels writes, '[a]fter fifty years of Nag Hammadi study we are finally learning . . . to drop generalizations about whatever it is thought we meant by the term "gnosticism" and speak instead about specific texts.'[33] Such critiques correctly remind one of the dangers of drawing rash, or even crass, generalizations. There is, however, a danger that in dispensing with broad labels we are throwing away helpful heuristic and taxonomical devices. The solution to bad use of categorization is not no categorization, but better categorization, which acknowledges diversity without falling into the trap of undifferentiated fragmentation. The label 'Protestant' covers a variety of religious phenomena with many varied beliefs and practices (perhaps more so than ancient 'Gnosticism'), but if this is recognized the term can still remain a helpful category. Logan argues for reclaiming the descriptor 'Gnostic' stating, 'we need not abandon the term *per se*, only recognize and correct the way that reinscribing the discourses of orthodoxy and heresy distorts our reading and reconstruction of ancient religion.'[34] It needs to be remembered that the term 'Gnostic' while used by opponents of the movement in antiquity, also reflects the self-definition of such groups with their claim to possess higher or secret knowledge, γνῶσις.

With its strong 'knowledge' motif, the *Gospel of Philip* stands in the broad stream of Christian movements which promote an élitist form of Christianity

31. Wilson, *The Gospel of Philip*, 153.

32. One of the seminal studies in addressing the appropriateness of this category is M.A. Williams, *Rethinking 'Gnosticism': An Argument for Dismantling a Dubious Category* (Princeton, NJ: Princeton University Press, 1996).

33. Pagels, 'Ritual in the *Gospel of Philip*', 280.

for those willing to learn and participate in the more esoteric expressions of belief that are presented. One of the key elements is the way knowledge liberates, but the text cautions against superior knowledge becoming a source of pride.

> He who has knowledge of the truth is a free man . . . in fact, he who is really free, through knowledge, is a slave, because of love for those who have not yet been able to attain to the freedom of knowledge. Knowledge makes them capable of becoming free. (78.15–16, 26–29)

From the perspective of the text, possession of knowledge needs to be recognized as a privilege that must be utilized in the service of others.

If the *Gospel of Philip* can be seen as part of the general phenomenon of Gnostic reflections on the Christian belief system, can a more specific definition be found? Scholars have increasingly seen this text as most closely aligned with the branch of Gnosticism known as Valentinian Gnosticism. Thus Isenberg succinctly states that the text is 'generally Valentinian in theology'.[35] Schenke outlines a fuller theory of composition and understanding of the circles in which the text originates. He suggests that the text joined both Valentinian and non-Valentinian sections, but that this redactional process was undertaken by Valentinian compilers.[36] Much of the preserved information concerning both the originator of the movement, Valentinus, and his teachings are transmitted through the polemic of his opponents, Irenaeus, Clement of Alexandria and Hippolytus of Rome. Apparently born in Alexandria around 100 CE, Valentinus moved to Rome at some point between 136 to140 CE and his teachings made a strong impact on the Christians in the imperial capital and further afield.[37] Valentinus was held in such regard among the Roman churches that he was a candidate for the office of bishop. One of the interesting counterfactual questions of history is the issue of how different Christianity may have been if he had been elected to that office. It is perhaps impossible to separate Valentinus' teachings from those of his followers. As the system of thought can be reconstructed from various writings it may be stated that 'Valentinian texts generally deal with three themes: salvation in history, redemption in ritual, and protology.'[38] All three of these themes are prominent in the *Gospel of Philip*. Despite the reservations of some recent scholars against using categorical labels, it appears that the *Gospel of Philip* does in general conforms to what is known of Valentinian teaching from other writings stemming from those circles, as well as from descriptions contained in the polemical writings of

34. Logan, *The Gnostics: Identifying and Early Christian Cult*, 2.

35. Isenberg, 'Gospel According to Philip', 131.

36. H. -M. Schenke, 'Das Evangelium nach Philippus. Ein Evangelium der Valentinianer aus dem Funde von Nag-Hamadi', *TLZ* 84 (1959) 1–26.

37. C. B. Smith II, *No Longer Jews: The Search for Gnostic Origins* (Peabody: Hendrickson, 2004) 142.

opponents. While the *Gospel of Philip* should be studied as an entity in its own right, and the category of 'Valentinian' should not force the interpretation of individual passages if they seem to be at odds with the teaching of this movement as reported elsewhere, nonetheless, this category provides a helpful context for approaching the text and appreciating who might have been reading it in antiquity.

4. *The Significance of the* Gospel of Philip

The *Gospel of Philip* presents a very different cosmology and world-view when compared to that of the four canonical gospels, or even to that contained in non-canonical texts such as the *Gospel of Peter*. Primarily it sees individuals living a ruptured state, with the male earthly part of the being divorced from the feminine spiritual angelic part. The promise of the *Gospel of Philip* is to enable initiates to undergo a process of reunification whereby these two alienated parts are brought together in the ritual of the bridal chamber. As part of this reformulation of the whole being, group members are encouraged to lead an encratic life of sexual continence. However, this life is also seen as being one of service to those Christians without this superior knowledge.

To enter the world of the *Gospel of Philip* is to further appreciate the diversity of early Christianity. Many who claimed allegiance to Christ were seen as heretical both by their contemporary opponents and later 'orthodoxy' in the Church. Yet they attempted to interpret the significance of the Christ-figure through their existing understandings of the universe as a multilayered structure that separated the perfect spiritual realm from the tainted earthly and material existence. In this way they integrated both Platonic and pre-Christian Gnostic ideas with their very real adherence to Jesus as the source of salvation. What, however, they needed saving from was conceived differently. Theirs was not a salvation from sin and death, but a soteriology enacted by the Saviour and based on the rescue of the wholeness of being from its separation and descent into the lower earthly realm.[39] For those who had undergone this reunification of being in the bridal chamber, there was a need to live as newly reconfigured spiritual entities. This meant laying aside certain physical practices and instead committing oneself to the spiritual existence that had been reborn within the Gnostic believer.

38. Thomassen, 'How Valentinian Is the *Gospel of Philip*?', 254.

39. Thomassen observes that 'although the incarnation and the crucifixion are both clearly taken for granted and possess obvious soteriological significance, there is no mention of suffering on the part of the Saviour in the whole of *Gos. Phil.* . . . In this sense, it may be argued that *Gos. Phil.* presents a somewhat more de-historicised Saviour.' See, Thomassen, *The Spiritual Seed: The Church of the Valentinians*, 102.

Bibliography

A. D. DeConick, 'The True Mysteries: Sacramentalism in the Gospel of Philip', *VC* 55 (2001) 225–261.

A. D. DeConick, 'The Great Mystery of Marriage: Sex and Conception in Ancient Valentinian Traditions', *VC* 57 (2003) 307–342.

W. W. Isenberg, 'Gospel According to Philip', in B. Layton (ed.), *Nag Hammadi Codex II, 2–7*, vol. 1: Gospel According to Thomas, Gospel According to Philip, Hypostasis of the Archons, and Indexes (Leiden: Brill, 1989) 129–217.

W. W. Isenberg, 'Philip, Gospel of', in D. N. Freedman, *Anchor Bible Dictionary*, vol. 5 (New York: Doubleday, 1992) 312–313.

H. -J. Klauck, *Apocryphal Gospels: An Introduction* (London: T&T Clark – a Continuum International imprint, 2003).

A. H. B. Logan, *The Gnostics: Identifying an Early Christian Cult* (London: T&T Clark – a Continuum International imprint, 2006).

H. -M. Schenke, 'Das Evangelium nach Philippus. Ein Evangelium der Valentinianer aus dem Funde von Nag-Hamadi', *TLZ* 84 (1959) 1–26.

H. -M. Schenke, 'Das Evangelium nach Philippus', in J. Leipoldt and H. -M. Schenke (eds), *Koptisch-gnostische Schriften aus den Papyrus-Codices von Nag-Hamadi* (Hamburg-Bergstedt: Reich-Evangelischer Verlag, 1960) 31–65.

C. B. Smith II, *No Longer Jews: The Search for Gnostic Origins* (Peabody: Hendrickson, 2004).

E. Thomassen, *The Spiritual Seed: The Church of the Valentinians* (NHMS 60, Leiden: Brill, 2006).

J. D. Turner and A. McGuire (eds), *The Nag Hammadi Library after Fifty Years: Proceedings of the 1995 Society of Biblical Literature Commemoration* (Leiden: Brill, 1997).

M. L. Turner, *The Gospel According to Philip. The Sources and Coherence of an Early Christian Collection* (Leiden: Brill, 1996).

R. McL. Wilson, *The Gospel of Philip* (London: A. R. Mowbray & Co., 1962).

CHAPTER 7

THE *GOSPEL OF JUDAS*: AN UNLIKELY HERO

Simon J. Gathercole

'One of the greatest historical discoveries of the twentieth century', wrote New Testament scholar Bart Ehrman.[1] 'Greatest archaeological discovery of all time', announced the *Mail on Sunday*.[2] In April 2006, when the English translation and a preliminary Coptic text of the *Gospel of Judas* was finally published, the work provoked a flurry of media attention in which journalists tried to talk scholars into saying that it would overturn the traditional picture of Christianity. Most scholars resisted the temptation, although Bart Ehrman went so far as to say that 'It will open up new vistas for understanding Jesus and the religious movement he founded.'[3]

What attracted the most attention in the publicity surrounding the *Gospel of Judas* was its apparently radical re-interpretation of the betrayal of Jesus. This betrayal did not, according to the original publication of this new Gospel, lead to Judas being cursed by God, but was in fact an action to which Jesus gave his blessing. Jesus tells Judas that, by comparison with the other disciples and the rest of humanity, 'You will be greater than them all. For you will sacrifice the man who carries me about' (codex p. 56).[4]

At the time of writing, I am aware of about a dozen books already published on the *Gospel of Judas*. The volume edited by Rodolphe Kasser, the first scholar to work in detail on the text, contains the first official translation and also has several essays on the interpretation of the text and its historical origins.[5] This has been published by National Geographic (who hold the copyright to the text), as has a journalistic account of the manuscript's discovery and tortuous journey from an Egyptian tomb to its final publication.[6] Another book, written

1. R. Kasser, M. Meyer and G. Wurst (eds), (with additional commentary by B. D. Ehrman), *The Gospel of Judas* (Washington, DC: National Geographic, 2006), back cover.

2. *The Mail on Sunday*, 12 March 2006.

3. B. D. Ehrman, 'Christianity Turned on Its Head: The Alternative Vision of the Gospel of Judas', in Kasser *et al.* (eds), *The Gospel of Judas*, 77–120 (80).

4. This translation is drawn from that in Kasser *et al.* (eds), *The Gospel of Judas*, 19–45.

5. Kasser *et al.* (eds), *The Gospel of Judas*, 19–45.

6. H. Krosney, *The Lost Gospel: The Quest for the Gospel of Judas Iscariot* (Washington, DC: National Geographic, 2006). See also the National Geographic DVD documentary *The Gospel of Judas*.

by James Robinson, appeared at the same time as the two 'official' publications and offered a very different side to the story.[7] Tom Wright, the Bishop of Durham, has written a short book arguing that the *Gospel of Judas* exposes just how incredible Gnostic portraits of Jesus are given that they detach Jesus from his Jewish origins.[8] By contrast, the famously sceptical Gert Lüdemann has written a much less traditional book, treating the *Gospel of Judas* alongside the *Gospel of Mary*.[9] Bart Ehrman, a contributor to both of the National Geographic volumes, has also produced his own book with the US division of Oxford University Press.[10] The year 2006 also saw a German translation of the text,[11] and a book in Dutch, by Egyptologist Jacques van der Vliet.[12]

Nor had the excitement died down by 2007, when there was a further flurry of books. Elaine Pagels and Karen King produced a volume which argued for a polemic against a theology of martyrdom in the work.[13] Stanley Porter and Gordon Heath have attacked the sensationalism surrounding the publication of the work.[14] My own book,[15] and that of April DeConick appeared towards the end of the year, the latter important for the criticisms it raises of the preliminary publication of the text published.[16] DeConick argues that the original published text distorts the picture of Jesus in the work by turning him into the hero, whereas in reality Judas is portrayed very negatively, even as a demon. Most important of the publications from 2007 for scholarly purposes, however, are the two critical editions.[17] There is also a very learned, almost book-length, article in German by Coptologist Peter Nagel.[18] The *Gospel of Judas* bibliography will no doubt continue to burgeon. Bart Ehrman's prediction will

7. J. M. Robinson, *The Secrets of Judas: The Story of the Misunderstood Judas and His Lost Gospel* (New York: HarperSanFrancisco, 2006).

8. N. T. Wright, *Jesus and the Gospel of Judas* (London: SPCK, 2006).

9. G. Lüdemann, *Das Judas-Evangelium und das Evangelium nach Maria. Zwei gnostische Schriften aus der Frühzeit des Christentums* (Stuttgart: Radius, 2006).

10. B. D. Ehrman, *The Lost Gospel of Judas Iscariot: A New Look at Betrayer and Betrayed* (New York: Oxford University Press, 2006).

11. U. -K. Plisch, 'Das Judasevangelium', in U. -K. Plisch (ed.), *Was nicht in der Bibel Steht: Apokryphe Schriften des frühen Christentums* (Stuttgart: Deutsche Bibelgesellschaft, 2006) 165–177, and for the translation with scholarly notes, U. -K. Plisch, 'Das Evangelium des Judas', *Zeitschrift für antikes Christentum* 10 (2006) 5–14.

12. J. van der Vliet, *Het Evangelie van Judas: Verrader of bevrijder?* (Utrecht/Antwerpen: Uitgeverij Servire, 2006).

13. E. Pagels and K. L. King, *Reading Judas: The Gospel of Judas and the Shaping of Christianity* (London: Penguin/Allen Lane, 2007).

14. S. E. Porter and G. L. Heath, *The Lost Gospel of Judas: Separating Fact from Fiction* (Grand Rapids: Eerdmans, 2007).

15. S. J. Gathercole, *The Gospel of Judas* (Oxford: Oxford University Press, 2007).

16. A. D. DeConick, *The Thirteenth Apostle: What the Gospel of Judas Really Says* (London: A Continuum imprint, 2007).

17. The English-language critical edition: R. Kasser, G. Wurst, *et al.* (eds), *The Gospel of Judas: Critical Edition* (Washington, DC: National Geographic, 2007); the German: H. -G. Bethge and J. Brankaer (eds), *Codex Tchacos: Texte und Analysen* (Berlin: Walter de Gruyter, 2007).

18. P. Nagel, 'Das Evangelium nach Judas', *Zeitschrift für die Neutestamentliche Wissenschaft* 98 (2007) 213–276.

certainly come true: 'Eventually there will be hundreds of scholarly books and articles written on the Gospel of Judas.'[19]

As already mentioned in connection with April DeConick's *The Thirteenth Apostle*, one of the recent twists of fate is that the question of whether Judas is a hero or a villain in the work has been opened. Bart Ehrman and the Pagels/King translation followed the National Geographic's initial interpretation of Judas as the hero of the work. On the other hand, April DeConick's book and the German critical edition have argued strongly for a negative portrayal of Judas – he is altogether too unlikely a hero after all. The earliest academic discussions of the *Gospel of Judas* have been dominated by this question, which is a pity: in fact the figure of Judas is by no means central to the work.[20]

1. *The Manuscript and Its Origins*

The *Gospel of Judas* is copied in the ancient Egyptian language of Coptic on 26 papyrus pages – 26 fairly short pages, since the surviving work is only about as long as Paul's epistle to the Ephesians. It is found in a codex, a bound volume similar to those found near Nag Hammadi in Egypt in 1945–1946. The papyrus has been carbon dated to the third or fourth century CE, and our copy seems to have been made somewhere not far from where it was discovered – about 100 miles south of Cairo. The language bears the influence of the dialect of Coptic local to this region.[21]

But in fact the *Gospel of Judas* goes back considerably earlier than the third or fourth century. Our Coptic version of the text is not the original; the first edition of the *Gospel of Judas* was almost certainly written in Greek, probably sometime between 140 and 200 CE. And there is a reasonable chance that we have reference to it in the church fathers, although this is by no means as certain as some of the literature so far has assumed. Irenaeus refers to a work of the same name, and to the group behind it, in his *Against Heresies*:

> Others again say that Cain came from a higher Power, and claim that Esau, Korah and the Sodomites and all such people are their ancestors. They also claim that because of this, they have been attacked by the creator, but that none of them has actually been harmed. For Sophia snatched away from them what belonged to her. They say that Judas the betrayer knew these things very well, and that he alone – more than the other disciples – knew the truth and so accomplished the mystery of the betrayal. So they say that through him all things, both earthly and heavenly, were dissolved. And they put

19. Ehrman, *The Lost Gospel of Judas Iscariot*, 100.

20. This was the main question which emerged in all three sessions on the *Gospel of Judas* at the 2007 Annual Meeting of the Society of Biblical Literature in San Diego.

21. On all this, see R. Kasser, 'The Story of Codex Tchacos and the Gospel of Judas', in Kasser *et al.* (eds), *The Gospel of Judas* (Washington, DC: National Geographic, 2006) 47–76.

forward a fabricated book to this effect, which they call the 'Gospel of Judas'. (*Against Heresies*, I, 31, 1–2)

Epiphanius then makes the next mention of the *Gospel of Judas*, in his *Medicine-Chest against the Heresies*, written in the 370s CE. He contributes the information that it was a 'short work' (*syntagmation*), and also notes the name of the group which made use of it – the Cainites, who derived their name from their reverence for Cain (*Panarion*, 38, 1.5).[22] Theodoret in the fifth century CE is the last of the Fathers to discuss the work, and seems to argue against its authenticity on the grounds that Judas hanged himself shortly after the betrayal, and so would not have had the opportunity to write a Gospel (*Compendium*, I, 15). It may well be that this *Gospel of Judas* talked about by the Fathers was substantially the same as our own. The mention of it as a short book might be a point in favour. But on the other hand, there are certain striking differences from the patristic accounts. Certainly the surviving *Gospel of Judas* has no interest in Cain: on the contrary, it is Seth who is the ancestor of the 'Gnostics' in our Coptic text. But a connection still can certainly not be ruled out.[23]

2. *The* Gospel of Judas*: Its Content and Meaning*

In fact, Judas and his betrayal of Jesus are by no means the central focus of the new Gospel, which is why – as already mentioned – it is rather frustrating that the original publication and the recent reactions against it have been dominated by this question. The main attention in the work is actually focused upon the secret revelation about the nature of the world and the message of salvation that is communicated by Jesus to Judas. The principal subject matter of the *Gospel of Judas* is *gnōsis* – the secret knowledge by which one is liberated from the slavery of this present ill-formed world and returned to the spiritual light from which one's true self came. Because of this misconception about the *Gospel of Judas*'s centre of gravity, some space is devoted here to expounding the content of the work. Thereafter we will address some of the claims made about its significance.

The *Gospel of Judas* can roughly be divided (as far as we can tell, given its fragmentary state) into two main sections. The first half consists of a dialogue between Jesus and all his disciples, and the second half principally of a dialogue with Judas – with one long stretch of that second half being a discourse by Jesus. Before the main body of the text there is a prologue and a summary

22. These Cainites are already known from third-century writers, but although their name is often included in modern editions of Irenaeus, it almost certainly does not go back to Irenaeus himself.

23. For more on the Cainites, see Gathercole, *Gospel of Judas*, 114–131.

of Jesus' ministry, and at the end an epilogue in which the 'betrayal' of Jesus is described, followed finally by the title of the work.

Prologue (codex p. 33)

The *Gospel of Judas* begins with an announcement of its contents: 'The secret message of the revelation which Jesus spoke to Judas Iscariot in the week leading up to the third day before he celebrated passover.' (codex p. 33). This makes clear the kind of work it is: a Gospel similar in some respects to the *Gospel of Thomas* and *Gospel of Mary*. It is not a narration of Jesus' public ministry, death and resurrection as *per* the four Gospels in the New Testament, but is instead a secret revelation to an individual. The revelation to Judas comes to an end 'on the third day before he celebrated passover' probably because the traditional account of the passion has the plot against Jesus being set in motion when passover is two days away (Mk 14.1).

Summary of Jesus' ministry (codex p. 33)

The *Gospel of Judas* is further introduced with a paragraph describing Jesus in reasonably orthodox terms as a wonder-worker and saviour, and mentioning the calling of the disciples.

Part I: Dialogue between Jesus and the disciples (codex pp. 33–43)

The action of the dialogue in Part I breaks naturally into three parts, each taking place on a different day. Day 1 involves Jesus coming upon the disciples celebrating 'eucharistia'. This is the first indication that elements of this new Gospel may be somewhat anachronistic, although one could take the disciples merely to be giving thanks over a meal. In any case, there is a bigger surprise in the shape of Jesus' response to the disciples here: he laughs. He is laughing, he says, not at the disciples themselves, but is rather pouring scorn upon their *practice*. They may think that they are worshiping the true God through this eucharist, but in fact their worship is really a form of idolatry. Here we encounter the all-important distinction in the *Gospel of Judas* between the true supreme divinity, called the 'Great Invisible Spirit', and the lesser, evil demiurge Saklas. The disciples here have been deceived, by errant heavenly powers, into worshipping this false deity. It does not require an overactive imagination to see the real-life backdrop to the text at this point. Clearly what we have is a polemic against what the pagan philosopher Celsus called 'the great church' – the Christianity which saw itself as founded upon the 12 disciples, and which claimed that its teaching was rooted in the doctrine of the apostles. The *Gospel of Judas*, on the other hand, reflects the voice of a dissident group implacably opposed to this 'great church'.

After the events of day 1, Jesus disappears. Day 2 begins with Jesus reappearing, and he explains that in his absence from the disciples he has been visiting a 'great and holy generation' – clearly a breed far superior to the idolatrous disciples. It is identified elsewhere in the work as the seed, or generation, of Seth. The disciples ask him about this generation, and Jesus laughs again, this time at the folly of the attempt to inquire into what is infinitely beyond them. This clearly continues the polemic: this generation – one might call them 'Gnostics' or 'Sethians' – are the superior race, incomprehensible to the inferior false believers who merely merit Jesus' mockery.

On the third day, the disciples receive the heaviest blow of all. They recount to Jesus a vision which they have collectively experienced, in which priests are offering sacrifices in a temple. These priests are no ordinary pious servants of God, however. They are seen in the vision as guilty of murder, homosexual behaviour, child sacrifice and other unsavoury activities. Jesus then delivers an interpretation of the vision: the priests are the disciples themselves. Again, then, the attack on the non-Gnostic church continues: the leaders of the unenlightened pseudo-Christians are corrupt priests who lead the poor ignorant masses astray.

In the course of these three days of rather strained discussions between Jesus and the disciples, there has nevertheless been one of the twelve who has begun to grasp Jesus' esoteric teaching. Judas has recognized who Jesus really is – not a son of the god worshipped in the eucharist, but rather an emissary from the aeon of Barbelo, despatched by the supreme deity. (Barbelo is a female or androgynous divinity, one of the highest in the Gnostic hierarchy, though not herself the supreme God.) Since Judas has proven himself worthy to receive further *gnōsis*, Jesus takes him aside: 'Step away from the others, and I shall tell you the mysteries of the Kingdom' (codex p. 35).

Part II: Dialogue between Jesus and Judas, including monologue on creation (codex pp. 43–57)

Judas, then, becomes detached from the hopeless band of disciples. Although he once shared in the eucharist, he has begun to see the error of his ways and separated himself from the others. (There is a strong contrast here with the account in Acts 1, which also talks of Judas defecting from the 12, but in very different terms.) It is this second half of the work which really seems to fulfil the promise of the prologue, and to deliver the secret revelation of Jesus to Judas.

The focus of the revelation is primarily on the events of creation. The drama of this creation opens with a great cloud of light, probably a representation of the Great Invisible Spirit, and from this cloud emerges a great angel called Autogenes (literally 'self-generated'). He is called the 'light-god', and is therefore another figure who embodies the supreme reality of the sacred. This Autogenes generates a number of luminaries (the term used for the sun and moon in Genesis), myriads of angels to minister to him, and – those distinguishing marks of this kind of creation account – the 'aeons'. These aeons are heavenly spheres or time-zones with a twist: they are also divine characters who in some sense have personhood. Twelve of these aeons, for example, coalesce to form a descendant of Autogenes, the heavenly primal Man 'Adamas'. This Adamas brings further creatures into being, and the luminaries further generate more luminaries as well.

So thus far there are two major differences between the account of creation here and that of Genesis. First, the focus is not on the creative activity of a single figure, God, but on successive creations who in turn become creators. It is more akin to a genealogy: A generates B, who generates C, and so forth. Second, our author considers that the author of Genesis has jumped far too precipitately into describing the creation of the physical world. As any good Platonist knows, there must be an ideal heavenly world before the material world, which it resembles, can come into being.

But there are still further divergences from the biblical version of events. At some point in the cascade of creations, things go bad. This might be because of a fall of some kind. Perhaps more likely, however, is that we have the other explanation of evil found in Gnostic accounts: not a single fall, but rather a gradual dilution of the light the further away one gets from the original source, the great luminous cloud. After the first few rounds of creation, we encounter the *cosmos* – not the physical world, because we are still in the realms of the heavenly idea of the physical world which will be a copy of it. Nevertheless, even this archetypal pattern of the *cosmos* is corrupt: the *Gospel of Judas* calls it 'the cosmos, that is, perdition' (codex p. 50). When the material form of this *cosmos* comes into being, it is populated by Adam and Eve, as one might expect. But Adam and Eve are not the products of the supreme benign deity as in the Old Testament. They appear on the production line just after the rulers of the underworld and chaos, all made by the evil deity Saklas (*sakla* is Aramaic for 'fool') and his angelic minions. As in Genesis, Adam and Eve are the final creatures to appear; but in the *Gospel of Judas* they are at the end because they are the dregs, rather than the pinnacle of creation.

But to return to happier things, we have already mentioned in passing the generative activity of Adamas. In Genesis, the earthly Adam's true heir was Seth, through whom the line of humanity continued. Adam*as*, the heavenly counterpart of Adam, also has a heavenly son called Seth, who in the *Gospel of Judas* – as in other similar works – is the first of the great holy generation mentioned by Jesus in Part I. The descendants of Adamas and Seth are no less than the true heavenly selves of Gnostic believers. The true holy generation which spiritually towers above the corrupt 'apostolic church' traces its real ancestry back to the primeval spirits descended from Adamas.

As has been noted, the question which has dominated scholarship thus far is whether Judas belongs to this holy generation, to the demonic realm, or to somewhere in between. The other disciples are described as 'those who offer up sacrifice to Saklas'; Judas will sacrifice the physical body which carries around the spirit of Jesus (codex p. 56). Is Judas here a true priest of the Great

Invisible Spirit, rather than a corrupt priest like the rest of the disciples in the temple vision of day 3 above? Is he an ideal servant because he will perform the ultimate sacrifice? Or does he, as DeConick argues, thereby do *worse* than the other disciples?[24] We do not have space to go into the matter here, but the text as it stands appears to present Judas ambiguously: he is neither portrayed in a straightforwardly negative or positive manner.

Epilogue: The Betrayal (codex p. 58)
After the abstruse revelation communicated to Judas and his subsequent leap into the great light-cloud, the action moves back to earth.[25] The betrayal is actually described very briefly, and so the conclusion to the text is quite abrupt. The high priests are looking out for a way to arrest Jesus, but are also nervous about his popularity among the people who consider him a prophet. They approach Judas, who takes his payment from them and delivers Jesus: 'Judas took some money, and he handed him over to them' (codex p. 58). End of story. This strikes us as odd if we are familiar with the New Testament Gospels, with their lengthy accounts of the cross and resurrection. But the apparent anticlimax in the *Gospel of Judas* only serves to highlight the point made in the preface: that the focus of the work is not historical events, but 'the secret message of the revelation'.

Title (codex p. 58)
The title 'the Gospel of Judas' is not a modern invention, but the title given – as is often the case in Coptic texts – at the end of the copy in the manuscript itself. So the 'good news' or 'Gospel' does not consist of Jesus dying for our sins, but rather of the 'knowledge' mentioned at several points in the text, expounded by Jesus to Judas particularly in the long discourse on the nature of the world and salvation. In taking the title of 'Gospel', the work locates itself among both canonical and non-canonical works similarly entitled. We do not know how many other accounts of Jesus had been produced prior to the *Gospel of Judas*, but its relationship to them would not have been the same in each case. The *Gospel of Judas* is clearly intended in large measure to supersede the four canonical Gospels, whereas it may have sat more happily alongside other Gnostic works such as the *Gospel of Mary*.

3. *The Significance of the* Gospel of Judas

We have already mentioned the stir caused by the publication of the *Gospel of Judas*, and so for many people it is clearly not just another Gnostic work

24. DeConick, *The Thirteenth Apostle*, 57–58.

25. Some scholars – notably those who see Judas in a negative light – read the text as saying that *Jesus* enters the light cloud. This does not appear to me to be the natural reading of the text, but this part of the text is precisely one of the areas of the debate over the portrayal of Judas.

contained in an Egyptian codex. We have a good number of these from the same period, and yet *Zostrianos*, *Hypsiphrone* and the *Trimorphic Protennoia* have not been the subjects of eye-catching books which have spent weeks on the *New York Times* best-seller list. Clearly the *Gospel of Judas* has caught the public imagination to some extent, while also attracting a lot of scholarly attention. Nevertheless, some of the claims that have been made on its behalf by its admirers need to be taken with a pinch of salt. We will begin by looking at that for which the *Gospel of Judas* is most direct evidence, and then work back in time to Jesus.

3.1 *The* Gospel of Judas *and Gnosticism*

One of the most complicated questions in the history of earliest Christianity is that of how the Gnostic creation myth develops. We know of it from the several different versions preserved – in Irenaeus' *Against Heresies*, in the various texts of the *Apocryphon of John* and in works newly discovered near Nag Hammadi such as *Eugnostos the Blessed* and the *Gospel of the Egyptians*.[26] Now the *Gospel of Judas* enters the picture. Those who favour the idea of a pre-Christian Gnostic mythology, such as Marvin Meyer, are likely to be interested in the question of what in the *Gospel of Judas* goes back to 'Jewish Gnostic lore'.[27] On the other side, scholars who are not convinced of the Jewish Gnosticism theory will be more interested in locating the *Gospel of Judas* in relation to other second-century versions of the myth.

3.2 *'Gnosticism' and 'Christianity' in the Second Century*

The reappraisal of Gnosticism in the past generation has argued strongly for the position that 'Gnostics' were Christians just as much were the orthodox – both groups were part of the great melting pot of earliest Christian faith. The problem with this thesis, however, is that often neither side really regarded the other as part of the same movement at all. Irenaeus, for example, certainly did not regard the Gnostics as Christians, but similarly neither did the Gnostics regard themselves and the 'orthodox' as together constituting one big (even unhappy) family. To impose the single category of 'Christian' upon all of them may serve a contemporary ideological purpose (as, to be sure, does keeping Gnostics and Christians distinct), but does little to help us understand them.

The *Gospel of Judas* is an interesting example of this tendency to highlight the ugly ditch between Gnostics and orthodox in the second century. The 'great church' is, as we have seen, lampooned as a corruption. It is noteworthy that while Jesus occupies a central place in the document, he is quite separate from

26. These traditions have been meticulously analysed above all in A. Logan, *Gnostic Truth and Christian Heresy: A Study in the History of Gnosticism* (Edinburgh: T&T Clark, 1996).

27. M. Meyer, 'Introduction', in Kasser *et al.* (eds), *Gospel of Judas*, 1–16 (10).

another figure called 'Christ': this title refers to one of the gods of the underworld created by Saklas. So Jesus' credentials as Jewish Messiah have been swept aside in preference for his role as Gnostic revealer.

3.3 *Evidence for First-Century Christianity?*

As is widely recognized in the scholarly work on the *Gospel of Judas* thus far, the chances of the document going back to, or even telling us anything new about, first-century Christianity are slim indeed. The overwhelming scholarly consensus is that the *Gospel of Judas* dates to the mid-second century.[28] The most telling evidence for the majority of scholars has been the presence of motifs such as the 'aeons', and of figures such as Barbelo, Autogenes and Adamas – all of which are the bread-and-butter of second-century Gnosticism but unknown in the literature of the first century.

To the evidence that has already been recognized by scholars one can add the picture of the church's structure presupposed by the *Gospel of Judas*. We have already mentioned the temple vision in which the disciples see themselves as depraved priests: here the leaders of the emerging Orthodox Church are portrayed as priests performing sacrifices in a temple at an altar. This characterization of Christian worship is hard to imagine before the end of the first century; we see the beginnings of it in the *Didache* and *1 Clement*.

Gregor Wurst has argued that the separation of Judas from the disciples and his subsequent replacement by another, shows that our author was aware of the account in *Acts of Matthias* taking Judas's place, and this may well be right.[29] Perhaps clearer, however, is the probable dependence of the *Gospel of Judas* on the *Gospel of Matthew*. This is suggested by influence of Matthean redaction at the end of the work: 'Some of the scribes were there looking out so that they might arrest him at prayer, for they feared the people, because they all held him to be a prophet' (codex p. 58; cf. Mt. 21.46). Another indication in this direction is the *Gospel of Judas*'s use of the phrase 'way of righteousness', found in the New Testament only in Mt. 21.32, and there are other similar examples.[30] So if the *Gospel of Judas* post-dates Matthew, this reinforces the view that it is a product of the second century.

3.4 *Evidence for Jesus?*

Given the evidence that the *Gospel of Judas* originates in the second century rather than the first, it is very difficult to have any confidence that it preserves

28. See for example, Meyer, 'Introduction', 5.

29. G. Wurst, 'Irenaeus of Lyon and the Gospel of Judas', in Kasser *et al.* (eds), *The Gospel of Judas*, 121–135 (132–133). The parallels are between Acts 1.21–26 and the top of page 36 in the codex.

30. On this, see further my discussion in *The Gospel of Judas*, 134–138.

any tradition about Jesus which is independent of the four NT Gospels. The eyewitnesses of Jesus' ministry had long since died out by the time the *Gospel of Judas* is composed. One particularly clear illustration of the distance between the *Gospel of Judas* and the historical Jesus is in his detachment from Judaism in the work. Jesus is not portrayed as in any sense the fulfilment of Jewish expectation, nor is Jesus' Jewishness integral to his personality at all.

In fact, humanity is not integral to Jesus' person either – this is another theological theme which shows that he has moved a long way from his Jewish roots. The already well-known reference to Judas's destiny of sacrificing the man who carries Jesus highlights the fact that we have a kind of docetic Christology in the *Gospel of Judas*: Jesus is not truly human, but remains a purely divine spirit uncontaminated with the flesh even in his earthly existence. As a result of this, the *Gospel of Judas* has nothing about Jesus' self-giving love on the cross. Indeed, there is no mention of love – divine or human – in the whole of the book.

4. *Conclusion*

The *Gospel of Judas* offers us, as we have said, a fascinating window into the turbulent relationship between the 'the great church' and some of her opponents in the second century CE, and its account of the Gnostic creation myth will no doubt add further complexity to the task of those brave souls who try to trace its development. However, one should be extremely sceptical of claims that 'it will open up new vistas for understanding Jesus'. It has very little that can be regarded as historically reliable: indeed nothing that is new in the *Gospel of Judas* can be said with any confidence to go back to historical bedrock. In addition, it is difficult to imagine a twenty-first-century reader who would find its vision of a somewhat loveless Jesus detached from a body in any way theologically attractive.

Bibliography

Critical Editions

J. Brankaer and H. -G. Bethge (eds), *Codex Tchacos: Texte und Analysen* (Texte und Untersuchungen zur Geschichte der altchristlichen Literatur 161; Berlin: Walter de Gruyter, 2007).

R. Kasser, G. Wurst, M. Meyer and F. Gaudard (eds), *The Gospel of Judas together with the Letter of Peter to Philip, James, and a Book of Allogenes from Codex Tchacos: Critical Edition* (Washington, DC: National Geographic, 2007).

Translations with Other Explanatory Material

A. D. DeConick, *The Thirteenth Apostle: What the Gospel of Judas Really Says* (London: A Continuum imprint, 2007).

S. J. Gathercole, *The Gospel of Judas* (Oxford: Oxford University Press, 2007).

R. Kasser, M. Meyer and G. Wurst (eds), *The Gospel of Judas*, with additional commentary by B. D. Ehrman (Washington, DC: National Geographic, 2006).

P. Nagel, 'Das Evangelium nach Judas', *ZNW* 98 (2007) 213–276.

E. Pagels and K. L. King, *Reading Judas: The Gospel of Judas and the Shaping of Christianity* (London: Penguin/Allen Lane, 2007).

U. -K. Plisch, 'Das Judasevangelium', in U. -K. Plisch (ed.), *Was nicht in der Bibel Steht: Apokryphe Schriften des frühen Christentums* (Stuttgart: Deutsche Bibelgesellschaft, 2006) 165–177.

U. -K. Plisch, 'Das Evangelium des Judas', *ZAC* 10 (2006) 5–14.

J. van der Vliet, *Het Evangelie van Judas: Verrader of bevrijder?* (Utrecht/Antwerpen: Uitgeverij Servire, 2006).

Other Secondary Literature

B. D. Ehrman, *The Lost Gospel of Judas Iscariot: A New Look at Betrayer and Betrayed* (New York: Oxford University Press, 2006).

H. Krosney, *The Lost Gospel: The Quest for the Gospel of Judas Iscariot* (Washington, DC: National Geographic, 2006).

J. M. Robinson, *The Secrets of Judas: The Story of the Misunderstood Judas and his Lost Gospel* (New York: HarperSanFrancisco, 2006).

N. T. Wright, *Jesus and the Gospel of Judas* (London: SPCK, 2006).

Chapter 8

The *Gospel of Judas*: A Parody of Apostolic Christianity

April D. DeConick

On the evening of 9 April 2006, the National Geographic Society aired a documentary, *The Gospel of Judas: The Lost Version of Christ's Betrayal.* The movie showed the scholars who were members of the National Geographic team tell their stories about the recovery, reconstruction and interpretation of the 'found' *Gospel of Judas*. They said that this gospel presents us with a very different story of Judas Iscariot, one in which Judas is the hero, not the villain. As Jesus' 'soul-mate', Judas was asked by Jesus to kill him in order to release Jesus' spirit and bring about salvation. This opinion formed the basis for the team's book, *The Gospel of Judas*, released on the same day.[1]

In many ways, this line of interpretation reclaimed and affirmed the opinion of Epiphanius who said that Judas, in his gospel, betrayed Jesus because he was a strong Power from above whose knowledge was supreme. Judas knew if he betrayed Jesus, that Christ's crucifixion would destroy the Archons, the gods who ruled this world. So Judas carried it out. Epiphanius writes, 'Knowing this, Judas made every effort to betray him, thereby accomplishing a good work for salvation. We should admire and praise Judas because through him the salvation of the cross was prepared for us' (*Pan.* 38.3.1–5).

This line of interpretation has been accepted and reaffirmed by many well-known scholars who quickly released their own interpretations, and in some cases translations, of the *Gospel of Judas*.[2] Unfortunately, these studies are based on the faulty provisional Coptic transcription originally posted by the National Geographic Society on its website and the English translation in the original popular English publication.[3] In some quarters, however, re-evaluation of the Coptic and a reassessment of the initial reading of the *Gospel of Judas*

1. R. Kasser, M. Meyer and G. Wurst, *The Gospel of Judas* (Washington, DC: National Geographic, 2006).

2. Cf. B. D. Ehrman, *The Lost Gospel of Judas Iscariot: A New Look at Betrayer and Betrayed* (Oxford: Oxford University Press, 2006); N. T. Wright, *Jesus and the Gospel of Judas* (London: SPCK, 2006); E. Pagels and K. L. King, *Reading Judas: The Gospel of Judas and the Shaping of Christianity* (New York: Viking, 2007).

3. Kasser, Meyer and Wurst, *Gospel of Judas.*

have been underway since April 2006, and the results are shocking. Judas is not a hero or a Gnostic, but is evil as ever.[4]

1. *The Tchacos Codex and the Qarara Books*

The *Gospel of Judas* is one manuscript within a bigger papyrus codex. The modern name of the codex derives from the name of the Zurich antiquities dealer, Frieda Nussberger-Tchacos, who purchased the book after it had been decaying in a bank vault in Hicksville, New York, for many years. In 2001, she brought the codex to Switzerland, met Professor Rudolphe Kasser, and established the Maecenas Foundation to aid in the codex's restoration. Eventually the National Geographic Society became involved, purchasing the right to publish the codex. The Society appointed a team of scholars to complete the restoration, translation and interpretation of the codex. Scholars who became members of the team were required to sign non-disclosure statements to keep the release of the documents secret.

Unfortunately this resulted in a situation in which the codex had not been analysed and discussed broadly by a community of scholars before the release of a 'definitive' translation or critical edition. This created an odd situation in which a handful of scholars released the official transcription and interpretation of a codex that the rest of scholars had not seen. National Geographic released the *Critical Edition* in the summer of 2007, while refraining from publishing useable full-size facsimile photographs.[5] This limited scholars in their ability to evaluate the official transcription and to make their own personal contributions.

The publication of the Tchacos Codex in the *Critical Edition* released by the National Geographic Society was further complicated by the fact that a

4. L. Painchaud, 'À Propos de la (Re)découverte de L'Évangile de Judas', *Laval théologique et philosophique* 62.3 (October 2006) 553–568; A. D. DeConick, *The Thirteenth Apostle: What the Gospel of Judas Really Says* (New York: Continuum, 2007); J. Brankaer and H -G. Bethge, *Codex Tchacos: Texte und Analysen* (Texte und Untersuchungen zur Geschichte der altchristlichen Literatur 161; Berlin: de Gruyter, 2007); G. S. Robinson, 'The Relationship of the Gospel of Judas to the New Testament and to Sethianism, Appended by a new English translation of the *Gospel of Judas*', *Journal for Coptic Studies* (forthcoming, 2008); A. D. DeConick, 'The Mystery of Judas' Betrayal: What the *Gospel of Judas* Really Says', in Madeleine Scopello (ed.), *The Gospel of Judas in Context. Proceedings of the First International Conference on the Gospel of Judas*. Paris, Sorbonne, October 27th–28th 2006, (Leiden, 2008). E. Thomassen, 'Is Judas Really the Hero of the Gospel?', in Madeleine Scopello (ed.), *The Gospel of Judas in Context. Proceedings of the First International Conference on the Gospel of Judas*. Paris, Sorbonne, October 27th–28th 2006, (Leiden, 2008). J. Turner, 'The Place of the *Gospel of Judas* in Sethian Literature', in Madeleine Scopello (ed.), *The Gospel of Judas in Context. Proceedings of the First International Conference on the Gospel of Judas*. Paris, Sorbonne, October 27th–28th 2006, (Leiden, 2008).

5. R. Kasser, G. Wurst, M. Meyer and F. Gaudard, *The Gospel of Judas together with the Letter of Peter to Philip, James, and a Book of Allogenes from Codex Tchacos: Critical Edition* (Washington, DC: National Geographic Society, 2007).

substantial portion of the ancient book, some 50 photographed fragments (a.k.a. the Ohio fragments), remain unpublished because this part of the book is being held hostage in a legal battle over ownership. So it is important for us to remember that we do not know yet the full extent of the contents of the Tchacos Codex. The portion that we do have appears to be the first 66 pages of the codex.

The *Gospel of Judas* is found on pages 33 to 58 of the Tchacos Codex. It is the only surviving copy from antiquity of the *Gospel of Judas*. The other documents within the book are another copy of the *Letter of Peter to Philip* (1–9; cf. NHC 8, 2 132.10–140.27), another version of the *First Apocalypse of James* (10–22; cf. NHC 5, 3 24.10–44.10) and a fragment of the beginning of another work whose central figure is named Allogenes (59–66). Two of the Ohio fragments (Ohio 4578, 4579) from *Corpus Hermeticum* 13.1–2 have also been identified. It remains to be seen whether they were part of this book.

The Tchacos Codex was not discovered alone. In the 1970s, it was found with three other ancient books in limestone box when a tomb near Jebel Qarara just north of Al Minya was looted. Like the Tchacos Codex, the three other books do not survive intact. They were divided into smaller portions by antiquities dealers who wanted to increase profits from their sale. One of these books was a fourth- or fifth-century papyrus codex containing a very important version of Exodus.[6] This codex survives in pieces scattered in private collections and university libraries.[7] The second codex, a book containing Paul's letters, has not resurfaced. What we know about it comes from the brief report written in 1983 by Stephen Emmel, who had the opportunity to view the codices when they were being offered for sale.[8] The third book in the limestone box was a Greek geometry book called the *Metrodological Tractate*. It was torn in half and was sold to two separate buyers – Lloyd E. Cotsen, who has donated his portion to Princeton University, and an anonymous private collector.[9]

Why was the Tchacos Codex buried in a tomb with these three other books? If nothing else, their burial together points to their privileged place in the life of an early Christian living in ancient Egypt, a Christian who seems to have had esoteric leanings. Whoever was buried with these books had no difficulty during his or her lifetime studying canonical favourites like Paul and Exodus alongside the Gnostic *Gospel of Judas*. Since both the Hermetics and the Gnostics studied mathematical theorems in order to map their universe, understand

6. D. A. DeSilva and M. P. Adams, 'Seven Papyrus Fragments of a Greek Manuscript of Exodus', *Vetus Testamentum* 56 (2006) 143–170.

7. A list of the whereabouts of these fragments is kept by Ernest A. Muro, Jr on the World Wide Web. See www.breadofangels.com/geneva1983/exodus/index/html (last accessed on 23 September 2007).

8. Reported in J. M. Robinson, *The Secrets of Judas: The Story of the Misunderstood Disciple and His Lost Gospel* (San Francisco: Harper, 2006) 117–120.

9. H. Krosney, *The Lost Gospel: The Quest for the Gospel of Judas Iscariot* (Washington, DC: National Geographic, 2006) 226–227, reports that both sections of the treatise will be published by A. Jones and R. Bagnall in 2008.

their place within it and route the spirit's journey home, the burial of the *Metrodological Treatise* with them should not come as a surprise. Knowledge of their contents may have provided the deceased assurance that his or her spirit would find the proper path to the divine realm and not become trapped in the hells and purgatories along the way.

2. *Setting Straight the Coptic Transcription of the* Gospel of Judas

National Geographic's involvement in the publication of the *Gospel of Judas* has complicated the work of scholars. On the one hand, the Society is to be commended for restoring the Tchacos Codex, and for bringing back to life 85 per cent of the *Gospel of Judas*. On the other hand, the rush to publish an English translation of the Gospel for public consumption has resulted in the distribution of faulty information. Part of the faulty information is the consequence of the fact that the scholars who made the first English translation based it on a *provisional unfinished* Coptic transcription. This transcription was released on the National Geographic website at the same time that the English translation was made available in bookstores.

Unfortunately, we now know that the provisional transcription was flawed in crucial areas of the text. These flaws were corrected a year later in the *Critical Edition*, but not before they became part of the academic discourse and the public consciousness. They skewed our perception of the Gospel's actual story and its presentation of Judas. Doesn't the Gospel say that Judas will ascend to the holy generation? Only in the flawed original transcription does Jesus say to Judas, 'In the last days, *they will curse your ascent to the holy generation*' (*Gos. Jud.* 46.24–47.1; italics mine).[10] This particular sentence was the result of a faulty parsing of the Coptic and an emendation of the sentence that resulted in the erasure of the negative future tense from the verb, *bôk*, 'to ascend'. What does the corrected transcription read? 'In the last days *they <will---> to you, and you will not ascend on high to the holy generation*.'[11]

Doesn't the Gospel say that it is possible for Judas to go to the Kingdom? Only in the flawed original transcription does Jesus say to Judas, 'I shall tell you the mysteries of the kingdom. *It is possible for you to reach it, but you will grieve a great deal*' (*Gos. Jud.* 35.25–27; italics mine).[12] What does the corrected transcription say? 'I shall tell you the mysteries of the kingdom, *not so that you will go there, but you will grieve a great deal*.'[13] This opposite reading is the consequence of re-examining the ink traces on the edges of a lacunae in line 26, and correctly adjusting the reading from *oun com*, 'it is possible', to *oukh hina*, 'not so that'.

10. Kasser, Meyer and Wurst, *Gospel of Judas*, 33.
11. Kasser *et al.*, *Critical Edition*, 211.
12. Kasser, Meyer and Wurst, *Gospel of Judas*, 23.
13. Kasser *et al.*, *Critical Edition*, 189.

What this means in terms of interpretation is that there is no evidence in the *Gospel of Judas* that would support an ascent by Judas to the holy generation or any realm beyond those contained within this cosmos. It is quite unfortunate that the faulty readings are now such a large part of the scholarly and public discourse, since the corrected readings present us with a Judas who never leaves this universe.

3. *The Thirteenth Daimon*

The faulty readings generated from the provisional Coptic transcription were compounded by substantial translation errors in the original English translation, many of which, unfortunately, have been retained in the English translation published in the *Critical Edition.* The most important in terms of identifying Judas is the statement found in the *Gospel of Judas* 44.18–21. Jesus mockingly laughs at Judas and says to him, 'Why do you compete (with them), *O Thirteenth Demon*?'[14] The Coptic behind 'demon' is *daimon*, which the National Geographic team rendered 'spirit' in their original publication, while wisely shifting to the more ambiguous '*daimon*' in the *Critical Edition.*[15] The 'spirit' translation was justified on the grounds of Plato's *Symposium* 202e–203a, and it was used to posit Judas as a positive figure.[16]

This may reflect the world-view of Plato and later Hellenistic philosophers, but it does not reflect the world-view closest to the author of the *Gospel of Judas* who was a Sethian Gnostic writing within the Christian tradition. All occurrences of the word *daimon* or a cognate in the New Testament are references to demons.[17] Christian literature in the early period as well as the medieval period contain hundreds of references to words built from the word *daimon.* The meaning of these words? They refer to demons, evil spirits, devils, demon possession, and devilish behaviour.[18] Of the Gnostic books from Nag Hammadi, I have located about 50 occurrences of the word *daimon* or its cognate. In every case, the word refers to an Archon or one of his demonic assistants.[19]

The reason for this sinister designation in Gnostic literature is the fact that the Gnostic cosmology was fairly consistent in terms of its view that a chief

14. DeConick, *The Thirteenth Apostle*, 48–51, 77.

15. Kasser, Meyer and Wurst, *Gospel of Judas*, 31; Kasser *et al.*, *Critical Edition*, 207.

16. Kasser, Meyer and Wurst, *Gospel of Judas*, 31 n. 74, 163–165.

17. Kittel, *TDNT*, 2, 16–19.

18. E. C. E. Owen, 'Daímon and Cognate Words', *JTS* 32 (1931) 133–153.

19. *Holy Book of the Great Invisible Spirit* 57.10–20; 59.25; *Apocalypse of Paul* 19.5; *Apocalypse of Adam* 79.15; *Authoritative Teaching* 34.28; *Trimorphic Protennoia* 35.17; 40.5; 41.6; *Testimony of Truth* 29.17; 42.25; *Apocalypse of Peter* 75.4; 82.23; *Concept of Our Great Power* 42.17; *Zostrianos* 43.12; *Paraphrase of Shem* 21.26; 21.36; 22.7; 22.25; 23.9; 23.16; 24.7; 25.9; 25.19; 25.22; 25.26; 25.29; 27.24; 28.7; 28.15; 29.10; 29.17; 30.1; 30.8; 30.23; 30.32; 31.16; 31.19; 32.6; 32.16; 34.5; 35.15; 35.19; 36.27; 37.21; 40.26; 44.6; 44.15; 44.31; 45.17; 45.23.

Archon, an arrogant and rebellious Demiurge, created and rules this world. Below him exists heavens or realms populated by his own wicked creations, an entourage of Archons and assistants who, alongside him, are rebelling against the supreme transcendent God. When the word *daimon* is used in Gnostic sources, it is applied frequently and consistently to these wicked Archons and their assistants. Its application to Judas in the *Gospel of Judas* should be understood no differently. Jesus is identifying Judas as a demon.

What is perhaps even more fascinating is that the Gospel tells us that Judas is a particular demon, the Thirteenth (*Gos. Jud.* 44.18–21). In another passage in the Gospel, Judas is connected with the Thirteenth realm and its star or planet, which is a reference to the particular Archon who resides there (*Gos. Jud.* 55.10–11). The Gospel physically places Judas in the Thirteenth realm in the near future (*Gos. Jud.* 46.19–24). These references are to Sethian cosmology which is mapped out in terms of thirteen realms. There are five hells or abysses and seven heavens ruled by the demon Archons. These twelve realms are the creations of Ialdabaoth, Saklas and Nebruel, the chief demon Archons who reside above them in the thirteenth realm. In Sethian literature, Ialdabaoth is known by the nickname, 'god of the thirteen realms' (*Gos. Egy.* 63.19). In this same text, Nebruel, one of Ialdabaoth's chief archons living in the thirteenth realm is twice called 'the great demon (*pnoc ndaimôn*)' (*Gos. Egy.* 57.10–20). This is the same Nebro(el) who is also known as Ialdabaoth in the *Gospel of Judas*. This is the particular demon that Judas has been identified with in the *Gospel of Judas*.

How and why this transparent reference to Ialdabaoth was missed in the initial interpretations of the *Gospel of Judas*, I do not know. But until someone can offer a better explanation about the identity of a 'thirteenth spirit' beyond an allusion to lucky numbers,[20] the most reasonable starting point for understanding who Judas is in the *Gospel of Judas* is what the Coptic actually tells us: he is the Thirteenth Demon, Nebro(el)-Ialdabaoth, who is also called the Apostate, the renegade and traitor (*Gos. Jud.* 51.12–15). Saklas, who is mentioned as a separate archon, appears toward the end of the goapel to be amalgamated with this figure too.

4. *Separation from the Gnostic Generation*

Another window into the character of Judas is a very important statement made by Jesus that Judas has been 'separated from' the holy generation (*Gos. Jud.* 46.14–18). The Coptic is very clear here, using the expression *pôrj e*. This expression is a Coptic unit with a fixed lexical meaning – that is, the preposition is bound to the verb in terms of meaning.[21] Although *e* as a lone preposition

20. Kasser, Meyer and Wurst, *Gospel of Judas*, 164–165.

21. Bentley Layton, *A Coptic Grammar* (2nd edn Wiesbaden: Harrassowitz Verlag, 2004) sec. 181.

might have a variety of meanings, including 'for', when it is bound with this particular verb it can only mean 'from'.[22]

This expression is found frequently in Coptic literature, including translations of Old and New Testament passages, and always indicates separation 'from', exclusion or opposition.[23] In Coptic translations of the Bible, it is used to render Paul's question in Rom. 8.35 (S) – 'Who shall separate us from the love of Christ?' – and the words of Jesus in Mt. 10.35 (SB) – 'For I have come to set a man against his father.'

It is chosen by the Coptic translator of the *Gospel of Philip* to indicate the separation of Eve from Adam (70.21) and woman from man (70.10).[24] The same is true of the translator of the *Tripartite Tractate* who wishes to discuss the powers that separate the Pleroma from the Logos (97.21). In *On the Origin of the World*, the expression is used to speak about the separation of Sabaoth from the darkness (106.12), while in two other passages the translator uses it to indicate the separation out of a part from the whole during the process of creation (103.3, 5). In the *Apocryphon of James* 14.33, it indicates the parting of two people – 'I shall depart from you.'

How has this been translated by the National Geographic team in the original publication and is retained in the *Critical Edition*? 'When Judas heard this, he said to him, 'What is the advantage that I have received? For *you have set me apart for that generation*.'[25] It makes a big difference whether Judas is set apart for the Gnostic generation or separated from it! But separated he is, just as we discover earlier when Jesus interprets Judas' dream to mean his exclusion from the holy generation (*Gos. Jud.* 44.15–46.4). In the *Gospel of Judas*, Judas is no hero, and certainly no Gnostic.

5. *Criticism of the Apostolic Church*

Because Judas is identified with the chief Archon, Ialdabaoth, there are a couple of passages in which he is told that he will rule in the thirteenth realm over the twelve Archons and their realms below him (*Gos. Jud.* 45.25–46.24; 55.10–11; cf. 46.2–4) and that he will be in control of the Archons (*Gos. Jud.* 46.5–7).

22. W. E. Crum, *A Coptic Dictionary* (Oxford: Clarendon Press, 1939) 271b–272a. It translates Greek expressions such as χωρίζω ἀπό, διχάζω, διαστέλλω, ἀφορίζω, and ῥήγνυμι.

23. Cf. 2 Kgs 1.23S; Prov. 18.1SA; Wis. Sol. 1.3S; Mt. 10.35; 1 Cor. 7.10; 2 Cor. 6.17; Rom. 8.35.

24. For additional usages, see *Gos. Phil.* 53.16, 64.18.

25. Kasser, Meyer and Wurst, *Gospel of Judas*, 32; Kasser *et al.*, *Critical Edition*, 211. The n. for lines 17–18 in *Critical Edition* offers '. . . from that generation' as an alternative. Unfortunately Marvin Meyer continues to perpetuate this faulty translation in the new international edition of the Nag Hammadi texts, and in his anthology of 'Judas' sources. See M. Meyer, *The International Edition of the Nag Hammadi Scriptures* (San Francisco: Harper, 2007) 765, with 'from' listed as an alternative reading in n. 63); M. Meyer, *Judas: The Definitive Collection of Gospels and Legends about the Infamous Apostle of Jesus* (San Francisco: Harper, 2007) 60, with 'from' listed as an alternative reading in n. 67.

This is not an exaltation of Judas, but a sinister association of him with the King of the Archons. It is an association that Judas resists and laments, while Jesus laughs and mocks (*Gos. Jud.* 46.6–13; 55.10–13; cf. 44.18–22).

Even more sinister is the Gospel's association of the twelve Archons that Judas will rule over with the twelve apostles of the Church who curse Judas and try to stone him (*Gos. Jud.* 44.24–26, 46.2–24). The *Gospel of Judas* is very clear that Judas has been replaced with a twelfth apostle so that their number will match the numerology of Ialdabaoth's realms (*Gos. Jud.* 36.1–4; cf. Acts 1:12–14). The association of the disciples with the twelve signs of the Zodiac is not unique to this text. Theodotus the Valentinian taught that 'the Apostles were put in place of the twelve signs of the Zodiac, as birth is governed by these signs, so is rebirth (governed) by the Apostles' (Clem. Alex., *Exc. Theo.* 25.2). For Theodotus, they are functioning positively. Closer to *Judas'* demonic interpretation of the Twelve, however, is the *First Apocalypse of James*, which explains that the twelve Archons, who are armed adversaries of Jesus, are a 'type' of the twelve disciples (NHC 26.2–27.25; NHC 36.1–3).

Whoever wrote the *Gospel of Judas* is lodging criticism against the Apostolic Church by identifying its authorities with ignorant and rebellious Archons, demons who curse the very demon who made possible their atonement. So this Gospel does not go easy on the Twelve. To begin with, Jesus does not approve of the disciples as they partake of the Eucharist (*Gos. Jud.* 33.22–34.10). In fact, he laughs at them in a very sinister way. They collectively respond by trying to defend the ritual, saying, 'Teacher, why are you laughing at our eucharist? We have done what is right.' Then Jesus tells them that he laughed at them because whenever they partake of the Eucharist, Ialdabaoth is receiving the benefit. It is he they are worshipping, and it is this they are ignorant of.

They continue to show off their ignorance when they are unable to confess correctly who Jesus is and are shown up by the worst demon of all, Judas Iscariot, who is able to proclaim Jesus' true identity and is demonstrably more perfect than they (*Gos. Jud.* 34.11–35.20). For an early Christian Gnostic text to say that Judas the demon 'got it' while the Twelve could not – and that even Judas, the wicked and cursed disciple, was more perfect than they – is a characterization of the Twelve that could not be more subversive or severe.

In the next appearance scene, the disciples want to know where Jesus goes when he leaves them (*Gos. Jud.* 36.11–37.20). They are informed by Jesus that he ascends to the holy generation. The Twelve are shocked. So out of their ignorance, they ask Jesus, 'Lord, who is the great generation more exalted and holier than us?' Again Jesus laughs at them. He explains to them that they are unable to associate with the holy Gnostic generation because they belong to the human generation, a generation which is ruled by the stars. They are troubled but keep silent.

Jesus joins the Twelve on another occasion when they recount a collective dream that they had experienced that night (*Gos. Jud.* 37.20–39.5). They claimed to have seen twelve priests executing their own children on the Temple's altar in Jesus' Name. Jesus offers a shocking interpretation of their dream. He tells them that it is their worst nightmare. They are the twelve priests who stand over the altar, invoke Jesus' Name, and present the sacrifices. But it is not an offering to the supreme God, but to the 'Deacon of Error', the 'Lord of the Universe', Ialdabaoth. Furthermore, on that final day of consummation when judgement is rendered, the Twelve will be guilty of worshipping this false god and leading astray countless generations of people who are yet to be born.

This portrait of the Twelve, although queer to modern Christian sensibilities, is not an *ex nihilo* fabrication of anti-Christians. Rather it is an interpretation dependent upon a very literal reading of the *Gospel of Mark*. As such, it is incredibly faithful to scripture. It is in the *Gospel of Mark* that the demons are the entities who recognize Jesus and confess him, including Peter who is rebuked as Satan (1.34; 3.11; 5.6–7; 8.31–33). The twelve disciples never fare well. They are faithless and ignorant straight through to the end of the Gospel even though they are handpicked by Jesus and given special teachings (3.13–19; 4.10–20; 4.37–41; 6.52; 8.15–21; 9.15–19; 9.33–35; 10.13–14; 14.50. At one point in the narrative, Jesus rebukes the disciples for their failure to heal an epileptic boy, 'O faithless generation, how long am I to be with you? How long am I to bear with you?' (Mk 9.15–19). The disciples' reputation is never redeemed, even in the longer ending of Mark where the disciples are chided by Jesus 'for their unbelief and hardness of heart, because they had not believed those who saw him after he had risen' (16.14).

The reason that the author of the *Gospel of Judas* portrays the apostles so harshly is not because he hates Christianity. Rather he worried that Christians were being led astray by the Apostolic Church, which claimed to rely on teachings derived from the Twelve. From his acquaintance with the Gospel of Mark, the author of *Judas* reasoned that the Twelve were so ignorant and faithless that even the demons – including Judas – were more knowledgeable than they were. So the author's purpose was to challenge the Apostolic Church's doctrines and practices, which were claimed by its leaders to be passed down as the authoritative teachings from the apostles to the current bishops in an unbroken chain of transmission. For the author of the *Gospel of Judas*, the foundational link in this chain was corrupt. Because the disciples were ignorant and faithless, whatever information they passed on was bogus. Following their teachings leads Christians astray, and joining in their rituals tricks them into worshiping the wrong god! The consequence of this horrible situation was the annihilation rather salvation of countless Christians.

Whoever wrote the *Gospel of Judas* was himself a Gnostic Christian who operated from a perspective informed by highly literal interpretations of biblical stories about the twelve disciples and was grounded in an apocalyptic cosmology in which Archons created and ruled the universe as opponents of the supreme God, Jesus' Father. According to these Gnostic Christians, the apostles did not possess God's mysteries, but like the Archons remained ignorant of the truth. They were leaders of the 'human generations' that belonged to the archonic kingdoms. Particularly loathsome to these Gnostics was the Church's doctrine of atonement and its re-enactment in the Eucharist. The reason that this doctrine and practice was so hideous to them was because it assumed infanticide – that a father would and should kill his own son. So heinous a crime was this, so immoral, that the Sethian Christians could not stomach it, and so in the *Gospel of Judas* the Twelve are accused of engaging in child sacrifice and understand Judas the demon as the one who initiated it.

But doesn't Jesus in the *Gospel of Judas* ask Judas to kill him in order to release his spirit? No. This conversation does not occur anywhere in the *Gospel of Judas*. What occurs is a short diatribe by Jesus in which he condemns all the sacrifices that are made to the Archons (*Gos. Jud.* 56.11–21). This appears to be a flashback to the twelve apostles' earlier nightmare when they are severely chastised by Jesus for making sacrifices to the lower god (*Gos. Jud.* 37.20–40.26) and when he commands them to stop sacrificing (*Gos. Jud.* 41.1–2). In the middle of the fragmented diatribe, Jesus declares that their sacrifices are evil. Then he tells Judas, 'You will do *more than* all of them. For the man which clothes me, you will sacrifice him.'

The question is, do more than what? The answer must be determined from the immediate context of the Coptic phrase, *er-houo eroou terou*, 'more than'. The context does not indicate that Judas will do a good thing as the National Geographic interpretation suggests in its original publication and maintains its *Critical Edition*: 'But you will *exceed* all of them. For you will sacrifice the man who bears me.'[26] Rather given the negative context, Jesus is telling Judas that his sacrifice will be the worse kind possible, because he will be sacrificing Jesus himself to the Archons.

The atonement was (and still is) a cherished interpretation of Jesus' death among Christians. Nonetheless, it is an interpretation that came after the fact of his death. Because of this, the interpretation did not align exactly with the way in which the Christian story remembered Jesus' death – that a demonic Judas was the one who actually made it happen. The Sethian Gnostics in the *Gospel of Judas* pointed out the obvious problem with this. If Jesus' death really was a sacrifice made by God for the purpose of salvation, why would a demon be the instrument? And why would Judas be cursed for his involvement?

The Apostolic doctrine struck them as dangerous and humorous at the same time, because they felt that it showed up the ignorance and ineffectiveness of the Apostolic faith. Judas was a demon, and the god who put out Jesus' death warrant was Ialdabaoth. Judas collaborated with him, and together they brought about Jesus' sacrifice, which was nothing less than apostasy and murder. The sacrifice was a sacrifice to Ialdabaoth, so all Eucharistic offerings serve only to worship and extol him. I find this to be a very clever and powerful argument given the premises of the Gnostic universe.

26. Kasser, Meyer and Wurst, *Gospel of Judas*, 43; Kasser *et al.*, *Critical Edition*, 231.

6. *The Apostolic Response*

Given what the *Gospel of Judas* has to say by way of critique of Apostolic doctrine and practices, I find it fascinating that the Apostolic Christians begin to become concerned about Judas in the literature produced by the Church Fathers in the late second and early third centuries. His actions appear to have become a liability for the Apostolic Christians.

It seems that the sophisticated Gnostic critique we find in the *Gospel of Judas* concerned a number of Apostolic Christian thinkers, who prior to the publication of the *Gospel of Judas* in the mid-second century rarely mentioned Judas beyond the mere repetition of his stories from the gospels or fanciful embellishments of these stories. Not only does the number of references to Judas in their writings increase in the late second century, but the Apostolic writers begin working hard to provide defences of and interpretations for Judas' actions, especially his connection with demonic forces. These apologies for Judas look like they are meant to resolve the exact problem articulated in the *Gospel of Judas* – that a demon is responsible for Jesus' death, and any atonement he may have brought about was by and for the Archons who rule this world.

Of particular interest is Origen's early-third-century discussion where, as he is thinking about God's bigger plan of redemption, he forges a link between Judas and the Devil. The terms of this plan is a ransom paid to the Devil, an idea rooted in the Gospels and Paul (cf. Mk 10.45; Mt. 20.28; Rom. 3.24; 8.23; 1 Tim. 2.5–6). What Origen begins insisting is that God – not Judas and not the Devil – is responsible for Jesus' sacrifice. He supports this by quoting the apostle Paul that God 'spared not his own son, but delivered him up for us all' (Origen, *Comm. Matt.* 13.8). How does Judas get involved? Judas, Origen says, was an evil person whose soul was already being eaten by a spiritual gangrene, a wickedness hidden deep within (Origen, *Comm. Matt.* 11.9). Because of this, Judas allowed the Devil to possess him fully, as it is written that after the supper, 'Satan entered into him' (Origen, *On First Principles* 3.2; *Comm. John* 10.30) and God delivered Judas to the demons. Then the Devil used Judas to deliver Jesus to those men who would crucify him. Jesus' blood was the ransom that bought the sinful dead from the Devil. But the Devil, when he accepted this purchase price, got a big surprise. Because Jesus' spirit was more powerful than his, Jesus was able to rise from the dead and conquer death. The Devil could not hold on to him so he was cheated out of his ransom. This, Origen thinks, is how God tricked the Devil and Jesus atoned for the sins of humanity (Origen, *Comm. Matt.* 12.40; 13.8–9).

What is striking to me is that the end of Origen's story is not so far removed from the Gnostic story, which centred around the moment when Jesus' powerful spirit conquered the Archons who tried to subdue him. The Gnostic interpretation of his death is victory over death and the Archons who enslave the human spirit. On this point, I think that Origen and the Gnostics were on common ground.

The Church Fathers also respond to the *Gospel of Judas* by directly taking on the text itself. The first to do this was Irenaeus around 180 CE in *Against Heresies* 1.31.1. In this passage, he does not give us much in terms of detail, only suggesting that the *Gospel of Judas* had Judas as its central figure, that Judas knew the 'truth' while the other disciples did not, and that his betrayal of Jesus was a 'mystery' that set the earth and heavens into chaos. He never says that Judas was characterized as 'good' or a 'hero' in the *Gospel of Judas*.

It is difficult to know from his description whether he actually read the version of the *Gospel of Judas* that we now possess, or was testifying to hear-say about its contents, or worst of all, was guessing at them. His description appears to me to be fairly accurate of the manuscript we possess, except that he identifies it as a Gospel belonging to people who declared that their ancestors were Esau, Korah and the Sodomites, and that Cain was an entity derived from a Power above.

Since the people who wrote the *Gospel of Judas* understood themselves to be descendants of the great Seth, son of Adam, not Cain nor any of the others whom Irenaeus mentions, this suggests to me two immediate possibilities. Either the *Gospel of Judas* was not originally Sethian, and this non-Sethian version is what Irenaeus knew, or his genealogy is fictitious, whose purpose is to undermine the Gospel's credibility. My analysis of the *Gospel of Judas* suggests that the subversive Sethian hermeneutic is not merely a surface patina, but integral to the entire narrative. So the former possibility is not very attractive to me. The latter is reasonable given Irenaeus' agenda against Gnostic groups and writings, where he embellishes and distorts 'facts', and creates polemics to undercut his opponents, including false genealogies tracing the many sprouting mushrooms back to Simon Magus.

Having said all of this, however, there is something about his description that causes me to pause. The Sethians did teach that Cain was a Power. In their system, however, he was not a benevolent Power, but an evil Archon, a Power ruling one of the cosmic realms. So if the Sethians taught that the human Cain owed his existence to a Power above, he owed it to an evil one, not a good one. Could it be that Irenaeus knew this and merely tweaked the 'facts' slightly to fit his polemical agenda?

The other Church Father to write about the *Gospel of Judas* is Epiphanius who leaves us a very elaborate discussion in *Panarion* 38.1.2–5 and 38.3.1.5, a discussion which at least has been influenced by Irenaeus. Epiphanius rids the Irenaean description of any ambiguity it might have had, so that Cain is said to be from 'the *stronger* power and dominion above' as are also Esau, Korah and the Sodomites. He adds that Abel is from 'the weaker power'. He gives the name Cainites to the authors of the *Gospel of Judas*, and says that they believed that Judas was their kinsman, knew about the upper Aeons, and possessed the highest of knowledge.

He goes into several elaborate schemes about how the crucifixion came about according to the Cainites (cf. Clem. Alex. *Strom.* 7.17.17; Tert. *Prescription* 33; Tert. *On Baptism* 1; Ps.-Tert. *Ag. Haer.* 2.5–6; Hipp. *Ref.* 8; Origen, *Contra*

Celsum 3.13; Philastrius, *Diverse Heresies* 34.1; Epiph. *Pan.* 38.1.5–2.3; 38.2.4–5; 39.1.1–2). One scheme sets up Judas as a strong power who triumphs over the weaker, Christ's body. Another scheme involves a wicked Christ who is betrayed by an admirable Judas in order to stop Christ from destroying 'sound teachings'. A final scheme understands Judas to betray Jesus because Judas was a high power who knew that the Archons power would be drained if Jesus was crucified. So Judas did everything he could to accomplish this good work of salvation and should be admired and praised for this. Of course, none of this is found in the *Gospel of Judas*. Epiphanius appears to be passing along a story that had been fabricated long before him about a fictitious group of Gnostic Christians called the Cainites. This invention was likely the result of (mis)reading Irenaeus in an attempt to further discredit the Gnostic *Gospel of Judas*.

7. *A Sethian Parody*

What I find especially valuable about the *Gospel of Judas* is that it preserves traditions that demonstrate just how close the Apostolic and Sethian Christians were, and yet how far apart. It appears to be a given of both types of Christianity that Judas is a demon. The dispute is over which one, the Devil or Ialdabaoth. Both forms of Christianity recognize the implications of this identification, because it means that a demon brought about salvation through atonement. It is this problem that Origen finally solves by fashioning the doctrine of the Devil's Ransom in the early third century.

For the Gnostic Christian, no apology was necessary. The tradition that Judas a demon brought about atonement proved to the Sethians that this doctrine was put into place by the demons as part of their plan to trick human beings into worshipping them instead of the supreme God. Every time people participated in Eucharist ceremonies, which re-enacted the bloody sacrifice of Jesus' body, they were making their offerings to the Demiurge not the transcendent God. Who else would want bloody offerings expect Ialdabaoth-Nebro(el) whose appearance was corrupted with blood (*Gos. Jud.* 51.11)?

The Gnostic Christians worried that the Apostolic Christians were being led astray by their leaders, whose ignorance and faithlessness could be traced back to the Markan characterization of the Twelve, their direct predecessors. If the Sethian Christians could not convince them of this, in the End the Apostolic Christians would be judged to be apostates and destroyed along with Judas-Ialdabaoth and his 12 underlings. It was the weight of this hidden tragic knowledge that likely seeded the idea to retell Judas' story as 'good news'. Parody The Sethian author rewrote Judas' story with both humor and satire so that the Apostolic Christians would be critiqued, corrected and hopefully saved.

Bibliography

J. Brankaer and H. -G. Bethge (eds.), *Codex Tchacos: Texte und Analysen* (Texte und Untersuchungen zur Geschichte der altchristlichen Literatur 161; Berlin: Walter de Gruyter, 2007).

A. D. DeConick, *The Thirteenth Apostle: What the Gospel of Judas Really Says* (New York: Continuum, 2007).

A. D. DeConick, 'The Mystery of Judas' Betrayal: What the *Gospel of Judas* Really Says', in Madeleine Scopello (ed.), *The Gospel of Judas in Context. Proceedings of the First International Conference on the Gospel of Judas*. Paris, Sorbonne, October 27th–28th 2006, (Leiden, 2008).

B. D. Ehrman, *The Lost Gospel of Judas Iscariot: A New Look At Betrayer and Betrayed* (Oxford: Oxford University Press, 2006).

S. Gathercole, *The Gospel of Judas* (Oxford: Oxford University Press, 2007).

R. Kasser, M. Meyer and G. Wurst (eds), *The Gospel of Judas*, with additional commentary by B. D. Ehrman, (Washington, DC: National Geographic, 2006).

R. Kasser, G. Wurst, M. Meyer and F. Gaudard (eds), *The Gospel of Judas together with the Letter of Peter to Philip, James, and a Book of Allogenes from Codex Tchacos: Critical Edition* (Washington, DC: National Geographic, 2007).

H. Krosney, *The Lost Gospel: The Quest for the Gospel of Judas Iscariot* (Washington, DC: National Geographic, 2006).

G. Lüdemann, *Das Judas-Evangelium und das Evangelium nach Maria. Zwei gnostische Schriften aus der Frühzeit des Christentums* (Stuttgart: Radius, 2006).

M. Meyer, *Judas: The Definitive Collection of Gospels and Legends about the Infamous Apostle of Jesus* (San Francisco: Harper, 2007).

P. Nagel, 'Das Evangelium nach Judas', *ZNW* 98 (2007) 213–276.

E. Pagels and K. L. King, *Reading Judas: The Gospel of Judas and the Shaping of Christianity* (New York: Viking, 2007).

L. Painchaud, 'À Propos de la (Re)découverte de L'Évangile de Judas', *Laval théologique et philosophique* 62.3 (October 2006) 553–568.

U. -K. Plisch, 'Das Evangelium des Judas', *ZAC* 10 (2006) 5–14.

S. Porter and G. Heath, *The Lost Gospel of Judas: Separating Fact from Fiction* (Grand Rapids: Eerdmans, 2007).

G. S. Robinson, 'The Relationship of the Gospel of Judas to the New Testament and to Sethianism, Appended by a new English translation of the *Gospel of Judas', Journal for Coptic Studies* (forthcoming, 2008).

J. M. Robinson, *The Secrets of Judas: The Story of the Misunderstood Disciple and His Lost Gospel* (San Francisco: Harper, 2006) 117–120.

E. Thomassen, 'Is Judas Really the Hero of the Gospel?', in Madeleine Scopello (ed.), *The Gospel of Judas in Context. Proceedings of the First International Conference on the Gospel of Judas*. Paris, Sorbonne, October 27th–28th 2006, (Leiden, 2008).

J. Turner, 'The Place of the *Gospel of Judas* in Sethian Literature', in Madeleine Scopello (ed.), *The Gospel of Judas in Context. Proceedings of the First International Conference on the Gospel of Judas*. Paris, Sorbonne, October 27th–28th 2006, (Leiden, 2008).

N. T. Wright, *Jesus and the Gospel of Judas* (London: SPCK, 2006).

Chapter 9

THE *PROTEVANGELIUM OF JAMES*

Paul Foster

The *Protevangelium of James* is a text that narrates events prior to and immediately following the birth of Jesus. Unlike the four canonical gospels the central character of this narrative is not Jesus, but his mother Mary. She is portrayed as a paradigm of purity. From the time she turns three until she reaches twelve she lives in the Temple and her role is patterned on that of the young Samuel serving in the Temple at Shiloh. The text strongly advocates the perpetual virginity of Mary and thus allows for some of the origins of this theological position to be identified. The text has little or no historical value in terms of the actual events it reports, but it does provide a fascinating window into the piety of late second-century or early third-century Christianity.

1. *The Textual Landscape of Early Christianity*

It is sometimes claimed by both ancient and modern writers that the non-canonical texts were products of small isolationist communities, that these texts were for internal consumption only and that they had little circulation outside the sectarian groups for which they were written. By contrast, the canonical gospels are represented as having an outward looking perspective, as being written for universal Christianity and in character being far removed from narrow sectarian tendencies. The falseness of this dichotomy, however, should be recognized both at the general as well as the specific level. At the general level the desire to see non-canonical texts as marginal is simply not supported by the record of the circulation of such documents. Furthermore, the fourfold gospel was not a feature of early Christianity from the first century onwards, but took time to establish itself as these four texts gained prominence in multiple Christian communities. More specifically, a canonical text such as the *Gospel of John* seems to have a very inward looking almost ghetto-like mentality, especially in the farewell discourses,[1] whereas texts like the *Gospel of Peter* and the *Gospel of Thomas*, which may both have originated in a Syrian

1. John Ashton, *Understanding the Fourth Gospel* (Oxford: Oxford University Press, 1991).

context have been found in manuscript discoveries in multiple locations in Egypt. This demonstrates at least a wide geographical circulation. The *Gospel of Peter* also takes a popularizing approach to Christian traditions and it is hard to imagine the author of this text engaging in his radical rewriting without the hope of wide circulation. Also at a specific level, there is one gospel text (if it is correct to call it a gospel) that demonstrably had huge popular appeal, wide circulation and made an indirect impact on some of the Christological debates of the fourth and fifth centuries. That text is now known as the *Protevangelium of James*. It narrates two birth stories, those of the Virgin Mary and of her son Jesus. Events commence with a description of the barrenness of Mary's parents and conclude with the notice of the death of Herod the Great. Between this temporal span of less than two decades, according to the narrative world of the text, many incidents are related – some of which have direct biblical parallels, although the majority describe events and background to the canonical infancy narratives which are otherwise unknown.

2. *Text, Manuscripts and Reception*

Although divided into 25 chapters in modern editions, the text of the *Protevangelium of James* is much shorter than any of the canonical accounts. It contains approximately 278 verses and can be read comfortably in twenty minutes.[2] The title *Protevangelium*, which indicates that the work is considered a prior or first gospel in chronological sequence with the canonical accounts, was given this title in the mid-sixteenth century by the French humanist scholar, Guillaume Postel, who 'rediscovered' a Greek manuscript of the text while on a visit to the East and then translated the text into Latin under this title. In Orthodox circles the text has retained its traditional title *Birth of Mary*, often with the appended description *Revelation of James*. Both these elements are contained in the most ancient surviving manuscript of the text.[3]

The range of manuscript witnesses to the *Protevangelium* is both rich and varied. To date more than 140 Greek manuscripts have been catalogued and these have been categorized as belonging to one of five separate textual families.[4] Most of the extant Greek manuscripts, however, are late, dating to after

2. As a comparison, the canonical gospels in order of ascending length contain the following number of chapters and approximate number of verses: Mark – 16 chapters, 666 verses; John – 21 chapters, 867 verses; Matthew – 28 chapters, 1071 verses; Luke – 24 chapters, 1151 verses. The difficulty in providing an accurate count of verses stems from a number of textual problems which affect the exact extent of the text. The two most famous of these involve the Longer Ending of Mark's gospel and the *Pericopae Adulterae* usually found in John's account. Hence the verse numbers are approximations only.

3. For more discussion on the title and variations see W.S. Vorster, 'James, Protevangelium of', *Anchor Bible Dictionary*, vol. III (New York: Doubleday, 1992) 631.

4. É. de Strycker, 'Die grieschischen Handschriften des Protevangeliums Iacobi', in D. Harlfinger (ed.), *Grieschische Kodikologie und Textüberlieferung* (Darmstadt: Wissenschftliche Buchgesellschaft, 1980) 577–612.

the tenth century.[5] The oldest surviving Greek manuscript of the text, Papyrus Bodmer V, is dated by Martin Testuz, the editor of the *editio princeps*, as probably being copied in the third century.[6] This text occupies the first 49 pages of a 56 page papyrus codex. Two other early Greek fragmentary texts of importance are the fifth-century PSI 1.6 which contains a highly broken text of Chapters 13–23, and the sixth-century P.Oxy. 3524 which contains a fragment of Chapter 25.[7] Although no ancient Latin manuscript of the text exists, the versional evidence in other ancient languages is multifaceted, including Sahidic Coptic, Syriac, Armenian, Georgian, Ethiopic, Slavonic and Arabic. In fact the Arabic text may have influenced Qu'ranic and later Islamic understandings of the place of Mary in the Christian tradition.

The lack of Latin manuscripts is a result of two factors. First, the *Protevangelium* was rejected in the West by the Gelasian Decree (c. 500 CE) where it is listed as an apocryphal writing that is not to be received as authoritative. Secondly, it was absorbed into two later and fuller works written in Latin, *The Gospel of Pseudo-Matthew* and *The Gospel of the Birth of Mary*. While the latter conveniently removes the theological problem of Joseph's prior marriage, this detail which is offensive in certain strands of the Christian tradition still remained present in *Pseudo-Matthew*.

The *Protevangelium* is mentioned in the writings of Church Fathers from as early as the first half of the third century. Origen, in his *Commentary on Matthew* exegeting the phrase 'They thought, then, that He was the son of Joseph and Mary' makes the following passing reference to a work he calls *The Book of James*, which is very likely the same text known to modern scholarship as the *Protevangelium*.

> But some say, basing it on a tradition in the *Gospel according to Peter*, as it is entitled, or *The Book of James*, that the brethren of Jesus were sons of Joseph by a former wife, whom he married before Mary. (Origen, *Comm. Matt.* 10.17)

Others have detected an even earlier allusion to the *Protevangelium* in the writings of Clement of Alexandria who died around 202.

> But, as appears, many even down to our own time regard Mary, on account of the birth of her child, as having been in the puerperal state, although she was not. For some say that, after she brought forth, she was found, when examined, to be a virgin. (Clem. Alex., *Strom.* 7.16.93)

5. J. K. Elliott, *The Apocryphal New Testament* (rev. reprinting, Oxford: Oxford University Press, 1999) 51.

6. M. Testuz (ed.), *Papyrus Bodmer V: Nativite de Marie* (Geneva: Bibliotheca Bodmeriana 1958) 10.

7. J. R. Rea (ed.), *The Oxyrhynchus Papyri*, vol. 50, Papyri numbers 3522–3600 (London: British Academy/Egypt Exploration Society, 1983).

There is little doubt that the same tradition is being described here as is found in the *Protevangelium* (19.18–20.4), where Mary is found to still have her hymen intact after giving birth to Jesus. Although these two texts share the same tradition it is not possible to show whether one is dependent upon the other, or if they have both inherited a common story.

Notwithstanding the uncertainty of the relationship between the tradition in Clement's writings, the explicit reference in Origen provides a *terminus ad quem* for the *Protevangelium* of no later than the second half of the third century. This is also strongly supported by the artefactual evidence of Papyrus Bodmer V. Furthermore, it has been suggested that the *Protevangelium* was written in response to Celsus' polemical work, *True Doctrine* written around 178 CE, in which he suggests that Jesus was the offspring of an illicit union with a Roman soldier and further that Mary was little more that a squalid peasant girl. Although this intriguing suggestion is beyond verification, what the writings of Celsus, Clement and Origen demonstrate is that such questions dealing with claims of Mary's virginity were being addressed between the last quarter of the second century and the first half of the third century and the composition of the *Protevangelium* plausibly falls within this period. Furthermore, it must have been composed prior to the fourth century because of the evidence of Papyrus Bodmer V. Thus a date of composition in the region of 170–250 CE appears highly likely, although it needs to be acknowledged that some would be happy to push it even earlier, extending the earliest possible date downward to around 150 CE.

3. *Contents*

The text, in its current form, can be divided into three major sections which relate to separate though related phases in the life of Mary, coupled with a brief epilogue giving details of pseudonymous author.[8]

SECTION	OVERVIEW OF CONTENTS
1.1–8.2	Mary's conception, birth and events until her adolescence
8.3–16.8	'Marriage' to Joseph, pregnancy, and preservation of virginity
17.1–24.14	Journey to Bethlehem, birth of Jesus, violent events
25.1–4	Epilogue: Putative author and circumstances of composition

3.1 *Mary's Conception, Birth and Events until Her Adolescence (Prot. Jas. 1.1–8.2)*

None of the events presented in the first section of this text finds a parallel in the infancy accounts of the canonical gospels. However, there are many places where the incidents in this section (and the rest of the text) are patterned on

8. R. F. Hock, *The Infancy Gospels of James and Thomas* (Santa Rosa, CA: Polebridge, 1995) 4–8.

existing stories from biblical narratives, especially those dealing with childlessness or barrenness. There has been a tendency to find an ever increasing number of allusions in early Christian texts, and a trend to detect ever fainter (non-existent?) echoes.[9] However, the *Protevangelium* signals such borrowings in a more demonstrable manner through shared terminology, the use of names from the Hebrew Bible, and a strong parallelism between events.

The text opens by narrating the story of a certain Joachim, an Israelite, whose piety and prosperity are exemplified by his gift offerings to the Lord. On an unspecified festival day Joachim is prevented from presenting his offering first, by a slightly officious individual called Reubel. Apart from his name, nothing is known of Reubel apart from his protest, 'you are not allowed to offer your gifts first because you have not produced an Israelite child' (*Prot. Jas.* 1.5). Joachim consults a work or record known as *The Twelve Tribes of the People* and discovers that all the righteous members of Israel indeed produced offspring. From frustration and bewilderment he retires to the desert fasting 'forty days and forty nights', and determines 'not to go back to food or drink until the Lord my God appears to me' (*Prot. Jas.* 1.11). Although readers are not given a direct account of a heavenly visitation to Joachim, in 4.3–4 there is a second-hand report from two messengers sent to his wife who relate the angelophany Joachim has received from none other than the angel of the Lord.

It is only in Chapter 2 that Anna, Joachim's wife, is introduced although she has been mentioned without name in 1.9. She too is lamenting her state. Her complaint is twofold: widowhood and childlessness. While the second condition is a physical reality, the first is a metaphor for her apparent abandonment by Joachim, perhaps with an expectation that he would die in the desert unvisited by the Lord. Anna reacts with much vitriol when she is presented with a headband by her slave-girl Juthine to wear at another unidentified religious festival (*Prot. Jas.* 2.2–6). There is much that is enigmatic in this incident. The headband bears a royal insignia – does this indicate something of Anna's pedigree? Why does Anna accuse the slave-girl of trickery and how will she share in the slave-girl's sin if she accepts the item? Finally, why does Juthine understand Anna of accusing her of attempting to curse her mistress by use of the headband? While the answers must remain in large part obscure, some of the parallels to Old Testament stories may cast a little light this strange incident. In the story of the birth of Samuel to the barren Hannah (= Greek *Anna*, see the LXX of 1 Sam. 1.2), her husband Elkanah gave her a double portion of

9. For works that advocate a maximalist position in relation to the detection of echoes and allusions see R. B. Hays, *Echoes of Scripture in the Letters of Paul* (New Haven: Yale University Press, 1989), and R. E. Watts, *Isaiah's New Exodus and Mark* (Tübingen: Mohr Siebeck, 1997).

10. This comparison holds regardless of whether the birth story in 1 Sam. 1 originally related the circumstances of the birth of Samuel or as perhaps appears more likely, that it told of the birth of Saul. See. P. Kyle McCarter, *1 Samuel*, AB 8 (New York: Doubleday, 1980) 62, 65.

his sacrifices.[10] This parallels Joachim's practice of doubling his offerings. Moreover, Elkanah's other wife Peninnah 'would provoke her [Hannah] bitterly to irritate her, because the Lord had closed her womb' (1 Sam. 1.6). The modelling of the story in the *Protevangelium* on the Samuel birth narrative is transparent. The other story that is directly referenced is that of the birth of Isaac to Sarah, with Anna explicitly praying 'bless me and hear my prayer, just as you blessed our mother Sarah and gave her a son, Isaac' (*Prot. Jas.* 2.9). Utilizing a similar type of narrative device Sarah is despised by her maidservant Hagar because of her inability to conceive (Gen. 16.4–5) in the same way that Juthine mocks Anna's sterility (*Prot. Jas.* 2.6). In Chapter 3, Anna sings a lament which is of a totally different tone to the joyous song of Hannah in (1 Sam. 2). This air of lamentation is soon transformed, as an angel immediately appears, Anna is promised a child and her response is to dedicate the child to the service of the Lord. Again the strongest resonances are with the actions of Hannah in the Samuel narrative, but there are also reminiscences of the events surrounding the birth stories in Lk. 1–2.

Virtually simultaneously Joachim returns home. Anna is told by two angels that Joachim has already been informed through his own angelophany that his wife will have a child (*Prot. Jas.* 4.4). This verse contains a significant text-critical problem with important theological ramifications. The Greek phrase in question reads:

> ἰδοὺ ἡ γυνή σου Ἄννα ἐν γαστρὶ εἴληφεν/λήψεται (*Prot. Jas.* 4.4)

The difference is the form of the final word. The first possibility εἴληφεν is a perfect verb so consequently the phrase would be translated 'Behold your wife Anna has conceived in the womb.' Alternatively, the second option is a future form. Hence, the verse would be rendered 'Behold your wife Anna will conceive in the womb.' If the future form were to be preferred, then the note in 4.10 that 'Joachim rested the first day at home' could be read euphemistically as the time when the predictive promise was brought to fruition.[11] The textual evidence, however, appears to favour the perfect form, since the earlier Greek manuscripts contain this reading.[12] This would then imply that Anna was already pregnant, miraculously, when Joachim arrived home. Such a reading would be in line with the piety of this document that goes to extraordinary lengths to affirm Mary's purity. It would be strange if its author had allowed the heroine of his story to be tainted with carnal concupiscence. Here it is possible to see the emergence of a theology of the immaculate conception of Mary, although it is not framed in such theologically developed terms.

11. Hock, *The Infancy Gospels of James and Thomas*, 39.

12. É. de Strycker, *La forme la plus ancienne du Protévangile de Jacques* (Bruxelles: Société des Bollandistes, 1961) 80.

Chapters 5 and 6 recount the birth of Mary, and in highly folkloric sentiments the text recounts the length to which Anna goes to preserve ritual purity for Mary. This includes not allowing her to walk on common ground (6.3), transforming the girl's bedroom into a sanctuary (6.4) and engaging 'undefiled' Hebrew females to entertain the infant Mary. Such tropes are not uncommon in the legends of the childhood years of sacred figures. Anna sings her second song in the narrative, no longer of mourning, but an outpouring of praise. Here is the more direct parallel to the song of Hannah contained in 1 Sam. 2, and simultaneously the counterpoint to Anna's earlier lament (*Prot. Jas.* 3.2–8). The remaining material in this opening section (7.1–8.2) describes the process by which Mary leaves the parental house to reside in the Temple. Again the parallels with the Samuel story are clear. The whole act of dedicating the child and handing it over to the priests is an obvious parallel, as is the reluctance of the two mothers who both seek a delay before the child is given to the Temple. In the *Protevangelium* the embellishments to the parallel with the Samuel birth story have an almost surreal character. The undefiled Hebrew women are summoned to form a lamp-lit procession accompanying Mary so her heart will not be 'captivated by things outside the temple' (7.5). The priest kisses and blesses Mary on her arrival (7.7). She is sat on the third step of the altar, she dances in the Temple and is the darling of the people of Israel (7.9–10). She is fed directly from the hand of an angel (8.2). Such characterization presents Mary in a manner that approaches that of a goddess being venerated in her own sacred shrine. Yet this situation of blissful veneration of childhood innocence is problematized as Mary approaches her adolescence.

3.2 *'Marriage' to Joseph, Pregnancy and Preservation of Virginity (Prot. Jas. 8.3–16.8)*

Having set up this idyllic sacral vision of the pure child serving in the Temple, the narrative jumps from the time when Mary is 3 years old to nearly a decade later, when Mary is 12. Upon her reaching this age of symbolic maturation, a meeting is convened between the priests. Their concern is that Mary will soon be in a state to pollute the Temple (*Prot. Jas.* 8.4). Although not stated explicitly, the priests of this narrative appear to be concerned about Levitical stipulations which prohibit a woman from approaching the sanctuary while she has a flow of blood related to childbirth or menstruation (Lev. 12.1–6; 18.19). With divine direction a plan is formulated to give Mary in matrimony to one of the widowers of Israel. The choice of a widower is intended to connote a man who can act as a guardian, but will presumably have no sexual feelings towards Mary. Again miraculously Joseph is selected to fulfil this role and although he initially protests, he finally acquiesces. Theologically, it is interesting that one of the reasons Joseph puts forward to demonstrate why he is unsuitable for the role is 'I already have sons and I am an old man' (*Prot. Jas.* 9.8). Thus the *Protevangelium* can be seen to support *in nuce* what became known as the

Epiphanian solution to the problem of the siblings of Jesus. In the New Testament (Mk 6.3; Mt. 13.55–56) there are instances where the text speaks in an unequivocal and unqualified manner about the brothers and sisters of Jesus. For those who affirm the perpetual virginity of Mary this creates an obvious problem. Although the 'solution' of calling these siblings stepbrothers and stepsisters is associated with Epiphanius, the fourth-century Bishop of Salamis on Cyprus, as the *Protevangelium* shows the idea was in circulation much earlier. Ultimately the ploy of casting the siblings as children of Joseph by an earlier marriage was rejected as incorrect. In part the growing cult of virginity in the fourth century accounts for the climate in which the 'stepbrother' explanation was rejected. Jerome 'seems to be the first Father of the Church to have suggested that the brothers of Jesus were actually cousins and that both Joseph and Mary were perpetual virgins.'[13] The *Protevangelium* has no concern to defend the notion of the perpetual virginity of Joseph, which was a theological novelty of the fourth century. However, at every possible point it reiterates and affirms the purity and virginity of Mary prior to conceiving Jesus, at his birth and afterwards. This is without doubt one of the most important theological concerns of the text.

The story then turns to an incident that is historically and factually inaccurate. The council of the priests determine to have a veil made for the Temple. This is not described as a replacement, but is most naturally read as being an innovation. However, veils have been used to shield parts of the various sanctuaries in the Israelite and Jewish cult. During the Exodus wanderings the tabernacle is made of ten curtains of blue, purple and scarlet material (Exod. 26.1), and a further curtain is used to screen the ark (Exod. 30.6). When Solomon orders the construction of the first Jerusalem Temple, a veil is made of the same coloured fabrics (2 Chron. 3.14). Josephus also mentions the veil in the second Temple when he describes the pillage undertaken by Antiochus IV Epiphanes: 'So he left the temple bare, and took away the golden candlesticks, and the golden altar, and table, and the altar; and did not abstain from even the veils, which were made of fine linen and scarlet.' (Jos. Ant. 12.5.4). This shows that the veils were not an innovation and that there was a long tradition of their use and of their colours. Rather, the story appears to be told to allow readers the potential to recognize the intertextual link with the rending of the Temple veil in the passion narrative, now armed with the startling piece of knowledge that the mother of Jesus actually helped make the same veil.

Before being called to participate in making the curtain, readers have been informed that Joseph has left Mary at home while he goes away to follow his business interests (*Prot. Jas.* 9.12). This leaves no possibility of Joseph being the father of the child she is about to bear. In Chapter 11, for the first time in

13. J. P. Meier, *A Marginal Jew: Rethinking the Historical Jesus*, vol. 1: The Roots of the Problem and the Person, ABRL (New York: Doubleday, 1991) 324.

the narrative, there is a direct parallel to events contained in the canonical infancy narratives. In line with the appearance story in Luke's gospel, Gabriel announces Mary's forthcoming conception. In the version contained in the *Protevangelium* Mary has the good sense to ask a few more questions – this is very helpful for the readers! Mary asks Gabriel if she will 'give birth the way women usually do' (*Prot. Jas.* 11.6). She is told 'no', but at this stage no further details are provided. On returning home Joseph leaps to the logical conclusion that another man has been involved. Mary protests her innocence (*Prot. Jas.* 13.8), but unhelpfully, as the narrative mentioned slightly earlier, she had forgotten the conversation with Gabriel (*Prot. Jas.* 12.6). No explanation is given as to how she could have failed to remember this memorable event. This lack of recollection does serve to heighten the tension that develops in the story. Joseph is brought before the Temple authorities and accused as being the one responsible for this heinous act. If there had been any doubt that the marriage was intended as an asexual union, the accusation that Joseph has 'violated the virgin' (*Prot. Jas.* 15.6) makes it clear that he was not expected to exercise any conjugal rites. In order to prove their innocence both Joseph and Mary are required to undergo the 'drink test' (*Prot. Jas.* 16.3–7). This involves drinking water, journeying into the wilderness and waiting to see if the accused returns unharmed. The outcome is positive for both, so they are acquitted of the charge. The rite seems to be a variant on the 'ritual of the water of bitterness' described in Num. 5.11–31.[14] Both husband and wife survive the test and thus are vindicated and acquitted of the charges brought against them.

3.3 *Journey to Bethlehem, Birth of Jesus, Violent Events (Prot. Jas. 17.1–24.14)*

This final major section in the *Protevangelium* most closely parallels events known from the Matthean and Lukan gospels, but the major difference is the tendency to expand known events, to add details and to modify existing stories. This is achieved by creating direct dialogue between characters which provides certain psychological insights into their *personas*, heightening miraculous elements and producing greater tension by more vividly describing the threat to Jesus from Herod. Such techniques appear to address the desire of the audience to know more of the details surrounding the lead-up to the birth of Jesus.

Chapter 17 opens with the notice concerning the edict of Augustus to conduct a census of the population be conducted. This parallels a detail unique to the Lukan birth story, but there are two significant differences. First the *Protevangelium* deletes the note that this was the first census when Quirinius was governor of Syria (Lk. 2.2), and secondly the geographical scope of the census

14. For a discussion of the similarities and differences between these two rites see Hock, *The Infancy Gospels of James and Thomas*, 61; J. K. Elliott, *The Apocryphal New Testament* (Oxford: Oxford University Press, 1993) 51.

is restricted. In the Lukan account Augustus orders a census of 'all the inhabited earth' (Lk. 2.1), whereas in the *Protevangelium* it is only the inhabitants of Bethlehem of Judea who are required to be enrolled (*Prot. Jas.* 17.1). No explanation is provided for calling for a census of one small village. It is tempting to view the removal of Quirinius from the description as an attempt to tidy up the conflict between Lukan and Matthean chronology. Quirinius was legate of Syria from 6 CE, approximately a decade after the death of Herod the Great, who was very much alive when Jesus was born according to the Matthean account. Such a motivation, however, may well be beyond the concerns of the *Protevangelium* and the omission of this problematic detail is probably purely coincidental.[15]

Labour pains halt the couple from actually reaching Bethlehem (*Prot. Jas.* 17.10). Joseph finds a cave and goes to look for a midwife to assist Mary (18.1–2). The birth of Jesus in a cave at some distance removed from Bethlehem is noticeably different from the synoptic accounts. The tradition that Jesus was born in a cave is also known in other sources in the late second and early third centuries. Responding to the arguments of his interlocutor Celsus, Origen appears to give evidence of an already flourishing tourist industry which showed travellers the site of the birth.

> If anybody wants further proof to convince him that Jesus was born in Bethlehem besides the prophecy of Micah and the story recorded in the gospels by Jesus' disciples, he may observe that, in agreement with the story in the gospel about his birth, the cave at Bethlehem is shown where he was born and the manger in the cave where he was wrapped in swaddling-clothes. What is shown there is famous in these parts even among people alien to the faith, since it was in this cave that the Jesus who is worshipped and admired by Christians was born. (Origen, *Contra Celsum* 1.51)[16]

As Joseph goes out to locate a midwife he is confronted with a series of amazing sights which result from the suspension of time, during which he is the only animate physical form. The clouds and birds are frozen in the sky, people are suspended in the middle of eating, water and animals are motionless and suddenly all returns to normal (18.3–11). The striking thing about this story is not the events themselves, although they are amazing, but the fact that the narrator does not explain their significance. Such a catalepsis of the natural realm, visible to Joseph alone, reflects the cosmological significance of the

15. R. E. Brown, *The Birth of the Messiah*, ABRL (rev. edn; New York: Doubleday, 1993) 394–396.

16. This translation is taken from H. Chadwick, *Origen: Contra Celsum* (reprinted and corrected; Cambridge: Cambridge University Press, 1965) 47–48. It is also noted that the birth of Jesus in a cave is mentioned by Justin, *Dial.*, 78 (cf. also 70); Eusebius, *D. E.* III, 2, 97c; VII, 2, 343b; *VC* III, 42, f; Epiphanius, *Panarion*, LI, 9, 6; Jerome, *Ep.* LVIII, 3; CXLVII, 4; Philoxenus of Mabbug, *de Trin. et Incarn.* 3. Furthermore, the cave was visited by pilgrims in the sixth century according to the itinerary of Antoninus of Placentia.

events that are transpiring in the cave. However, as Bovon notes, the very term 'cosmic' is 'a pretentious word for the little scene that is shown us. (Only in the beginning and at the end does the vocabulary in our text take on a philosophical hue.)'[17] The limitation of the cosmic horizon is of significance according to Bovon. He argues that the temporary nature of eschatological immobility reveals that salvation history has not yet reached completion, but that this is nonetheless a decisive moment in its unfolding.[18]

The next two chapters relate the experiences of an unnamed midwife and a second female observer called Salome. The midwife arrives at the cave in time to witness events, but not soon enough to assist with the birth. Interestingly, no actual physical birth is seen. A dark cloud obscures sight and the scene changes from that with a pregnant Mary, to one with mother suckling the child at her breast. The obscuring of sight is not best a device to protect modesty (the next chapter shows that is not a concern of the author), rather it creates an ambiguity about the physical process of the birth which is not resolved at this stage. The story then has the midwife leave the cave only to encounter Salome a sceptical passer-by. Unpersuaded by the midwife's testimony, Salome demands physical evidence: 'unless I insert my finger and examine her, I will never believe that a virgin has given birth' (*Prot. Jas.* 19.9). This physical test reveals that Mary's hymen is not ruptured. Salome bewails her unbelief and also sees her hand being eaten away with flames as punishment. A quick prayer of repentance results in an angelic messenger appearing and commanding Salome to hold out her hand to the child. This results in instant healing, and an accompanying warning from the angel not to speak of these things until the child has been taken to Jerusalem. The incident has certain parallels with the judgement against Miriam the sister of Moses (Num. 12.9–15). The anger of the Lord is kindled against Miriam for speaking against Moses, a cloud overshadows the tent of meeting, she is left leprous (not just her hand) and Moses prays for her restoration. Although the parallel is not exploited, it may have served as a generic type for the judgement against Salome.

The remaining material in this section elaborates upon the Matthean story of the visit of the Magi and the slaughter of the innocents. In reaction to Herod's murderous fury against the infants, Mary wraps Jesus in cloth and hides him in a feeding trough. Thus the manger tradition from the Lukan account (2.7, 12) is recycled by the author and inserted in the Matthean context of the story of the flight from Herod.[19] The *Protevangelium* also adds an account of John the Baptist's life being threatened by Herod's attempt to eradicate all children less than 2 years old. Herod summons Zechariah to ascertain the whereabouts

17. F. Bovon, 'The Suspension of Time in the Protevangelium Jacobi', in B. A. Pearson, *The Future of Early Christianity: Essays in Honor of Helmut Koester* (Minneapolis: Fortress, 1991) 403.

18. Bovon, 'The Suspension of Time in the Protevangelium Jacobi', 403.

19. Brown, *The Birth of the Messiah*, 399.

of his recently born son. When Zechariah refuses to provide the information he is murdered at the entrance to the Temple. This aetiological story is based on the misidentification of Zechariah the father of the Baptist with the Zechariah of Q 11.51 (see Mt. 23.35).[20]

3.4 *Epilogue: Putative Author and Circumstances of Composition (Prot. Jas. 25.1–4)*

The final chapter of the *Protevangelium* contains a brief authorial note which describes the circumstances of composition and expresses a doxological outpouring of praise from the author. Next it salutes all faithful readers and records two epitaphs that have been used as titles of this work. Because of its brevity of this epilogue it can be cited in full.

> [1]Now I, James, am the one who wrote this history in Jerusalem, there being an uproar when Herod died, [2]I took myself into the desert until the uproar in Jerusalem ceased. [3] I praise the Lord God who gave me the wisdom to write this history. [4]Grace shall be with all those who fear the Lord, Amen.
> Birth of Mary. Revelation of James.
> Peace to the writer and to the reader.

The identity of the putative author is not unambiguous, but the James in question is usually taken to be the brother of Jesus mentioned in Mk 6.3. Within the narrative world of the *Protevangelium* this person would strictly be Jesus' older stepbrother, the son of Joseph by a former marriage. The intended identity of 'Herod' is far more certain. This is Herod the Great who prior to the epilogue was slaughtering children less than 2 years old and executing Zechariah the father of John. Hock although seeing the case for Herod the Great as being stronger, nevertheless claims that 'Herod Agrippa, the grandson of Herod the Great, who died in 44 C.E., cannot be ruled out, especially since he persecuted the Jerusalem church and even killed another James, the brother of John, the son of Zebedee.'[21] While strictly speaking this is true, it would be very poor authorial practice to have mentioned Herod the Great in the previous section, then to not only change the reference to another Herod, but also to jump nearly half a century without any signal to the readers. Taking Herod the Great as the intended character, then the narrative purports to have been written shortly after his death in 4 BCE.

The twin epitaphs 'Birth of Mary' and 'Revelation of James' have been used as titles for this work, either with the first standing alone (as is common in the

20. For a discussion of the figure intended by the Matthean narrative see W. D. Davies and D. C. Allison, *The Gospel according to Matthew*, vol. 3, chs XIX–XXVIII, ICC (Edinburgh: T&T Clark, 1997) 317–319; H. T. Fleddermann, *Q: A Reconstruction and Commentary*, BiTS 1 (Leuven: Peeters, 2005) 547.

21. Hock, *The Infancy Gospels of James and Thomas*, 77.

Greek Orthodox tradition) or sometimes with the two in tandem as a fuller title. The term 'revelation' may put this text in the category of 'revelation gospels' where the emphasis is upon the mystical communication of the events to the author by a divine fiat.[22] If there is any sense that the material is revelatory, this may stand in some tension with the desire to associate it with James the step-brother of Jesus who supposedly legitimates the events by functioning as an eyewitness.

4. *Theological Perspectives and Historical Value*

For those who read the text in its entirety there can be little doubt that the central concern revolves around the person of Mary. In particular, her purity is vigorously asserted prior to her adolescence, during the process of the conception of Jesus, even through the actual birth process and for the rest of the narrative. No doubt there is a strong tendency to valorize and glorify Mary, but it is necessary to seek the purpose in doing this. For Vorster, what the text states about Mary is used to assert something of the theological significance of the birth of Jesus.

> The author of *Prot. Jas*. used the annunciation stories of the NT to convince his readers of the extraordinary birth of Jesus. The story was written with an apologetic interest to defend the virgin birth and origin of Jesus, and to refute accusations that he was an illegitimate child.[23]

However, while this may be part of the author's purpose, the text seems to be more interested in the story of Mary for its own sake, rather than just using it as a vehicle for declaring something unique about the birth of her son. The focus in the narrative falls very heavily on the matriarch and not on her offspring, and while the motivation suggested by Vorster for interest in Mary in the birth stories may account for the origin of infancy traditions, by the stage of the composition of the *Protevangelium* the focus had shifted very much onto Mary as a figure of religious significance in her own right.

More helpful is Hock's classification of the work as having an encomiastic purpose. The term encomiun (ἐγκώμιον) refers to an oral or written form that is intended to convey praise of its subject. Hock states, 'The most important part of an ἐγκώμιον, however, is the presentation of the person's virtuous deeds, and the importance of Mary's virtues is shown narratively by the amount of space devoted to documenting her virtue, especially her σωφροσύνη, or self-control.'[24] The *Protevangelium* seeks to lavish praise on Mary by

22. On the generic differences between various texts labelled as gospels see C. M. Tuckett, 'Forty other Gospels', in M. Bockmuehl and D. A. Stanton, *The Written Gospel* (Cambridge: Cambridge University Press, 2005) 238–253.

23. Vorster, 'James, Protevangelium of', 631.

24. Hock, *The Infancy Gospels of James and Thomas*, 19.

expanding on her fleeting role in the canonical gospels and instead making her the central character in this literary work.

Before addressing the question of the historical value of the *Protevangelium*, it is worth considering how similar questions have been answered in relation to the infancy narratives contained in the Matthean and Lukan accounts. Numerous scholars and critics of Christianity have found the traditions of Jesus' birth to be historically unconvincing and certain aspects scientifically unbelievable. Even a scholar as sympathetic as Raymond Brown states baldly that a detailed comparison of the canonical narratives means that one must rule out the possibility 'that both accounts are completely historical'.[25] Notwithstanding this concession, Brown finds eleven points that are shared by the evangelists. Without citing all eleven, these include the names of the parents, the fact they had not come to live together or had sexual relations, Joseph being of Davidic descent, the birth in Bethlehem, a chronological relationship to the days of Herod, angelic appearances and the rearing of the child in Nazareth.[26] While some of these shared items such as angelic heralds or virgin birth have huge confessional significance and one could imagine the possibility of them being invented for theological ends, this is not the case with all the details. In fact certain details are not only mundane, but actually prove problematic in the tradition. The names Joseph and Mary are of little significance in either narrative; the association with Nazareth not only causes aspersions to be cast on Jesus' messianic credentials during his ministry, but it also leads Matthew to invent a scriptural citation to explain his upbring in that city (Mt. 2.23). These somewhat neutral or even embarrassing features lead to the suspicion that such details are unlikely to have been created *de novo*, since they serve no theological purpose.

By contrast, when one turns to the *Protevangelium* there is very little that does not have a strong theological motivation. The names of Mary's parents are far from coincidental. In Jewish tradition a certain Joachim is depicted as a very rich man (*Sus* 4), paralleling the wealth of the father of Mary. As has been noted Mary's mother Anna has the Greek form of the name Hannah, the barren mother of Samuel. The patterning of the birth of Mary on the story of the birth of Samuel is to say the least totally transparent and blatantly obvious. The folkloric portrayal of Mary's childhood and the preservation of her purity serve only to further the glorification of the central character. Her role in weaving the very veil that will be ripped asunder at Jesus' death is a bitter irony and hence the historicity of this incident cannot be sustained. The birth of Jesus without rupturing Mary's hymen and the subsequent examination with accompanying miracles is motivated by a desire to suggest that her perpetual virginity had been witnessed by one who was originally sceptical of the claim. The death of

25. Brown, *The Birth of the Messiah*, 36.
26. Brown, *The Birth of the Messiah*, 34–35.

Zechariah towards the end of the text is clearly not a reliable historical detail, but arises from a misidentification of the Zechariah of Luke's infancy narrative with a different character of the same name mentioned in both the Lukan and Matthean accounts (Q 11.51). One interesting detail that requires consideration is the tradition that Jesus was born in a cave. This aligns with traditions recorded by other early Christian writers; however, in contrast to such sources the cave is not located in Bethlehem, but at some distance from the village. The claim that Jesus was born in a cave may, however, derive ultimately from knowledge of a site shown to tourists making a pilgrimage to Bethlehem from the second century onwards, rather than reflecting a historical memory of the actual birthplace of Jesus.

So it must be adjudged that the *Protevangelium* contains no material of independent historical value and very little of historical value even where it parallels the canonical accounts. Its author expands existing traditions and creates others to serve the theological agenda of the text, which radically asserts the purity of Mary (not only sexual purity) and steadfastly preserves her virginity even after the birth of her son. Beyond this, the text does little to explore the theological implications of such perspectives for viewing Mary as an important soteriological figure in her own right. Such developments belong to a later period. Thus, while the text may be of little or no historical value, apart from being a literary artefact that reflects a certain strand of Christian spirituality in the late second century, it proved to be of major theological significance in more than one branch of Christianity.

5. *Conclusions*

The *Protevangelium* is a text which was most probably written in the final quarter of the second century or the first quarter of the third century. In one sense it may even be incorrect to call this text a 'gospel' since the now common title, *Protevangelium*, is a modern construct, and the text itself never uses the term 'gospel'. However, if a wide definition is given to the term 'gospel', without asking questions of the historicity of the text, then the traditions it conveys do relate to events in the life of Jesus (and earlier) and its narrative structure and apparent genre match that of the canonical gospels.[27] Although this text is not in the canon of any denomination, it would be a misrepresentation to classify it as being apocryphal or non-canonical for all branches of Christianity. It may be better to describe it as 'sub-canonical', or even 'almost canonical', at least for some Church traditions. In Orthodoxy it is still viewed as a text that relates important teaching. In Roman Catholicism the failure of the text to preserve the virginity of Joseph alongside that of Mary led to its rejection, but despite this apparent rejection its theology has had a strong impact on the Mar-

27. See Tuckett, 'Forty other Gospels', 238–253.

iology of the Roman church. At an academic level this influence may seem to be misguided since the historical value of the text is virtually naught. Yet this raises the larger epistemological question of whether theological truth must be predicated on historical reality. Perhaps, however, such an issue, like the *Protevangelium* itself, is something that is better left pondered than definitively answered.

Bibliography

F. Bovon, 'The Suspension of Time in the Protevangelium Jacobi', in B. A. Pearson, *The Future of Early Christianity: Essays in Honor of Helmut Koester* (Minneapolis: Fortress, 1991) 393–405.

R. E. Brown, *The Birth of the Messiah*, ABRL (rev. edn; New York: Doubleday, 1993).

J. K. Elliott, *The Apocryphal New Testament* (rev. reprinting, Oxford: Oxford University Press, 1999) 48–67.

R. F. Hock, *The Infancy Gospels of James and Thomas* (Santa Rosa, CA: Polebridge, 1995).

J. P. Meier, *A Marginal Jew: Rethinking the Historical Jesus*, vol. 1: The Roots of the Problem and the Person, ABRL (New York: Doubleday, 1991).

J. R. Rea (ed.), *The Oxyrhynchus Papyri*, vol. 50, Papyri numbers 3522–3600 (London: British Academy/Egypt Exploration Society, 1983).

É. de Strycker, *La forme la plus ancienne du Protévangile de Jacques* (Bruxelles: Société des Bollandistes, 1961).

É. de Strycker, 'Die grieschischen Handschriften des Protevangeliums Iacobi', in D. Harlfinger (ed.), *Grieschische Kodikologie und Textüberlieferung* (Darmstadt: Wissenschftliche Buchgesellschaft, 1980) 577–612.

M. Testuz (ed.), *Papyrus Bodmer V: Nativite de Marie* (Geneva: Bibliotheca Bodmeriana, 1958).

W. S. Vorster, 'James, Protevangelium of', *Anchor Bible Dictionary*, vol. III (New York: Doubleday, 1992) 629–632.

Chapter 10

The *Infancy Gospel of Thomas*

Tony Chartrand-Burke

The *Infancy Gospel of Thomas* (IGT) is one of the most well-known texts of the Christian Apocrypha. Its stories of the young Jesus shaming teachers and maiming playmates are sufficiently titillating and theologically challenging that many scholars and writers enjoy discussing the text, but few seek to understand it in its original historical and literary contexts. Few also have been willing to grapple with its complex transmission history. And so, 400 years after its initial publication, IGT remains a neglected text – a surprising and regrettable situation given its importance, for this gospel likely is one of the earliest pieces of Christian writing outside of the New Testament and its stories had a tremendous impact on art, literature and piety throughout the medieval period.

1. *The Recovery of the Original Text*

A description of the contents of the gospel must wait for a detailed discussion of the manuscript tradition, for the shape of the text depends on how one interprets the evidence. And there have been many interpretations. Each new manuscript discovery or edition of a version has been accompanied with a claim that the newly-published evidence best preserves the original form of the text. Alas no single witness holds that distinction. But, together, the growing number and variety of the witnesses has brought that elusive original text into view. And it is much different from what many expected.

The initial interest in manuscripts of IGT began in the late seventeenth century. The first of these, Vienna *Phil. gr. 162 (144)* from the fifteenth century (= O), was described in a 1675 catalogue by P. Lambeck.[1] The manuscript was subsequently lost; all that remains now are Lambeck's brief excerpts. The second manuscript, Paris *A. F. gr. 239 (2908/2279)* also of the fifteenth century (= P), was mentioned by Lambeck and a few other scholars. It was published in its entirety by J. B. Cotelier in his 1698 edition of the *Apostolic*

1. *Commentariorum de augusta bibliotheca caesarea vindobenensi*, vol. 7 (Vienna: Typis M. Cosmerovii, 1675) 270–273.

Constitutions[2] before reaching a larger audience in J. Fabricius' 1703 apocrypha collection.[3] The fragmentary manuscript features an introduction ascribing the text to 'Thomas the Israelite Philosopher' and promising to tell readers the miracles, Jesus did as a child in Nazareth. Several stories follow of the five-year-old Jesus breaking Sabbath regulations to fashion birds out of clay and animate them, cursing the son of Annas the scribe for disturbing his work, slaying a boy for bumping into him in the marketplace, blinding his critics and amazing a teacher with his knowledge. The text finishes prematurely in the middle of a story in which Jesus encounters a dyer.

Early commentary on the text identified IGT either as the 'Gospel of Thomas' (mentioned by Origen, Hippolytus, and others)[4] or as the Childhood of Jesus (mentioned by John Chrysostom, Epiphanius of Salamina, and others),[5] or both. A *terminus ante quem* for the text was established by Irenaeus' discussion of the episode of Jesus and the Teacher, a tale he attributes to the Marcosians (*Adv. Haer.* 1.20.1). The patristic citations led scholars to associate IGT with Gnosticism, an association which has endured to today despite the fact that IGT is not the 'Gospel of Thomas' known to the early writers, nor was it valued only by Gnostics – the anti-Gnostic *Epistle of the Apostles* (ch. 4) cites the same story of the Teacher, and other 'orthodox' apocrypha such as the *Gospel of Bartholomew* (2.11) and the *History of Joseph the Carpenter* (ch. 17) refer to episodes from the text. The lack of Gnostic elements in IGT has been no barrier to this mischaracterization. To explain their absence, an 'expurgation theory' was devised stating that the offending Gnostic material had been removed from the text by orthodox revisers (a process similar to what occurred with the Apocryphal Acts).

Subsequent manuscript discoveries led to the publication of longer and longer forms of IGT, though none of these longer forms were any more Gnostic than the Paris manuscript. C. von Tischendorf constructed a critical edition of the text based primarily on two other manuscripts – Dresden *A 187* (= D) and Bologna *Univ. 2702* (= B),[6] both from the fifteenth century – comprising the 19-chapter form of the text (= Greek A) well-known today.[7] Tischendorf also

2. *SS. Patrum qui temporibus apostolicis floruerunt*, vol. 1, (2nd edn; Antwerp: Huguetanorum sumtibus, 1698) 345–346.

3. *Codex Apocryphus Novi Testamenti*, vol. 1 (Hamburg: Schiller, 1703) 128–167.

4. A complete overview and discussion of the citations can be found in H. Attridge, 'The Greek Fragments: Introduction', in B. Layton (ed.), *Nag Hammadi Codex II, 2–7*, vol. 1, NHS 20 (Leiden: E. J. Brill, 1989) 95–112.

5. For an overview and discussion see T. Chartrand-Burke, 'The *Infancy Gospel of Thomas*: The Text, Its Origins, and Its Transmission' (Ph.D. diss., University of Toronto 2001) 11–17.

6. D was published for the first time by Tischendorf; however, B was published first in a diplomatic edition by G. L. Mingarelli, 'De Apocrypho Thomae Evangelio . . . epistola', in A. Calogiera (ed.), *Nuova Raccolta d'opuscoli scientifici e filologici*, vol. 12 (Venice 1764) 73–155 and then it was used along with D, P and O in a critical edition by I. C. Thilo, *Codex apocryphus Novi Testamenti*, vol. 1 (Lipsius: Vogel, 1832) lxxiii–xci and 277–315.

7. *Evangelia Apocrypha* (2nd edn; Leipzig: H. Mendelsohn, 1876) 140–157.

published a shorter form of the text (= Greek B) based on a manuscript he found during his famous visit to St Catharine's monastery in the Sinai (*Cod. Sinait. gr. 453*, fourteenth/fifteenth century; = S).[8] At the same time, Tischendorf brought attention to several Latin witnesses to the text: an expanded version of the *Gospel of Pseudo-Matthew* that features the IGT material as its *pars altera* (= Lm), a related fifth-century palimpsest (*Vindobonensis 563*; = Lv), and a second Latin translation featuring several introductory chapters detailing episodes from the Holy Family's sojourn in Egypt (*Vat. lat. 4578*, fourteenth century; = Lt).[9] The Greek manuscript base of IGT was expanded further in 1927 with A. Delatte's publication of a third form of the text from *Cod. Atheniensia gr. 355* (= A; fifteenth century).[10] This recension, labelled Greek D by subsequent scholars, is a second witness to the form of the text found in Lt.[11] Since Tischendorf's day, the body of evidence for IGT has expanded considerably with the publication of versions in Syriac,[12] Georgian,[13] Ethiopic,[14] Slavonic[15] and Irish.[16]

8. Ibid., 158–163.

9. Ibid., 93–112, xliv–xlvi and 164–180 (respectively).

10. 'Évangile de l'enfance de Jacques: Manuscrit No. 355 de la Bibliothèque Nationale', in *Anecdota Atheniensia*, vol. 1, *Textes grecs inédits relatifs à l'histoire des religions* (Paris: Edouard Champion, 1927) 264–271.

11. The earliest scholarship on the recension (as well as my own study of the Greek manuscript tradition in T. Chartrand-Burke, 'The *Infancy Gospel of Thomas*') used the designation Greek C. Greek D, the designation begun by S. J. Voicu, 'Notes sur l'histoire du texte de L'Histoire de l'Enfance de Jésus', *Apocrypha* 2 (1991) 119–132, has since become standard.

12. The first Syriac manuscript (BL *Add. 14484*; sixth century) was published by W. Wright, *Contributions to the Apocryphal Literature of the New Testament* (London: Williams & Norgate, 1865) 6–16. Since then three additional manuscripts have seen publication: Göttingen *syr. 10* of the fifth or sixth century (collated against Wright's manuscript by W. Baars and J. Heldermann, 'Neue Materielen zum Text und zur Interpretation des Kindheitsevangeliums des Pseudo-Thomas', *Oriens Christianus* 77 (1993) 191–226; 78 (1994) 1–32), a version of the Syriac *Life of Mary* published from a thirteenth-/fourteenth-century Alqoš manuscript by E. A. W. Budge, *The History of the Blessed Virgin Mary and the History of the Likeness of Christ* (2 vols; London: Luzac & Co., 1899) and Vat. *syr. 159* from 1622/1623 published in a partial French translation by P. Peeters, *Évangiles apocryphes*, vol. 2, Textes et documents pour l'étude historique du Christianisme 18 (Paris: Librairie Alphonse Picard & Fils, 1914) 291–311. A large number of Syriac manuscripts remain unpublished. A partial list of these manuscripts (though with a few infelicities) can be found in A. Baumstark, *Geschichte der syrischen Literatur mit Ausschluss der christlich-palästinensischen Texte* (Bonn: A. Marcus & E. Webers Verlag, 1922) 69–70 n. 12 and 99 n. 4 and S. C. Mimouni, 'Les Vies de la Vierge: État de la question', *Apocrypha* 5 (1994) 239–242. The Syriac tradition also spawned two offspring: the *Arabic Infancy Gospel*, which combines IGT with other infancy traditions, and an unrelated Arabic translation of IGT alone published by S. Noja, 'L'Évangile arabe apocryphe de Thomas, de la 'Biblioteca Ambrosiana' de Milan (G 11 sup)', in A. Vivian (ed.), *Biblische und Judistische Studien. Festschrift für Paolo Sacchi*, Judentum und Umwelt 29 (Paris: Peter Lang, 1990) 681–690.

13. From a single, fragmentary manuscript (Tblisi, *Cod. A 95*) copied around the end of the tenth century. The text was published by Russian scholars early in the twentieth century but was given wider exposure in a Latin translation by G. Garitte, 'Le fragment géorgien de l'Évangile de Thomas', *RHE* 51 (1956) 513–515.

As important as the Greek recensions are to the transmission history of IGT, it has been shown persuasively that the earliest versions are, collectively, a better witness to the original form of the text. In 1980 L. van Rompay demonstrated that the Syriac, Georgian, Ethiopic and Old Latin (represented by Lm, Lv and the Irish manuscript) versions all derive from a form of IGT comprised of only Chapters 2–9, 11–16 and 19.[17] This shorter text also has a number of abbreviations within chapters and features a speech made by Jesus in Chapter 6 that is absent in Greek A and B but has some parallel in the Greek D, Lt and Slavonic texts. Further evidence for an originally shorter IGT was bolstered by S. Voicu's discussion of yet another Greek recension – Greek S, based on *Cod. Sabait. 259* (= H; eleventh century) – which he describes as an 'intermediate' form of the text standing between the early versions (for it too lacks chs. 17 and 18 and contains the speech from ch. 6) and the other Greek recensions (as it includes chs. 1 and 10, the latter placed between chs. 16 and 19).[18] Voicu's knowledge of Greek S was based on a collation made available to him by J. Noret;[19] Voicu declined to publish the text as he felt the Greek manuscript tradition on the whole was not useful for determining the original form of IGT – indeed, he believed the Ethiopic text to be superior to all other witnesses.[20]

14. Found in Chapter 8 of *Ta'amra 'Iyasus (Miracles of Jesus)*, a large biographical work compiled from various canonical and non-canonical sources. There are 25 known manuscripts of the text; S. Grébaut, 'Les miracles de Jésus: Texte éthiopien publié et traduit', *PO* 12.4 (1919) 625–642 used five of these for his edition of the IGT section of the *Miracles.*

15. The Slavonic tradition comprises six medieval manuscripts in Middle Bulgarian, Serbian, Croatian and Russian, and ten in Ukrainian from the eighteenth/nineteenth century. The initial translation of the text is dated to the tenth or eleventh century. For more on the Slavonic tradition see the two major studies by A. de Santos Otero, *Das kirchenslavische Evangelium des Thomas*, PTS 6 (Berlin: De Gruyter, 1967) and T. Rosén, *The Slavonic Translation of the Apocryphal Infancy Gospel of Thomas*, Acta Universitatis Upsaliensis, Studia Slavica Upsaliensia 39 (Uppsala: Almqvist & Wiksell International, 1997).

16. Published from a single manuscript (Dublin, National Library of Ireland, *MS G 50*) by J. Carney, 'Two Old Irish Poems', *Eriu* 18 (1958) 1–43 and more recently by Maire Herbert and Martin McNamara in M. McNamara *et al.*, *Apocrypha Hiberniae*, t. 1: *Evangelia infantiae*, vol. 1, CCSA 13 (Turnhout: Brepols, 2001) 443–483. Though the manuscript is dated to the seventeenth century, the translation is believed to have been made directly from the Old Latin IGT (found in Lv and incorporated in *Ps.-Matt*) around 700 CE.

17. 'De ethiopische versie van het Kindsheidsevangelie volgens Thomas de Israëliet', in A. Théodoridès, P. Naster and J. Riesl (eds), *Enfant dans les civilisations orientales* (Leuven: Editions Peeters, 1980) 119–132.

18. 'Notes sur l'histoire', 128–129.

19. Noret ('Pour une édition de l'Évangile de l'enfance selon Thomas', *AnBoll* 90 ([1972] 412) had earlier mentioned the manuscript in an announcement of a planned critical edition of IGT that never materialized. Readings from the collation were incorporated (albeit in Italian) in Voicu's second work on the text, 'Verso il testo primitivo dei Παιδικὰ τοῦ Κυρίου Ἰησοῦ "Racconti dell' infanzia del Signore Gesù"', *Apocrypha* 9 (1998) 7–95.

20. This assessment of the Ethiopic version is shared by L. van Rompay ('De ethiopische versie', 131–132).

Greek S finally was published, along with additional Greek manuscripts, in my 2001 Doctoral dissertation.[21] The dissertation features a critical synopsis of each of the four recensions. The Greek S column of the synopsis is simply an edition of the Jerusalem manuscript. Greek A is based on two new manuscripts – Vienna, *Cod. hist. gr. 91* (= W; fourteenth/fifteenth century) and *Cod. Vatopedi 37* (= V; fourteenth century) – and incorporates all previously published Greek A manuscripts as well as evidence from the related Slavonic tradition. Two other Greek manuscripts similar to B and D are employed also: Samos, B. Metropoleos *MS gr. 54* (= M; fifteenth/sixteenth century) and *Cod. Lavra Θ 222* (= L; fifteenth century). Tischendorf's Greek B manuscript is accompanied by a second manuscript from Sinai: *Cod. Sinait. gr. 532* (= C; fifteenth/sixteenth century). And Greek D is reconstructed using A, Lt and two fragmentary manuscripts: Vienna, *Cod. theol. gr. 123* (= T; thirteenth century) and Vat. *Palat. gr. 364* (= R; fifteenth century). The dissertation aims to prove that Greek S may not be a perfect witness to IGT's original form, but it is the earliest known Greek manuscript and, aside from its additional chapters, follows closely the readings of the early versions. If read alongside the early versions, Greek S can be used to establish the original text of IGT with some confidence.

2. *The Origins of the Text*

Though Tischendorf's 19-chapter Greek A version of IGT remains popular in scholarship, it does not represent well the contents of the original text – indeed, the manuscripts he used for his edition do not even represent well the text of Greek A. Greek S and the early versions offer a much different text than all other Greek recensions of IGT; it is this much different text that must be used in future analyses of the gospel.

2.1 *Original Content*

The original title of IGT appears to have been simply 'The Childhood of the Lord'. It begins, not with the introduction ascribing the text to Thomas, but with the Animation of the Sparrows (Greek A chs 2–3). This tale concludes with Jesus withering the son of Annas but does not include the demand by the child's parents that Joseph 'teach him to bless and not to curse'. Then follows the Curse on the Careless Boy (ch. 4) and Joseph Rebukes Jesus (ch. 5). Jesus' behaviour attracts the attention of the teacher Zacchaeus (ch. 6) who wishes to teach this 'wicked boy' manners and respect. Joseph questions his ability to do

21. Chartrand-Burke, 'The *Infancy Gospel of Thomas*', 134–244. Details of all the Greek manuscripts are provided also in Chartrand-Burke, 'The Greek Manuscript Tradition of the *Infancy Gospel of Thomas*', *Apocrypha* 14 (2004) 129–151.

so, but Zacchaeus persists. So Jesus delivers a speech in which he declares his strangeness to this world and his superior knowledge and in which he predicts his demise on the cross. Then Jesus demonstrates his otherworldly wisdom with an esoteric description of the letter alpha. Zacchaeus is humbled by the boy and confesses his inability to fathom the nature of Jesus ('For what great thing this boy is – either a god or an angel or whatever else I might say – I do not know', ch. 7). In response to Zacchaeus' confession, Jesus restores those he had cursed (ch. 8). Several beneficent miracles follow: the Raising of the Child Zeno (ch. 9), Carrying Water in a Cloak (ch. 11), the Miraculously Great Harvest (ch. 12) and the Miraculous Repair of a Bed (ch. 13). In the later witnesses, these miracles elicit praise from his parents and the townspeople; but originally only the Zeno story included such a response. The text continues with Joseph taking Jesus to another teacher, who, angered by Jesus' insolence, strikes the boy. He is then cursed (ch. 14). In the later witnesses, this teacher is subsequently restored to life, but not in the early versions. A third teacher escapes harm only because he recognizes Jesus' superior knowledge (ch. 15). Jesus then saves his brother James from a snakebite (ch. 16). Finally, the text comes to a close with the story of Jesus in the Temple from Lk. 2:41–52. But whereas Luke has Jesus sitting among the teachers listening intently, IGT has Jesus teach *them* about the Law.

If this arrangement is indeed closer to the original form of the text, then IGT lacks many of the elements that have impaired previous commentary on the gospel. Distracted by the additions present in the later witnesses, scholars have remarked that the gospel shows few signs of a coherent arrangement or plot. The synoptic-like healing miracles of Chapters 10, 17 and 18 always seemed out-of-place in the text and obscured what scholars saw as a hint of progression in the boy Jesus' behaviour from cursing to blessing. But the shorter text form contains fewer references to the need to rehabilitate Jesus and more of a focus on the theme of teaching. The original author appears intent on demonstrating that Jesus is a being of power, wisdom and authority, and that these attributes must be recognized and respected – by both those who encounter Jesus in the stories and, presumably, the gospel's readers. It is not Jesus who needs to change, but those around him. The teaching stories highlight this theme. The Teacher story stands at the centre of the text and continues for three chapters; two sequels follow and the text culminates in the story of Jesus in the Temple. There the boy demonstrates his acumen and receives proper acknowledgement from the scribes and Pharisees who declare to Mary, 'Blessed are you, because the Lord God has blessed the fruit of your womb. For such present wisdom and glory of virtue we have never seen nor heard.'

The focus on the original text of IGT should not lead to the neglect of other childhood stories that weave in and out of the tradition over the centuries. Such tales as Jesus Rides the Sunbeam, Jesus and the Dyer, Jesus in the Temple of Idols and the episodes in Greek D's Egyptian Prologue testify to the continuing efforts to invent and compile stories of Jesus as a child. These additions and other variations in the manuscript traditions show also how views of Jesus' childhood and childhood in general change over time.

2.2 *Time and Place of Origin*

As with many of the non-canonical gospels, the origins of IGT are difficult to determine. It evokes both Jewish and non-Jewish literature, making its cultural affinities uncertain. And it bears no stamp of sectarian identification – neither in a reliably early apostolic attribution nor by titles assigned to Jesus. Early scholars of the text placed its origins in Syria, based on the Thomas attribution and similarities with childhood tales of Krishna and Buddha from India.[22] Some even suggested that IGT was composed in Syriac.[23] But we now know that the introduction was added to the text late in its transmission and in a non-Syrian milieu. Knowledge of Buddhist stories and Hindu ascetics by Clement of Alexandria (*Strom.* 1.15) and Philo (*Abr.* 182; *Dreams* 2.56) indicate that geographical proximity is not required for literary borrowing. And Syriac composition is unlikely – first, because it is extremely rare for early Christian apocryphal literature to be written in a language other than Greek,[24] and second, IGT (at least in the form that we have it in Greek S) bears none of the characteristics we find in Greek translations of Semitic texts.[25] Egypt has been offered as another place of origin.[26] So too has Palestine[27] – due to the existence

22. The connections were discussed first among scholars of the *religionsgeschichtliche Schule* of the late nineteenth century. A more recent case for IGT's reliance on the Indian tales was made by Z. P. Thundy, *Buddha and Christ: Nativity Stories and Indian Traditions*, SHR 60 (Leiden: E. J. Brill, 1993).

23. The first scholar to advance seriously a theory of Syriac composition was P. Peeters, *Évangiles apocryphes*, xvii–xxii as part of an idiosyncratic theory that IGT, *Arab. Gos. Inf.* and *Arm. Gos. Inf.* all derive from a Syriac infancy gospel similar to Budge's *Life of Mary* text.

24. Of all first- and second-century gospels only the *Gospel of the Hebrews* and the *Gospel of the Nazareans* are believed to have been written in a Semitic language. The third-century *Abgar Legend* and the *Acts of Thomas* were composed in Syriac. S. Brock, 'Greek into Syriac and Syriac into Greek', *Journal of the Syriac Academy* 3 (1977) 11–16 lists the few Semitic texts (Christian and non-Christian) esteemed enough in antiquity to be translated into Greek.

25. R. A. Martin, *Syntactical Evidence of Semitic Sources in Greek Documents*, Septuagint and Cognate Studies 3 (Cambridge: Society of Biblical Literature, 1974) 5–43 details 17 criteria by which one can determine whether a text was composed in Greek or was translated from a Semitic source. By these criteria, Greek S meets well the expectations of Greek composition. In addition, Greek S clearly draws upon a Greek version of Luke in the Temple story, not a translation from Syriac, whereas the same story in Wright's Syriac text exhibits no verbatim agreement with Old Syriac Luke. For the complete study see Chartrand-Burke, 'The *Infancy Gospel of Thomas*', 247–254.

26. L. Conrady, 'Das Thomasevangelium: Ein wissenschaftlicher kritischer Versuch', *Theologische Studien und Kritiken* 76 (1903) 377–459; A. Meyer, 'Kindheitserzählung des Thomas', in E. Hennecke (ed.), *Neutestamentlichen Apokryphen*, (2nd edn Tübingen: J. C. B. Mohr, 1924), 96; Baars and Heldermann, 'Neue Materialien', 30.

27. The most vigorous proponent for the location is B. Bagatti, 'Nota sul Vangelo di Tommaso Israelita', *Euntes Docete* 29 (1976) 482–489.

of several Jewish parallels to the tales[28] and of pilgrimage sites related to two of the IGT miracles (Antonini Placentini, *Itinerarium* 5 and 13), and the possibility that the teacher Zacchaeus is intended as a parody of the rabbi Yohanan ben Zakkai.[29] S. Voicu goes so far as to suggest that the text reflects Ebionite Christology.[30] But, as near as can be determined from the patristic evidence, the Ebionites are a poor fit as they believed Jesus had a normal human birth and childhood (see Epiphanius, *Pan.* 30.13.7–8).

IGT's time of origin is generally considered to be the late second century. This date is based primarily on Irenaeus' knowledge of the Teacher story (*Adv. Haer.* 1.20.1), though the same tale is reproduced in the *Epistula Apostolorum* which is convincingly dated also to the late second century. It is not certain whether the two authors knew the complete IGT or simply an isolated story. It is secure, however, that a collection of childhood tales was known to several authors of the fourth century. Chrysostom refers to miracles of Jesus' childhood (παιδικά) (*Hom. Jo.* 17), and Epiphanius, too, mentions miracles, Jesus 'is said to have performed in play as a child' (*Pan.* 51.20.2–3). And the fourth-century *Gos. Bart.* and *Hist. Jos. Carp.* contain allusions to several chapters of IGT. Further evidence for the date of origin for IGT can be gleaned from the text itself. First, borrowings from the NT are rare. The expanded Greek manuscripts of IGT draw material from the Synoptics and John. However, all of the NT parallels in Greek S could be derived solely from Luke-Acts.[31] The text also features some elements of Lucan redaction. These details indicate not only a close tie between IGT and Luke, but also perhaps a time of composition before the wide dispersion of other NT texts. And second, the absence of any claims of authorship in the text suggests an early dating. Anonymity in Christian compositions is far more common to those written in the first and second centuries.[32]

The cumulative weight of the evidence indeed suggests that IGT was composed in the second century. Its use of Luke provides the text with a *terminus*

28. The Miraculous Stretching of a Beam and the Healing of James recall similar tales told of Rabbi Hanina ben Dosa (*b. Ta'an* 25a; *t. Ber.* 3:20; *b. Ber.* 33a; the texts are excerpted in C. A. Evans, *Noncanonical Writings and New Testament Interpretation* [Peabody: Hendrickson Publishers, 1992] 234) and Carrying Water in a Cloak has a parallel in an apocryphal childhood tale of Ezra from a Jeremiah Apocryphon (discussed most recently by K. H. Kuhn, 'A Coptic Jeremiah Apocryphon', *Le Muséon* 83 (1970) 95–135, 291–350).

29. J. Neusner, 'Zacchaeus/Zakkai', *HTR* 57 (1964) 57–59.

30. Voicu, 'Verso il testo primitivo', 50.

31. For more on the relationship between IGT and Luke see T. Chartrand-Burke, 'Completing the Gospel: The *Infancy Gospel of Thomas* as a Supplement to the Gospel of Luke', in L. DiTommaso and L. Turcescu (eds), *The Reception and Interpretation of the Bible in Late Antiquity. Proceedings of the Montréal Colloquium in Honour of Charles Kannengeiser, 11–13 October 2006* (Leiden: Brill, in press).

32. See further K. Aland, *The Authorship and Integrity of the New Testament* (London: SPCK, 1965) 1–13.

a quo of around 90 CE and the few internal indications of its antiquity point to a time of composition that allows for its possible use by Irenaeus and *Ep. Apos.* IGT's connection with Luke suggests it was written in a place where Luke was held in high esteem; unfortunately, it is not known exactly where Luke originated, though Palestine seems unlikely. Syrian Antioch or Asia Minor may be the best candidates for IGT's place of origin: both regions have been suggested for the composition of Luke, they allow for its speedy dissemination into both the West and the East, and it is in Antioch where Chrysostom, the earliest secure witness to the παιδικά, came into contact with the text in the late fourth century.

3. *Genre and Meaning*

For many years IGT's identification as a once-lengthier Gnostic text has hampered serious investigation into its contents. There is now no reason to think it has been edited over time – indeed it has been expanded – nor to associate it with Gnosticism.[33] Nevertheless, these theories continue to influence much of modern commentary. But in recent years a few scholars have set aside the earlier negative assessments of the text and now seek to properly understand the text by observing affinities between IGT and Greco-Roman biographies.[34]

Childhood tales of the great men, and sometimes women, of history are plentiful. Such tales are found not only among ancient Mediterranean cultures but throughout the world. Biographies of gods (Hermes, Krishna), heroes (Hercules), leaders (Cyrus the Great, Alexander), philosophers (Plato) and holy men (Apollonius, the Buddha) all contain childhood tales. Such tales were prominent also in Hellenistic Jewish literature (e.g. in tales of Moses, Samson, Abraham, Malachi, Elijah, Solomon and Isaac) and continue into later Christian literature (e.g. in tales of Mary, Origen, Ambrose, Athanasius and a host of other saints). The primary purpose behind the tales is to foreshadow the adult career of their protagonist. This motif is permissible given how the ancient world viewed character and personality. Discussing Plutarch's work, C. Pelling reveals that the ancients tended to reconcile a person's various personality traits into one character 'type' and that they believed personality is inherited and remains consistent throughout one's life.[35] An esteemed figure, therefore, would have ascribed to him or her stories of beneficence, or signs of

33. For lists of apparent Gnostic elements in IGT see De Santos Otero, *Kirchenslavische*, 172–184 and Baars and Heldermann, 'Neue Materialien', 30–31.

34. Most effectively by R. F. Hock, *The Infancy Gospels of James and Thomas*, The Scholars Bible 2 (Santa Rosa: Polebridge Press, 1995) 95–97 which draws heavily on T. Wiedemann, *Adults and Children in the Roman Empire* (New Haven: Yale University Press, 1989) 49–83. For a more detailed discussion see Chartrand-Burke, 'The *Infancy Gospel of Thomas*', 380–394.

35. 'Childhood and Personality in Greek Literature', in C. Pelling (ed.), *Characterization and Individuality in Greek Literature* (Oxford: Clarendon Press, 1990) 235–240.

intelligence, military skill, or whatever quality for which they were known in adulthood, while notorious figures were portrayed as cruel, calculating or coddled, even as children. Childhood thus becomes a choice time in a person's life for exploitation in propaganda.[36]

The childhood tale was such a popular motif in antiquity that rhetoricians provided advice to writers on the process of composing the stories. In his treatise on constructing a panegyric, Quintilian instructs his readers to praise a subject with descriptions of his background, his beauty and with accounts of his education: 'it has sometimes proved the more effective course to trace a man's life and deeds in due chronological order, praising his natural gifts as a child, then his progress at school' (*Inst.* 3.7.15). Quintilian's instructions are echoed by the early fourth-century rhetorician Menander, who advises speakers to include in their praises such miracles as the recognition of an emperor's future role by children at play:[37] 'If there is anything like this in connection with the emperor, work it up; if it is possible to invent, and to do this convincingly, do not hesitate' (*Treatise* II.371.10–15). He recommends also to praise the subject's beauty and to emphasize his excellence at school: 'Then you must speak of his love of learning, his quickness, his enthusiasm for study, his easy grasp of what is taught him. If he excels in literature, philosophy, and knowledge of letters, you must praise this' (*Treatise* II 371.26–372.1). For nefarious figures, however, the schoolroom motif was used to illustrate the subject's intellectual shortcomings.

The emphasis biographers placed on presenting their subjects as children should not be credited to an interest in childhood as a stage of development – indeed, the majority of references in ancient writings to children and their qualities are disparaging. Greek and Roman writers characterize children as ignorant, capricious, foolish and quarrelsome. They spoke nonsense, lacked judgement, were physically frail, and easily frightened.[38] Adolescence, too, was often denounced. Biblical texts, for their part, describe children as ignorant, capricious and in need of strict discipline (see 2 Kgs 2.23–24; Isa. 3.4; Wis. 12.24–25; 15.14; Prov. 22.15; Sir. 30.1–13). The later rabbis associate the young with deaf mutes and the weak-minded, thereby indicating that children, too, lack their full faculties (*'Erub.* 3.2; *Šeqal.* 1.3; *Sukkah* 2.8; 3.10, etc.).[39] This negativity towards childhood contributes to the motifs we find in the

36. On biographies as propaganda see Pelling, 'Childhood and Personality', 217; P. Cox, *Biography in Antiquity: A Quest for the Holy Man* (Berkeley: University of California Press, 1983) xiv–xv; as negative propaganda, 10–12.

37. Such a tale is told of Jesus in *Arab. Gos. Inf.*, 41. More well-known is the example from the life of Cyrus recorded by Herodotus (*Hist.* 114–115).

38. See further Wiedemann, *Adults and Children*, 17–19, 24.

39. The following references are taken from J. M. Gundry-Volf, 'The Least and the Greatest: Children in The New Testament', in Marcia Bunge (ed.), *The Child in Christian Thought* (Grand Rapids: Eerdmans, 2000) 35.

childhood stories. None of the protagonists of these tales act like children. They all demonstrate a wisdom and maturity that belies their age. They excel at school, sometimes surpassing even the abilities of their teachers. They are praised for their seriousness. When they play, it is only in games that prophesy their future roles. The biographers appear uneasy with attributing typical childhood qualities to their subjects.

This uneasiness is not restricted to the educated elite who were responsible for biographies and other literature. Even ordinary children, some from very humble origins, were remembered for being wise beyond their years. Sarcophagi and funerary altars, primarily used by the lower classes, often contain images and inscriptions that portray the prematurely deceased as young adults. J. Huskinson labels this form of depiction 'proleptic' – that is, the images either present the children as they would have appeared had they not met an untimely death, or feature symbolic representations of the qualities which they (allegedly) possessed.[40] For example, young boys are found depicted as adult military men or budding orators (what Huskinson calls 'the proleptic figure par excellence'[41]) or as adherents to religious cults they would not be able to join until adulthood. Girls are portrayed as adult mythical figures, such as Diana or Venus. Inscriptions, too, testify to this need to exaggerate the commemorated child's maturity. For example, one inscription from Rome mentions Kritiès who died at the age of two and a half; for his intelligence, it is said, he should be compared to someone of grey wisdom.[42] The idealized intelligent, mature child – commonly referred to as the *puer senex* motif – appears also in Pliny's panegyric for Minicia Marcella (*Ep.* 5,16) and in Quintilian's portrayals of his own deceased children (*Inst.* 6.7, 10 and the *proemium*). These same literary and iconographic motifs can be found also in Christian funerary sources.[43]

All of these sources – the literature, inscriptions and reliefs – from high and low social strata betray an uneasiness with childhood. Deceased children are portrayed as they would have been had they lived to adulthood, and important historic figures are depicted as adult-like in childhood. It seems that any child of note, whether an emperor, a hero, a saint, or simply one's prematurely deceased child, did not act like children do. And IGT's Jesus is no exception. The wisdom and precocity he exhibits in the childhood tales are evidence not for Gnostic Christology as many scholars on the text maintain, but for the prevalence of the *puer senex* motif in ancient Mediterranean societies. This is

40. *Roman Children's Sarcophagi: Their Decoration and Its Social Significance* (Oxford: Clarendon Press, 1996) 2 and similarly H. I. Marrou, *Mousikos anér. Étude sur les scènes de la vie intéllectuelle figurant sur les monuments funéraires romains* (Rome: Brettschneider, 1964) 200.

41. *Roman Children's Sarcophagi*, 93.

42. For this and other examples see M. Kleijwegt, *Ancient Youth: The Ambiguity of Youth and the Absence of Adolescence in Greco-Roman Society* (Amsterdam: J. C. Gieben, 1991) 126–130 and Marrou, *Mousikos anér*, 201–207.

43. See further Chartrand-Burke, 'The *Infancy Gospel of Thomas*', 379–380.

particularly evident in IGT's interest in the theme of teaching; the Teacher and Temple stories allow Jesus to demonstrate his otherworldly nature while at the same time illustrating his shortage of childlike qualities and foreshadowing his future accomplishments. Furthermore, given the affinities between IGT and other biographical literature, readers should not expect to see the young Jesus grow and mature as the text progresses – indeed, Jesus is here presented as a cursing wonderworker because the author considers the adult Jesus to have been a cursing wonderworker. As it happens, the early Christian text that features such characters most prominently is Luke-Acts,[44] a text already shown to have been a great inspiration to the author of IGT.

4. *Conclusions*

Scholarship on IGT has progressed significantly in the last decade. The Slavonic and Greek traditions have been treated to in-depth analyses. Similar work is underway on the Old Latin and Syriac traditions, the results of which may clear up problems in establishing the original text.[45] E. Norelli has contributed a study of the much-overlooked Egyptian Prologue. He finds in the material a core narrative traceable to post-1970 Palestine and reflecting conflicts between Christian groups or between Jewish and Christian groups.[46] L. Paulissen has published two articles examining IGT's use of the theme of teaching.[47] And in 2008 Reidar Aasgaard will see the release of his study of the text – the first monograph devoted to IGT to be published in 40 years. Unfortunately, little of this scholarship ever makes its way to those authors who write entries in collections of non-canonical texts, or university textbooks, or popular-market overviews of early Christian literature. So, the majority of readers of the text still encounter it in new editions or translations of Tischendorf's Greek A and learn from introductions that IGT was once a

44. It has been noted that Luke's gospel in particular evokes the figure of Elijah, who was also a cursing wonderworker. See M. M. Faierstein, 'Why Do the Scribes Say Elijah Must Come First?', *JBL* 100 (1981) 75–86 and the responses by D. C. Allison, 'Elijah Must Come First', *JBL* 103 (1984) 256–258 and J. A. Fitzmyer, 'More about Elijah Coming First', *JBL* 104 (1985) 295–296.

45. See S. Voicu, 'La tradition latine des *Paidika*', *Bulletin de l'AELAC* 14 (2004) 13–21; as for the Syriac version, I have begun the process of assembling the known manuscripts and have already found better witnesses than those published.

46. 'Gesù ride: Gesù, il maestro di scuola e i passeri. Le sorprese di un testo apocrifo trascurato', in E. Franco (ed.), *Mysterium regni ministerium verbi (Mc 4, 11; At 6, 4). Scritti in onore di mons. Vittorio Fusco*, Supplementi alla Rivista Biblica 38 (Bologna 2001) 653–684.

47. 'Jésus á l' école. L'enseignement dans l' *Évangile de l'Enfance selon Thomas*', *Apocrypha* 14 (2003) 153–175; and 'Jesus, enfant divin: processus de reconnaissance dans l' *Évangile de l'Enfance selon Thomas*', in L. Couloubaritsis and B. Decharneux (eds), *Aux origiens théologico-politiques de l'humanisme européen. Actes du colloque international de l'Université Libre de Bruxelles et des Facultés Universitaires Saint-Louis, 15–18 mars 2000* (Ousia, Bruxelles, forthcoming).

longer, Gnostic text. Hopefully, that trend will soon come to an end and more and more readers will turn from denigrating the text to recognizing its proper place in the development of Christian thought and literature.

Bibliography

W. Baars and J. Heldermann 'Neue Materielen zum Text und zur Interpretation des Kindheitsevangeliums des Pseudo-Thomas', *Oriens Christianus* 77 (1993) 191–226; 78 (1994) 1–32.

T. Chartrand-Burke, 'The *Infancy Gospel of Thomas*: The Text, Its Origins, and Its Transmission' (Ph.D. diss., University of Toronto, 2001).

T. Chartrand-Burke, 'The Greek Manuscript Tradition of the *Infancy Gospel of Thomas*', *Apocrypha* 14 (2004) 129–151.

A. De Santos Otero, *Das kirchenslavische Evangelium des Thomas*. Patristische Texte und Studien 6 (Berlin: De Gruyter, 1967).

S. Gero, 'The Infancy Gospel of Thomas: A Study of the Textual and Literary Problems', *Novum Testamentum* 13 (1971) 46–80.

R. F. Hock, *The Infancy Gospels of James and Thomas*. The Scholars Bible 2 (Santa Rosa: Polebridge Press, 1995).

M. McNamara, 'New Testament Apocrypha in the Irish Church', in Elizabeth A. Livingstone (ed.), vol. 6 of *Studia Evangelica* (Berlin: Akademie-Verlag, 1973) 333–340.

E. Norelli, 'Gesù ride: Gesù, il maestro di scuola e i passeri. Le sorprese di un testo apocrifo trascurato', in E. Franco (ed.), *Mysterium regni ministerium verbi (Mc 4, 11; At 6, 4). Scritti in onore di mons. Vittorio Fusco*, Supplementi alla Rivista Biblica 38 (Bologna, 2001) 653–684.

L. van Rompay, 'De ethiopische versie van het Kindsheidsevangelie volgens Thomas de Israëliet', in A. Théodoridès, P. Naster and J. Riesl (eds), *Enfant dans les civilisations orientales* (Leuven: Editions Peeters, 1980) 119–132.

T. Rosén, *The Slavonic Translation of the Apocryphal Infancy Gospel of Thomas*. Acta Universitatis Upsaliensis, Studia Slavica Upsaliensia 39 (Uppsala: Almqvist & Wiksell International, 1997).

C. von Tischendorf, *Evangelia Apocrypha* (2nd edn; Leipzig: H. Mendelsohn, 1876).

S. J. Voicu, 'Notes sur l'histoire du texte de L'Histoire de l'Enfance de Jésus', *Apocrypha* 2 (1991), 119–132.

S. J. Voicu, 'Verso il testo primitivo dei Παιδικὰ τοῦ Κυρίου 'Ιησοῦ "Racconti dell' infanzia del Signore Gesù"', *Apocrypha* 9 (1998), 7–95.

Chapter 11

Papyrus Egerton 2

Tobias Nicklas

Papyrus Egerton 2, often called the 'unknown Gospel', is one of the oldest Christian manuscripts – dating to around 200 CE. Five fragmentary scenes from this important text survive, which are described and commented upon here. Then follows an investigation of the theological profile of the text, its date and its literary dependency (or otherwise) on the canonical gospels. The text which may date to the first half of the second century reflects arguments between (Jewish-) Christian groups and wider Judaism.

1. *Discovery, Publication and Significance*

Papyrus Egerton 2, also known as Papyrus London Christ. 1, came into the possession of the British library through an Egyptian dealer in antiquities. In London it soon got the attention of experts. Its publication in 1935 was considered a sensation.[1] The fragment was dated by its editors H. I. Bell and T. C. Skeat to the middle of the second century AD and therefore was regarded as the oldest extant Christian manuscript.[2] Although P. Egerton 2 lost this rank some months later to P.Ryl. 3.457 (P^{52}; Manchester, John Rylands Library, Gr.P. 457) which contains fragments of Jn 18.31–33, 37–38 that were dated to the beginning of the second century, it is astonishing that one of the oldest extant Christian manuscripts contains fragments of an otherwise unknown apocryphal text.

Papyrus Egerton 2 consists of fragments of three leafs of a codex. On both pages of each of these leafs there is one column of text. Only two of them (fragment 1: 11.5 × 9.2 cm; fragment 2: 11.8 × 9.7 cm) however, offer at least partly coherent pieces of text. The third one contains just a few words – it is simply too small to reconstruct more text (6 × 2.3 cm). Papyrus Egerton 2 is not just

1. H. I. Bell and T. C. Skeat, *Fragments of an Unknown Gospel and Other Early Christian Papyri* (London: British Museum, 1935).

2. Bell and Skeat, *Fragments*, 1, wrote: '. . . it is unquestionably the earliest specifically Christian manuscript yet discovered in Egypt.' Some months later Papyrus Rylands 3.457 (= P52) was edited which is considered to be older than Papyrus Egerton 2.

interesting because of its text. Even the manuscript itself and its palaeography offer several surprising insights:

1. The fragments attest that from very early times Christians seem to have used the codex for their writings instead of the scroll.[3]
2. Papyrus Egerton 2 is one of the earliest extant witnesses for the Christian practice of using so-called *Nomina Sacra*, that is, shortened forms of important holy names such as 'God', 'Lord', 'Jesus' and 'Christ'.[4] Papyrus Egerton 2, however, not only contains the most common forms of *Nomina Sacra*, but also shortened forms of words such as 'Father', 'Moses', 'Isaiah' and 'Prophets'.

Half a century after the publication of Papyrus Egerton 2, another fragment of the same codex was found in the papyrus collection of Cologne/Germany. In 1987 M. Gronewald published Papyrus Cologne 255, a fragment of 6.5 × 3 cm size, which can be connected to the first leaf of Papyrus Egerton 2 and offers additional five lines of text.[5] Palaeographical observations on Papyrus Cologne 255[6] also helped to revise the original dating of Papyrus Egerton 2 (now better known as Papyrus Egerton 2 + Papyrus Cologne 255). The codex now is dated around the year AD 200.

This date, of course, is just a *terminus ante quem* for the text found on the manuscript. Before the discussion of its contents some preliminary remarks are necessary:

1. It must always be borne in mind that we are working here with fragments of a text that was once more extensive than what is now extant. Therefore every conclusion from the nature of the fragmentary text to the nature of the whole must be questioned.
2. The reconstruction of a continuous text of the fragments is sometimes very problematic. In some cases it is possible to fill the gaps with the help of (mainly) biblical parallels. However, at least in one important case, the verso of fragment 2, very different reconstructions are possible.

3. For more information see G. N. Stanton, *Jesus and Gospel* (Cambridge: Cambridge University Press, 2004) 165–191.

4. For an introduction into the present discussion around *Nomina Sacra* see L. W. Hurtado, 'The Origin of the Nomina Sacra. A Proposal', *JBL* 117 (1998) 655–673; C. M. Tuckett, '"Nomina Sacra": Yes and No?', in: J. -M. Auwers and H. -J. De Jonge (eds), *The Biblical Canons* (BETL 163; Leuven: Peeters, 2003) 431–458.

5. M. Gronewald, 'Unbekanntes Evangelium oder Evangelienharmonie (Fragment aus dem "Evangelium Egerton")', in *Kölner Papyri, Papyrologica Coloniensia* vol. 7, Band 6, Universität Köln (1987) 136–145.

6. Concretely the newly found part of the manuscript has an apostrophe between two consonants at the new line 44, a scribal practice otherwise not attested during the second century CE.

A distinction therefore always has to be made between the extant and reconstructed text.

3. Another problem that should not be underestimated is that we even do not know the original sequence of the fragments in the original whole of the 'unknown Gospel'.

2. *The Fragments: Contents, Sequence and Significance*

In the following interpretation of the text I have arranged the fragments in the following sequence: fragment 1 verso, fragment 1 recto, fragment 2 verso and fragment 2 recto. However, I will at least consider some implications of a possible other sequence of the single texts.

2.1 *Fragment 1 + Papyrus Cologne 255*

VERSO

In the text of fragment 1 verso we find Jesus in a dispute with (very probably) Jewish opponents. The first sentences of the text obviously want to be understood as the conclusion of an argument between Jesus and experts of the law. Jesus' statement unfortunately cannot be reconstructed with absolute security – but it obviously has to do with a dispute between Jesus and a person (or persons) who have violated the law. Is this a reaction to the reproach not to act according to the law? Possibly yes, but a safe answer cannot be given.

Now a conversation between Jesus and the rulers of the (Jewish) people follows. It is not clear whether and how this dispute relates to the previous argument. The text at least tells that Jesus 'turns around' to his new opponents:[7]

> *Turned towards the leaders of the people, he [Jesus, TN] said the following word: Search the Scriptures, in which you think you have life. These are the ones which bear witness about me. Do not think that I have come to make accusations against you before my Father. There is already someone who accuses you; Moses, in whom you have hope. But when they said: 'We know that God has spoken to Moses, but of you we do not know where you come from', Jesus responded to them and said: 'Now your unbelief towards what he gave testimony of will be charged. For if you believed Moses, you would also have believed me. Because he has written about me to your forefathers . . .'*

Despite far reaching parallels between this apocryphal dialogue and Johannine texts (e.g. Jn 5.39, 45; 9.29),[8] the unknown gospel shows a very independent profile here. The discussion is concerned with the question of whether the

7. My own translation. See T. Nicklas, 'Papyrus Egerton 2', in T. J. Kraus/M. Kruger/ T. Nicklas (eds), *Gospel Fragments* (OECGT; Oxford: Oxford University Press, 2008).

8. The most important parallels from canonical texts already were collected by L. Cerfaux, 'Parallèles canoniques et extra-canoniques de l'évangile inconnu (Papyrus Egerton 2)', in *Muséon* 49 (1936) 55–77; here, 57–58.

Scriptures of Moses, to which the Jewish leaders refer, bear witness to Jesus or not. While Jesus' opponents think that they have 'life' in the Scriptures, Jesus expresses that the Scriptures testify him. According to this text not Jesus but Moses, the one in whom they place their hope, will accuse the Jewish leaders. This short passage already makes clear what it means to interpret a fragmentary text. If the original 'unknown gospel' like Jn 11.25 called Jesus 'the life', this short passage would take on a profoundly ironical dimension. In this case Jesus would impute to his opponents that they rightly considered the Scriptures as having to do with 'live' (and salvation) but that they did not know *in which manner* this was the case. However, we simply do not know whether Jesus was called 'the life' by the unknown gospel and it is therefore not possible to decide the matter. We simply have to acknowledge that the text is fragmentary. Nevertheless we should always be aware of the fact that we are interpreting a fragment which perhaps – at least at first sight – seems to be of a less literary quality than its canonical counterparts, simply because it lacks a context that could prove its quality.

During the further discussion between Jesus and the Jewish rulers two different ideas of the meaning of Israel's Scriptures come to the fore. These two ideas stand for two perspectives of reading these texts.[9] Although the rulers of the people admit that 'God spoke through Moses', they are described as being ignorant of Jesus' origins. Jesus' reply, on the contrary, interprets the Scriptures as an *unequivocal* witness about him. Someone who does not acknowledge this testimony therefore cannot really believe in Moses, its author. In other words: if Moses wrote about Jesus, then they must be read in the light of the coming of Jesus. The text thus regards any other reading of Israel's Scriptures as a sign of unbelief that leads to (eschatological) accusation by Moses.

RECTO

The recto of fragment 1 starts with the (partly reconstructed) conclusion of a scene where (probably) the crowd attempts to stone Jesus:[10]

> . . . stones together, . . . him. And the leaders laid their hands on him, to arrest him and the crowd . . . But they could not arrest him, because the hour of his deliverance had not yet come. But the Lord himself got out from their hands and withdrew himself from them.

Although it is planned to hand Jesus over to the crowd, he cannot be seized, 'because the hour of his deliverance had not yet come'. Jesus, who is called 'the Lord' here, evades.

9. More detailed: T. Nicklas, 'Christliche Apokryphen als Spiegel der Vielfalt frühchristlichen Lebens: Schlaglichter, Beispiele und methodische Probleme', *ASE*, 23 (2006) 27–44.

10. My own translation. See T. Nicklas, 'Papyrus Egerton 2'.

Again several parallels to the *Gospel of John* are obvious – the clearest one is Jn 7 where Jesus is told to go from Galilee to Jerusalem. As he begins to speak about his being sent from the Father (7.28–29), the 'Jews' try to arrest him (see 7.30; cf. also 7.44).

Papyrus Egerton 2 not only talks about an attempt to stone Jesus (cf. Jn 8.59; 10.31) and Jesus' sovereign escape here (Jn 10.39; but also compare Lk. 4.30), it also mentions the motif of the 'hour' (cf. Jn 8.20)[11] – here the 'hour of his deliverance'.

But what can be said about the relation to the verso of fragment 1? It is possible that the conclusion of the verso-scene is given here.[12] In that case the dispute between Jesus and his opponents has led the crowd to attempt to stone Jesus. But this is not necessarily the case. It is also perfectly possible that fragment 1 recto offers the conclusion of an otherwise lost scene here. Then the recto has to be read before the verso. In any case the parallel to the Fourth Gospel remains, but its function in the 'unknown Gospel' cannot be determined any more.

It is also quite difficult to say anything certain about the motif of the 'hour of his deliverance'. Perhaps, as in the Fourth Gospel this motif originally had to be connected with the 'hour of Jesus glorification'. However, it must be considered that the unknown Gospel connects the word 'hour' with the term 'deliverance' – so perhaps Mk 14.41 is a better parallel here. In any case the passage about the 'hour of deliverance' seems to offer us a small insight into the nature of lost passages of the 'unknown Gospel'. Although we cannot be absolutely sure, speaking about Jesus' deliverance only makes sense if the 'unknown Gospel' knew about Jesus' passion and – contrary to, for example, the *Gospel of Thomas* – told its own version of it.

Fragment 1 recto also recounts a further scene:[13]

> And see: a leper comes to him and says: Teacher Jesus, I wandered together with lepers and ate with them in the inn, and then I myself became leprous. If you now will, I will be clean. And the Lord said to him: I will, be clean! And immediately his leprosy left him. Then Jesus said to him; Go, and show yourself to the priests and for the sake of your purification offer as Moses commanded and do not sin again.

Although this story strongly resembles the Healing of the Leper according to Mk 1.40–44 par., a closer look to the text again reveals that the 'unknown Gospel' offers its own version of the story and sets its own priorities.

11. For further information on this motif see: T. Nicklas, 'Wiederholung und Variation: Das Motiv der Stunde im Johannesevangelium', in: G. van Belle (ed.), *Repetition and Variation in the Fourth Gospel* (BETL; Leuven: Peeters, forthcoming).

12. For further discussion of this sequence of the fragments see D. Lührmann, *Die apokryph gewordenen Evangelien* (NovTSup 112; Leiden: Brill, 2004) 125–143.

13. My own translation. See T. Nicklas, 'Papyrus Egerton 2'.

The leper approaches Jesus and addresses him – contrary to the synoptic parallels Mt. 8.2 and Lk 5.12 – not as 'Lord', but as 'teacher'. This is already a first surprise – actually Jesus' qualities as a healer and not as a teacher are necessary now. But more differences to the synoptic accounts emerge. The leper now begins to speak about the reasons of his disease. Because he had travelled around with leprous people and had eaten with them at the inn, he contracted leprosy, too. Must this sentence be considered a superfluous 'novelistic addition' to older traditions?[14] A comparison of the 'unknown Gospel' with a fragment of the so-called *Gospel of the Nazoraeans* is helpful here. In his commentary in Mt. 12.9–14 Jerome cites the words of the man with a withered hand according to that apocryphal text: 'I was a mason and earned (my) bread with the work of (my) hands: I pray to you, Jesus, to restore my health, that I don't have to beg for my bread in disgrace.' At least at first sight this addition of the original miracle story seems to parallel the words of the leper according to the 'unknown Gospel'. A closer look, however, reveals several differences. While the speech of the mason illustrates the extent of his need (and characterizes him in a positive way), the statement of leper does not work in the same way. Moreover, the leper's behaviour has to be considered imprudent and, if we take Lev. 13 into account, even sinful.[15] The leper ends his speech, as in the synoptic parallels Mk 1.40 par Mt. 8.2 par Lk. 5.12 (probably)[16] with the words 'If you are willing, I will be made pure.'

The story progresses in a way that again shows the profile of the scene according to the 'unknown Gospel':

1. Contrary to the synoptics, the 'unknown Gospel' does not mention that the leper falls down before Jesus.
2. The 'unknown Gospel' neither mentions that Jesus reaches out his hand nor that he touches the sick person (but compare Mk 1.41 par. Mt. 8.3, Lk. 5.13). The leper is healed just by the word of Jesus, who is now called 'the Lord': 'I am willing, become pure.'
3. Contrary to the *Gospel of Mark*, the 'unknown Gospel' neither speaks about Jesus' compassion for the sick (Mk 1.41) nor his excitement (Mk 1.43).

At the end of the scene Jesus orders the healed person to show himself to the priests, as Moses commanded, and thus to undergo the rites for reintegration into the community according to Lev. 14. The last extant sentence of the fragment resembles Jn 5.14 (cf. also the apocryphal scene in Jn 8.11): 'And do not sin any more.'

14. Cf. R. Pesch, 'Jesu ureigene Taten? Ein Beitrag zur Wunderfrage', *QD* 52 (1970) 112.

15. Cf. J. B. Daniels, 'The Egerton Gospel. Its Place in Early Christianity' (diss. Claremont, 1989) 144: 'The leper's explanation clearly illustrates his negligence (or ignorance) of Levitical notions about behavior concerning purity and impurity.'

16. The text here is lacunous, again.

Perhaps this last sentence could serve as a key to a proper understanding of the whole scene. It at least opens the possibility for the following interpretation of the extant text. Quite probably the text understands the disease of the leper as a result of his sin, his violation of God's instruction, the Torah. Jesus, the teacher of the Torah, commands the leper to act according to the Torah now. The account of the leper's former story then would serve to tell about his violation of the Torah. After all, the leper had been in contact with unclean persons and therefore himself was in danger of becoming impure. In this case the fact that the story neither tells about Jesus touching the sick nor speaks about an emotional excitation on his side also makes perfect sense. It could be interpreted to the effect that Jesus, the 'Lord' and teacher, does not want to become impure by performing the miracle. The healing of the leper then was a prerequisite for his liberation from sin through the priest's ritual of purification. And this again could be connected with Jesus' command not to sin any more.[17]

SEQUENCE OF THE SCENES OF FRAGMENT I

Nevertheless, many questions remain unanswered. One decisive problem in particular cannot be solved with certainty. What was the original sequence of the texts of fragment 1? If the text started with fragment 1 verso, then the attempt to stone Jesus on the recto could be understood as a reaction to the debate on the verso. But a reversed order would be perfectly possible, too. In that case the story about Jesus' attempted stoning would be the conclusion of a unit that is no longer extant. But the dispute told on the verso could have evolved from the healing of the leper recounted on the recto.

2.2 *Fragment 2*

VERSO

It is almost impossible to give a proper interpretation of the 'text' of fragment 2 verso. There are two reasons for this. On the one hand the manuscript is in a very bad condition here offering only fragments of words and sentences. On the other hand there are no extant (biblical and/or extra-biblical) parallels that would enable us to fill the gaps with at least some degree of certainty. It is not possible to discuss all the more or less probable reconstructions this fragment has seen.[18] All of them remain hypothetical. It is only possible to say that the original text very probably told about a miracle. Jesus seems to sow (probably) a kind of seed in the river Jordan or on its banks which immediately

17. But compare D. Lührmann, *Die apokryph gewordenen Evangelien*, 135–136, who neglects a relation to the saying of the leper, and points to the common relationship between sin and disease.

18. The most important reconstructions of the text can be found in D. Lührmann, *Fragmente apokryph gewordener Evangelien in griechischer und lateinischer Sprache* (MThSt 59; Marburg: N. G. Elwert, 2000) 153.

bears fruit.[19] The message of the story must remain open to interpretation. Should the text to be regarded as a kind of 'nature miracle' designed to prove Jesus' power over natural processes? Or does it concern a miracle, which tells about the abundance of God's grace? Is the sprouting of the fruit to be regarded as a symbol of overcoming death, or is the text referring to mysterious powers of the waters of Jordan (then perhaps a symbol for the waters of baptism)? Unfortunately there are only questions. No reliable answers are possible in this case.

RECTO

Fragment 2 recto, the other page of the leaf, is also full of gaps. But the fact that this text is partly parallel to Mk 12.13–17 (par. Mt. 22.15–22, Lk. 20.20–26) and concludes with a citation of Isaiah allows a far-reaching reconstruction of the text:[20]

> . . . they tested him and said: 'Teacher Jesus, we know that you have come from God. For what you do bears witness beyond all the prophets. So tell us: Is it allowed to hand over to the kings what belongs to their government? Shall we pay them or not? But since Jesus knew their intention, he became angry and said to them: Why do you call me teacher with your mouth, but do not hear what I say! Well did Isaiah prophesy about you: This people honours me with their lips but their heart is far away from me – in vain do they worship me' . . . commandments.

An unnamed group of persons wants to test Jesus. Of course, this conjures associations with synoptic parallels such as the demand for a sign according to Mk 8.11 par. or the question regarding divorce according to Mk 10.2 par. (cf. also Mk 12.28; Mk 12.15 par.). The speakers address Jesus not just as 'teacher', but also point out that they 'know', that he has come 'from God'. The parallels to the introduction of Nicodemus's speech according to Jn 3.2 are clear.[21]

Does the choice of the word 'to know' (instead of the much more appropriate 'to belief') already indicate a negative characterization of the speakers? At least in the context of the motif of testing Jesus, this seems to be the case.

The reader increasingly gains the impression that there is a certain discrepancy between the words of the speakers and their real intentions. This becomes even clearer with their words, 'What you do is a testimony beyond all the prophets'. This sentence can be interpreted as an allusion to Deut. 34:10–12 LXX in the speech of Moses. In that case the speakers call Jesus a prophet greater than Moses. Another interesting discrepancy between the words of

19. Cf. also H. -J. Klauck, *Apocryphal Gospels: An Introduction* (London: T&T Clark, 2003) 25.

20. My own translation. See T. Nicklas, 'Papyrus Egerton 2'.

21. See also J. W. Pryor, 'Papyrus Egerton 2 and the Fourth Gospel', *ABR* 37 (1989) 1–13.

these speakers and the Jewish rulers who according to fragment 1 recto[22] had said 'We do not know where you have come from' emerges.

So it is possible that the question of Jesus' origins and differing answers in the 'unknown Gospel' played a role comparable to that in the *Gospel of John*. It is also conceivable that the author of the 'unknown Gospel' at least sometimes described Jesus' opponents ironically. The extant text, however, does not allow too far-reaching conclusions.

Although the speakers' actual question evokes the canonical parallels Mk 12.13–17 par. the text of Papyrus Egerton could be understood in two different ways. The following interpretations are possible:

1. We are free to give the kings what belongs to their government. Shall we give them or not?

Or:

2. Is it right to give the kings what belongs to their government? Shall we give them or not?

In any case the profile of the apocryphal text becomes clear. The central subject of the scene according to the 'unknown Gospel' is not the problem of Roman rule over Israel, but more generally the relation to public power. The idea that God, the Lord, has to be regarded the real king of Israel and the world (cf. for example, Ps. 24; 29; 47; 93; 95–99; Isa. 52.7–10; Zech. 14) probably forms the main background here. The point of the story then can be formulated in the following way: Jesus as God's envoy is asked whether Jews have to perform obligations against worldly powers. In this case the question is a kind of test of whether Jesus truly has been sent by God, the actual king of the world.

Jesus' reply consists of two parts. In his first sentence, which resembles Lk. 6.46, he deals with the hypocritical intention of his opponents: 'Why do you call me a teacher with your mouth, but do not listen what I say?'

Then Jesus progresses with a citation of Isa. 29.13 LXX: 'This people honours me with their lips, but their heart is far removed from me. In vain do they worship me.'[23] Unfortunately the fragment ends with this sentence which again deals with the intention of the questioners, but not with their actual question. It must remain unresolved whether the original text contained a longer answer – and, if so, what kind of answer it offered. Again the lacunas in the text set the limits of its interpretation.

22. G. Mayeda, *Das Leben-Jesu-Fragment Papyrus Egerton 2 und seine Stellung in der urchristlichen Literaturgeschichte* (Bonn: 1946) 37, suspects that the speakers here are the same as the speakers on fragment 1 recto.

23. See also G. Mayeda, *Leben-Jesu-Fragment*, 49.

2.3 *Fragment 3*

Fragment 3, finally, does not offer a coherent text, merely a few fragments of words. The only thing that can be said is that the text possibly contained a parallel to Jn 10.30–32.

3. *Conclusion: The Character of the 'Unknown Gospel' on Papyrus Egerton 2*

Previous research on the 'unknown Gospel' frequently concentrated on the question of its literary relationship to the canonical Gospels. While some authors intensely defended the literary independence of the 'unknown Gospel' and opted for an early date of its text,[24] a vast majority of scholars assume literary dependency of the text to some, if not all of the four canonical gospels.[25] I tend towards the thesis that the 'unknown Gospel' is literary dependent on John's Gospel and that its author knows at least traditions in synoptic style (and quite probably also synoptic texts in written form).[26] That is why the 'unknown Gospel' should not be taken as one of our primary witnesses for a reconstruction of the historical Jesus.[27] I also would hesitate to date its text earlier than the first half of the second century CE. However, it should not be overlooked that the fragments of the 'unknown Gospel' offer us parts of an original own version of the story of Jesus of Nazareth.

Despite its many parallels to canonical texts the 'unknown Gospel' neither should be considered a Gospel harmony nor a testimony of an emerging 'Four-Gospel Canon'. Moreover, its very existence shows that it was still possible to create new 'Jesus stories' besides the texts that later became canonical. Besides, Papyrus Egerton 2 at least partially offers traditions not to be found in the canonical texts (see, fragment 2 verso!).

Today we can no longer know whether the 'unknown Gospel' contained a story about Jesus' infancy, while it is at least probable that the text was concerned with Jesus' passion and offered its own account of the events. After all the question of Jesus' origins and his deliverance play a role in the extant text.

24. Cf. J. B. Daniels, *Egerton Gospel*; H. Koester, *Ancient Christian Gospels. Their History and Development* (Harrisburg: TPI, 1990) 205–215.

25. Cf. For example, F. Neirynck, 'Papyrus Egerton and the Healing of the Leper', in F. Neirynck, *Evangelica II: Collected Essays 1982–1991* (BETL 99; Leuven: Peeters, 1991) 773–783; F. Neirynck, 'The Apocryphal Gospels and the Gospel of Mark', in F. Neirynck, *Evangelica II*, 715–772. For a well-argued middle-position see also E. Norelli, 'Le Papyrus egerton 2 et sa localisation dans la tradition sur Jésus. Nouvel examen du fragment 1', in D. Marguerat *et al.* (eds), *Jésus de Nazareth: Nouvelles approches d'une enigme* (MoBi 38; Genève: 1998) 397–435.

26. For more information on this topic see my T. Nicklas, 'Papyrus Egerton 2'.

27. For more details cf. T. Nicklas, 'Jesustraditionen in apokryphen Evangelien (außer dem Thomasevangelium)', in T. Holmén and S. E. Porter (eds), *The Handbook of the Study of the Historical Jesus* (Leiden: Brill, forthcoming).

Jesus is seen as the 'Lord' who performs miracles and is able to escape his persecutors in a sovereign way. Besides, Jesus is called the 'teacher' (of the law) – perhaps the text does not consider this category as adequate. Jesus speaks about God as his father; he is compared to the prophets (perhaps indirectly even with Moses). The Scriptures of Israel, too, play an important role for the interpretation of the text. The gospel does not merely reflect the early Jewish-Christian dispute around the question whether Israel's Scriptures refer to Jesus. Several passages of the text allude to the Old Testament or at least evoke Old Testament backgrounds. Simultaneously Jesus' Jewish opponents are painted in dark colours. This even goes so far that the crowd wants to stone Jesus. Comparable to the apocryphal *Gospel of Peter* at least once the crowds and the leaders of the people work together in their attempt to arrest Jesus.

Papyrus Egerton 2 thus offers us the remains of an otherwise 'unknown Gospel' that could date back to the first half or perhaps the middle of the second century CE. Although the condition of the manuscript does not allow for more than very cautious conclusions on the text's origins at least some suggestions can be made. The text is interested in the role of Israel's scriptures for a proper understanding of Jesus of Nazareth; it describes Jesus as a pious Jew observing the Law, but is also open to higher Christology: Jesus is called 'the Lord' and 'Son of God' (fragment 3!). While it is thus possible that this text was used by a group of (Jewish?) Christians in a situation of some disharmony with Judaism, this group shows no appropriate knowledge of concrete locations, dates and historical figures of Jesus' first-century Palestinian context.

Whether this text originated in Syria, Egypt or any other place of the Roman Empire must remain a matter of speculation.

Bibliography

H. I. Bell and T. C. Skeat, *Fragments of an Unknown Gospel and Other Early Christian Papyri* (London: British Museum, 1935).

L. Cerfaux, 'Parallèles canoniques et extra-canoniques de l'évangile inconnu (Pap. Egerton 2)', in *Muséon* 49 (1936) 55–77.

J. B. Daniels, 'The Egerton Gospel. Its Place in Early Christianity' (diss. Claremont, 1989).

M. Gronewald, 'Unbekanntes Evangelium oder Evangelienharmonie (Fragment aus dem "Evangelium Egerton")', in *Kölner Papyri, Papyrologica Coloniensia* vol. 7, Band 6, Universität Köln (1987) 136–145.

H. -J. Klauck, *Apocryphal Gospels: An Introduction* (London: T&T Clark, 2003).

H. Koester, *Ancient Christian Gospels. Their History and Development* (Harrisburg: TPI, 1990) 205–215.

D. Lührmann, *Fragmente apokryph gewordener Evangelien in griechischer und lateinischer Sprache*, (MThSt 59; Marburg: N.G. Elwert, 2000).

D. Lührmann, *Die apokryph gewordenen Evangelien* (NovTSup 112; Leiden: Brill, 2004).

T. Nicklas, 'Papyrus Egerton 2', in T. J. Kraus/M. Kruger/T. Nicklas (eds), Gospel Fragments (OECGT; Oxford: Oxford University Press, 2008).

Chapter 12

The Fayum Gospel

Thomas J. Kraus

This small papyrus fragment housed in the 'Papyrus Collection of the National Austrian Library' in Vienna (thus, abbreviated as *Papyrus Vindobonensis Graecus*, inventory number 2325, in short *P.Vindob.G* 2325) is part of almost every collective edition of manuscript fragments of potential unidentified Gospels. This popularity originated with its early publication in 1885, which at the time caused a huge stir. *P.Vindob.G* 2325, also known as 'Fayum Gospel' or 'Fayum Fragment', was first regarded as a pre-stage of, or as a potential parallel text to the synoptic Gospels. Many scholars hoped that with the help of this new fragment the Synoptics and the traditions behind them could be understood better. The initial sensation died away quite soon, after there were no significant conclusions gained from the papyrus and its text in relation to this issue. In a variety of publications I have attempted to re-evaluate this interesting and important attestation of early Christian history.[1]

1. *Description of the Papyrus*

The papyrus fragment is at most 3.5 cm high and 4.3 cm wide. The papyrus is slightly discoloured in the upper left and lower right area, probably due to its partial decomposition in the earth. The strong black ink is well preserved with the exception of the first two lines where the writing is partly worn away, so

1. See T. J. Kraus, 'P.Vindob.G 2325: Das sogenannte Fayûm Evangelium – Neuedition und kritische Ruchschlüsse', *JAC/ZAC* 5 (2001) 197–212; updated with *addenda*, '*P.Vindob.G* 2325: The So-Called Fayûm Gospel – Re-Edition and Some Critical Conclusions', in T. J. Kraus, Ad fontes: *Manuscripts and Their Significance for Studying Early Christianity* (TENT 3; Leiden: Brill, 2007) 69–94; '*P.Vindob.G* 2325: Das sogenannte Fayûm Evangelium', in T. J. Kraus und T. Nicklas (eds), *das Petrusevangelium und die Petrusapokalypse. Die grieschen Fragmente mit deutscher und englisher Übersetzung* (GCS.NF 11 = Neutestamentliche Apokryphen 1; Berlin: de Gruyter, 2004) 65–69; '*P.Vindob.G* 2325: Einige Modifikationen von Transkription und Rekonstruktion', *JAC/ZAC* 10 (2007) 383–385. This study is also dependent on a forthcoming discussion of *P.Vindob.G* 2325 to be published in a volume about several potential fragments of unidentified Gospels in the series *Oxford Early Christian Gospel Texts* (OECGT), edited by Christopher Tuckett and Andrew Gregory and published by Oxford University Press.

that some letters are lost in the middle of the first line. The scribe also used red ink to write the letter sequence 'PET' in line five, though the 'P' is slightly blackish now. Unfortunately, there is no margin left, which makes it hard to reconstruct the rest of the seven lines preserved. Although, assumptions about the reconstructed numbers of letters per line must remain hypothetical, the completion of words and phrases to form a meaningful context seems to suggest lines with up to 31 letters as realistic. The exact original line length, however, is unknown and thus the suggested reconstruction never gets beyond its tentative and hypothetical nature.

The scribe's hand forms regular letters parallel to the horizontal fibres (recto →) that are written rather fluently and slightly sloping to the right. Although some of the letters are in contact with each other, real ligatures and juxtapositions are missing, so that the letters are formed rather separately and individually. Every letter takes roughly equal space. The scribe has left small spaces before and after 'PET' and also after 'night' in line two and after 'and' in line five. There are no diacritical signs (for instance, any form of punctuation), but the three letters that form 'PET' in red ink have dots above the initial *pi* and the final *tau*, which indicate that they abbreviate a word, probably in the form of a suspension.

The other side with the vertical fibres (verso ↓) is blank, so that the papyrus can be regarded as a fragment from a roll, of which the width of the column for the writing is unknown. Nonetheless, the possibility that the fragment is originally part of a free-standing leaf with only writing on the recto and not more text than what one page (whatever its dimensions then would have been) can contain, cannot be ruled out completely.

2. *History of Research*

Gustav Bickell first published the fragment in 1885, but afterwards he revised his transcription and reconstruction of the first line several times. First he suggested the reading '[After] supper as he told . . .', next '[After] supper as was the custom . . .' and finally '. . . [ex]change likewise . . .'[2] However, he did not distinguish between letters he regarded as uncertain and certain. Bickell's second alternative was the most influential one: it was taken over and can still be found in re-editions and collections and as the source of translations. In 1906 Karl Wessely corrected the first line on the basis of palaeographical considerations to '[After] going [out] as . . .' (or '[After] being led [out] as . . .') by reading *xi* for Bickell's *phi* and then *lambda*.[3] In 2001, I published a

2. Cf. G. Bickell, 'Ein Papyrusfragment eines nichtkanonischen Evangeliums', *ZKTh* 9 (1885) 498–501; G. Bickell, 'Das nichtkanonische Evangelienfragment Raineri', *MPER* 2–3 (1887) 41–42; G. Bickell, 'Ein letztes Wort über das Papyrus-Evangelium', *MPER* 5 (1892) 79.

3. Cf. K. Wessely, *Les plus anciens monument du christianisme écrits sur papyrus* (*PO* 4.2; Paris 1906 [Turnhout: Brepols, 1985]) 174.

re-edition of *P.Vindob.G* 2325 on the basis of a close examination of the original papyrus in Vienna, in which I accepted Wessely's reading of *xi* for the remnants of the first letter in the first line. In the meantime I have readdressed this small papyrus fragments several times and proposed an improved reconstruction.[4]

According to Karl Wessely, in the 'Art der Auffindung, das Format, die Schrift und die paläographischen Eigentümlichkeiten' ('way of discovery, the format, the writing, and the palaeographical peculiarities') the likely date of the writing of the text for the papyrus fragment is the third century, and perhaps even as early as the beginning of that century as Gustav Bickell had suggested. This date is confirmed by the discovery of the fragment in the middle of a layer of papyri that are all earlier than the reign of Diocletian.[5] In addition, the individual papyri of the layer suggest the district of Heracleopolites in Middle Egypt as the provenance, that is, Heracleopolis (Magna) at the south-eastern part of the oasis with the name 'Fayum'.

After the temporary stir caused by the publication of the *editio princeps*, interest in the papyrus rapidly died down until Dieter Lührmann suggested that *P.Vindob.G* 2325 might be a potential witness to the *Gospel of Peter*,[6] a connection already referred to by Gustav Bickell in 1895.[7] Although I have palaeographical reservations about the reasoning in favour of such an identification (see below), this proposal has led scholars to devote more attention to the small 'Fayum Gospel' than had been the case previously since its initial publication.

3. *English Translation and Commentary*

During my visits to the Papyrus Collection of the Austrian National Library in Vienna, I was able examine the papyrus fragment in detail. The transcription, the reconstruction and the English translation presented here is based upon my own analysis of the papyrus undertaken in Vienna.

→

1 While going out[8] as he said: 'All
of you will be ashamed of me this night,

4. See n. 1.

5. K. Wessely, 'Ueber das Zeitalter des Wiener Evangelienpapyrus', *ZKTh* 11 (1887) 507–515, mentions a lease from 225 CE (from the period of Severus Alexander) that was found together with *P.Vindob.G* 2325.

6. Dieter Lührmann formulates this proposal in several of his publications, last in *Die apokryph gewordenen Evangelien. Studien zu neuen Texten und neuen Fragen* (NovTSup 112; Leiden-Boston: Brill, 2004) 87–90.

7. See *Papyrus Erzherzog Rainer. Führer durch die Ausstellung mit 20 Tafeln und 90 Textbildern* (Vienna 1895) no. 541. See the reference to Bickell by Lührmann, *Die apokryph gewordenen Evangelien*, 89, n. 103.

8. Or 'While being led out'. The place implied here is the Mount of Olives, cf. Mk 14.26 (par. Mt. 24.30).

according to what is written: I will strike the shepherd and the sheep will be dispersed.'

Peter said: 'If all, not I.'
Jesus said: 'Before the cock will have cried twice,[9]
you will deny me three times today.'

Of course, an English translation cannot readily imitate the Greek original. For this reason the above translation requires some comments and clarifications. Syntax and word order of the Greek text differ from their English equivalents, so that the distribution of the English words in every line does not minutely correspond to the Greek. Nevertheless, a readable and comprehensible English text serves the purpose of this study much more than a slavishly exact rendering (see, for example, lines six to seven with 'three times' in line seven though the equivalent Greek word is at the end of line six).

What is legible and can be reconstructed on a sound basis reads as follows:

. . . [will be] ashamed . . . this night . . . to what is written: I will strike the . . . sheep will be dispersed . . . Peter . . . if all . . . the cock [will have] cried twice . . .

Based upon the letters preserved it is highly plausible to reconstruct future forms for 'ashamed' and 'cried' corresponding to 'will be dispersed' for which the rest of the future ending can be easily completed. Moreover, 'according' before 'to what is written' seems to be probable.

The text preserved on *P.Vindob.G* 2325 has certain affinities with Mk 14.26–30 and Mt. 26.30–34. Consequently these texts are readily taken as providing a helpful basis for plausible reconstruction of the seven lines of Greek text. This approach has been followed by several other scholars. The 'Fayum Gospel', however, apparently lacks the reference to Jesus' resurrection and the meeting with the disciples in Galilee (Mk 14.28; Mt. 26.32). On the one hand *P.Vindob.G* 2325 is very close to the Markan version of the scene on the Mount of Olives: for instance, both mention the two cockcrows before Peter's denial (Mk 14.30: 'before the cock crows twice'; but see Mt. 26.34: 'before the cock crows') and the exact word order of the citation of the Septuagint version of Zech. 13.7 (in harmony with Mk 14.27: 'I will strike the shepherd and the sheep will be dispersed'; but see the Septuagint text: 'strike the shepherds and the sheep shall be scattered'). On the other hand, it differs from both Matthew and Mark as far as style and vocabulary are concerned. Among the most striking differences are the use of different Greek words for 'cock' and 'to cry' than those which occur in the canonical Gospels. The term for cock in the 'Fayum Gospel' is only used once in the Greek Bible (see 3 Macc. 5.23) and although this term was quite usual in classical texts, it stands in contrast to the common

9. Alternatively 'will cry twice' or 'cries twice'.

biblical word for 'cock', which reflects the vernacular Greek of the first three centuries CE. The 'Fayum Gospel' offers another rare word with the onomatopoetic Greek verb for 'to cry'. Originally and more literally 'cuckoo!' or 'to cry like a cuckoo', this term is not used in the Greek Bible at all. This verb is semantically stronger than the more common 'to cry' (or 'to sound') and is determined by its subject 'cock' as 'to crow' or 'to cry (like a cock)'. Thus, *P.Vindob.G* 2325 preserves two rare words that are more conspicuous and more complicated than those used in the canonical Gospels.

Further, the scribe evidently left some space for the name of Peter to fill later by using red ink. Probably, the space was too small to write Peter in full, so it was abbreviated in one of the common ways: the scribe wrote the first letters of the word and then placed dots above the initial and final letters. Alternatively the scribe originally intended to abbreviate 'Peter' that way by emphasizing it with red ink. Both explanations may be right. Be that as it may, the scribe had to interrupt the writing process to take up another writing implement or to use the red ink; and that means some additional effort for the scribe to write the manuscript.

P.Vindob.G 2325 thus offers some remarkable peculiarities that have to be taken into account when judging its original purpose. These specific features are that it is probably from a roll and that it preserves the short form 'PET' in red ink. The fragmentary text on the papyrus offers some striking vocabulary, it shows affinities with and differences from Mk 14.26–30 (and to a minor degree from Mt. 26.30–34), and it lacks the interlude of Jesus and the disciples in Galilee (Mk 14.28; Mt. 26.32). Besides these features, the quotation from Zech. 13.7 is apparently identical with that in Mk 14.27 (see the different word order in Mt. 26.31), though the introductory phrase used to identify it as a Biblical quotation is different ('it is written' in Mark and Matthew in contrast to 'according to what is written' in the 'Fayum Gospel').

4. *The Historical and Theological Character of the Fayum Gospel*

Some central questions may help to determine the historical and theological characters of the 'Fayum Gospel'. Has *P.Vindob.G* 2325 preserved the remains of a harmonization? Is the text a paraphrase of, or an excerpt from synoptic material? Is it part of a Gospel we do not know anything else about? Or is it a passage of the *Gospel of Peter*? The last hypothesis has repeatedly been suggested by Dieter Lührmann, but always with some advisable and adequate caution. However, his proposal to reconstruct lines four to five as 'I, Peter, said' instead of 'Peter said' causes some significant problems: the additional letters required for Lührmann's reconstruction (he proposes to put a first person pronoun where others place the Greek article) would lengthen line five on the left-hand side to such an extent that the first part of the line might become too long in comparison to the rest of the text. Besides, the first person narrative, which Lührmann interprets as an indication that this fragment might belong to the *Gospel of Peter*, is not exclusively a feature of the text of the *Gospel of Peter* and so does not point unambiguously exclusively to that apocryphal text. Although, there is no parallel text with which to collate that of the papyrus, the manuscript of the *Gospel of Peter*, the Akhmîm-Codex also does not have any reference to Galilee. Through this shared geographical omission the Fayum Gospel also does not make mention of Galilee although the Markan text which it parallels states that Galilee will be the place of meeting for Jesus and his after his resurrection. The significance of this shared omission should perhaps not be overstated and is due to coincidence rather than literary dependence or shared traditions. However, in addition, the text of *P.Vindob.G* 2325 can be plausibly reconstructed on the basis of the existing text of Mk 14.29–30.[10]

Consequently, the text on the small papyrus fragment can be regarded as an excerpt from synoptic material, which it shares with Matthew and, above all, with Mark. The use of the striking terms for 'cock' and 'to cry' makes it less likely that *P.Vindob.G* 2325 is a harmony or a paraphrase of the canonical gospels, although these possibilities cannot be ruled out. Basically, it is more probable to simplify a text than to make it more complex and to lift it on a higher semantic level than the texts it might have been derived from. The papyrus may thus have preserved the text of an unidentified Gospel. The 'Fayum Gospel' would then be parallel to, and different from, the synoptic tradition in the same way, and on an equal scale, as Mk 14.26–30 and Mt. 26.30–34 are similar to, and different from, each other. In sum, the papyrus may have preserved a textual fragment that could be a tradition historically parallel to that of the Synoptics. Theologically it does not offer any different interpretation from Mark and Matthew, even if the missing reference to Jesus' resurrection and the meeting with the disciples in Galilee (see Mk 14.28; Mt. 26.32) might have any significance. But the fragment is too small or, in other words, the text that survived is too short for any sound speculations about the theological background and importance of the 'Fayum Gospel'. *P.Vindob.G* 2325 is a unique artefact of early Christianity and an indispensable witness to the flexibility and vividness of the traditions and transmission of early Christian literary history.

Bibliography

A. E. Bernhard, *Other Early Christian Gospels. A Critical Edition of the Surviving Greek Manuscripts* (Library of New Testament Studies 315; London-New York 2006) 4, 50, 98–99, 104–105.

10. Cf. T. Nicklas, 'Ein `neutestamentliches Apokryphon´? Zum umstrittenen Kanonbezug des sog. `Petrusevangeliums´', *VC* 56 (2002) 266, and Kraus/Nicklas, *Das Petrusevangelium und die Petrusapokalypse*, 63, 68. The text of the papyrus can be plausibly reconstructed on the basis of the existing text of Mk 14.29–30. See also P. Foster, 'Are There Any Early Fragments of the So-Called Gospel of Peter?', *NTS* 52 (2006) 19–22.

J. K. Elliott, *The Apocryphal New Testament. A Collection of Apocryphal Christian Literature in an English Translation* (Oxford: Clarendon Press, 1993 [Paperback edition 2005]) 43–45.

H. Förster, 'Apokryphen', in J. Henner/H. Förster/U. Horak (ed.), *Christliches mit Feder und Faden. Christliches in Texten, Textilien und Alltagsgegenständen aus Ägypten* (Nilus 3; Vienna: Österreichische Verlagsgesellschaft, 1999) 15–16 (no. 13).

T. J. Kraus, Ad fontes: *Manuscripts and Their Significance for Studying Early Christianity* (TENT 3; Leiden: Brill, 2007) 69–94 (with black and white image).

D. Lührmann, *Die apokryph gewordenen Evangelien. Studien zu neuen Texten und neuen Fragen* (NovTSup 112; Leiden-Boston: Brill, 2004) 87–90.

J. Schefzyk (ed.), *Alles ECHT. Älteste Belege zur Bibel aus Ägypten* (Mainz: Philipp von Zabern, 2006) 123 (no. 60; with colour image).

Chapter 13

Papyrus Oxyrhynchus 840

Michael J. Kruger

In December 1905, in a rubbish heap at Oxyrhynchus, Egypt, a small fragment was discovered containing 45 well-preserved lines from an uncanonical gospel. The manuscript – commonly dated third or fourth century – consists of one vellum leaf from a miniature codex that contains the remains of a discourse between Jesus and his disciples and also a confrontation between Jesus and a Pharisee in the temple. Roderick Dunkerley referred to this fragment as 'the longest, best-preserved, and most valuable of the Oxyrhynchus fragments'.[1] Joachim Jeremias declared that the fragment 'in substance ranks as high as the Synoptic accounts'.[2] Henry Swete said the origin of this gospel 'may with probability be assigned to the first half of the second century'.[3] Assuming that these scholars are accurate in their assessments, P.Oxy. 840 is one of the most valuable sources we have for evaluating extra-canonical gospel traditions in the second century, their relationship to the canonical gospels and the role they played in early Christian communities.

1. *History of Interpretation*

Despite the initial interest in P.Oxy. 840, it has been consistently overlooked when it comes to research on the apocryphal gospels. Indeed, it has been over a century since its original discovery in 1905 and there has only been a small number of articles written on the text (most very brief) and only one full-length work.[4] This development is quite peculiar in light of the enormous advances

1. Roderick Dunkerley, *The Unwritten Gospel* (London: George Allen & Unwin Ltd, 1925) 8.

2. Joachim Jeremias, 'An Unknown Gospel of Synoptic Type', in E. Hennecke and W. Schneemelcher (ed.), *New Testament Apocrypha* (3rd edn; London: Lutterworth Press, 1963) 57–58.

3. Henry Barclay Swete, *Two New Gospel Fragments* (Cambridge: Deighton, Bell & Co., 1908) 3.

4. Michael J. Kruger, *The Gospel of the Savior: An Analysis of P.Oxy. 840 and Its Place in the Gospel Traditions of Early Christianity* (TENT 1; Leiden: E.J. Brill, 2005).

during the last century in the study of apocryphal gospels. Much of the neglect of P.Oxy. 840 can be attributed to the doubts raised by some scholars about the historical accuracy of some of its descriptions of the temple and its associated rituals. These doubts were first raised in the original edition of Grenfell and Hunt in the 1908 volume of the *Oxyrhynchus Papyri* (printed later as a separate work titled, *A Fragment of an Uncanonical Gospel*[5]). Over the next 5 years, this initial negative assessment was supported in brief articles by Schürer, Sulzbach, Zahn, Dräseke, Jülicher and Smith.[6] Others, however, were more positive in their outlook on P.Oxy. 840. Swete, Goodspeed, Lagrange and Harnack, while acknowledging some historical problems, were all more optimistic than the original assessment of Grenfell and Hunt, arguing that P.Oxy. 840 probably reflects some authentic Jesus tradition.[7] In addition to these more moderate reactions, a number of scholars stepped forth to defend the historicity of P.Oxy. 840. Büchler and Presuchen were its most significant defenders in the years following its discovery, but it was also defended later by Davies, Lietzmann, Marmorstein and Blau.[8]

Although P.Oxy. 840 received some scholarly attention between 1908 and 1914, the initial negative verdict of Grenfell and Hunt against the fragment proved too much to overcome. Despite the efforts of those defending the authenticity and value of P.Oxy. 840, it would suffer substantial neglect for nearly the next 70 years. Aside from the periodic article here and there – such

5. Bernard P. Grenfell and Arthur S. Hunt, *The Oxyrhynchus Papyri*, vol. V (Oxford: Horace Hart, 1908) 1–10; Bernard P. Grenfell and Arthur S. Hunt, *Fragment of an Uncanonical Gospel* (London: Oxford University Press, 1908). The two publications are virtually identical in every way.

6. E. Schürer, 'Fragment of an Uncanonical Gospel from Oxyrhynchus', *TLZ* 33 (1908) 170–172; A. Sulzbach, 'Zum Oxyrhynchus Fragment', *ZNW* 9 (1908) 175–176; Th. Zahn, 'Neue Bruchstücke nichtkanonischer Evangelien', *NKZ* 19 (1908) 371–386; Johannes Dräseke, 'Zum neuen Evangelienbruchstück von Oxyrhynchos', *ZWT* 50 (1908) 485–489; Adolf Jülicher, 'Ein neues Jesuswort?', *Christliche Welt* 8 (1908) 201–204; David Smith, *Unwritten Sayings of Our Lord* (London: Hodder and Stoughton, 1913) 133–143.

7. Henry Barclay Swete, *Zwei Neue Evangelienfragmente herausgegeben und erklärt* (Bonn: A. Marcus und E. Weber, 1908) 3–9; also published with an English title, *Two New Gospel Fragments*, as seen above in n. 3; Edgar J. Goodspeed, 'The New Gospel Fragment from Oxyrhynchus', *BW* 31 (1908) 142–146; M. -J. Lagrange, 'Nouveau Fragment non canonique relatif a l'Évangile', *RB* 5 (1908) 538–553; Adolf von Harnack, 'Ein Neues Evangelienbruchstück', in *Aus Wissenschaft und Leben, Band II* (Giessen: Alfred Töpelmann, 1911) 239–250.

8. Adolf Büchler, 'The New "Fragment of an Uncanonical Gospel"', *JQR* 20 (1908) 330–346; E. Preuschen, 'Das neue Evangelienfragment von Oxyrhynchos', *ZNW* 9 (1908) 1–11; W. W. Davies, 'A Fragment of Another Gospel', *Methodist Review* 90 (1908) 815–818; Hans Lietzmann, 'Das neugefundene Evangelienfragment und seine Vorgänger', *Beilage zur allgemeinen Zeitung* 31 (1908) 662–672; A. Marmorstein, 'Einige Bemerkungen zum Evangelienfragment in Oxyrhynchus Papyri, vol. V, n. 840, 1907', *ZNW* 15 (1914) 336–338; Ludwig Blau, 'Das neue Evangelienfragment von Oxyrhynchos buch- und zaubergeschichtlich betrachtet nebst sonstigen Bemerkungen', *ZNW* 9 (1908) 204–215.

as Riggenbach and Dunkerley – the only significant contribution during this time was by Joachim Jeremias who vigorously defended the fragment as Jesus tradition on par with the Synoptics.[9]

In the last 20 years there has been some renewed interest (although still relatively minor) with articles by Schwartz, Tripp and Bovon.[10] These articles have bypassed the standard historical questions and have focused on which community (or historical circumstances) may have given rise to this Jesus story. The palaeography of P.Oxy. 840 has received some recent attention in articles by myself and Kraus.[11] In 2005, I published a full-length study of P.Oxy. 840 titled, *The Gospel of the Savior: An Analysis of P.Oxy. 840 and Its Place in the Gospel Traditions of Early Christianity*. This study was a comprehensive examination of this fragment – from a palaeographical, historical and theological perspective – and argued that the stories contained in the fragment were produced by a second-century Jewish-Christian group (possibly the Nazarenes), who were reacting against the rabbinic (Pharisaic) Judaism of their day. In addition, the study argued that the text of P.Oxy. 840 demonstrates knowledge of the redactional portions of five key texts from the canonical gospels: Lk. 11.37–52; Mt. 23.1–39; Jn 7.1–52; Jn 13.1–30; and Mk 7.1–23.

2. *Palaeography and Codicology*

As noted above, the palaeography and codicology of P.Oxy. 840 has been much neglected over the years. This has been unfortunate because such features can shed considerable historical light on the purpose for which this manuscript was created and the way it may have functioned within early Christian communities. Moreover, careful analysis of the fragment itself can help establish a more definitive date for our manuscript, which has been assigned dates ranging from the third century to the fifth century – a 300-year span.[12]

9. E. Riggenbach, 'Das Wort Jesu im Gespräch mit dem pharisäischen Hohenpriester nach dem Oxyrhynchus Fragment v. 840', *ZNW* 25 (1926) 140–144; Dunkerley, *The Unwritten Gospel*, 113–117; Joachim Jeremias, 'Der Zusammenstoss Jesu mit dem pharisäischen Oberpriester auf den Tempelplatz. Zu Pap. Ox V 840', *Coni. Neotest.* 2 (1947) 97–108; and the later English contribution in Joachim Jeremias, *Unknown Sayings of Jesus* (London: SPCK, 1964) 47–60, 104–105.

10. Daniel R. Schwartz, 'Viewing the Holy Utensils (P. Ox. V, 840)', *NTS* 32 (1986) 153–159; David Tripp, 'Meanings of the Foot-Washing: John 13 and Papyrus Oxyrhynchus 840', *ExpT* 103 (1992) 237–239; François Bovon, 'Fragment Oxyrhynchus 840, Fragment of a Lost Gospel, Witness of an Early Christian Controversy Over Purity', *JBL* 119 (2000) 705–728.

11. Michael J. Kruger, 'P.Oxy. 840: Amulet or Miniature Codex?', *JTS* 53 (2002) 81–94; Thomas J. Kraus, 'P.Oxy. V 840--Amulett oder Miniaturkodex? Grundsätzliche unde ergänzende Anmerkungen zu zwei Termini', *ZAC* 8 (2005) 485–497.

12. J. K. Elliott, *The Apocryphal New Testament* (Oxford: Clarendon Press, 1993) 31; and M. R. James, *The Apocryphal New Testament* (Oxford: Clarendon, 1924) 29, both suggest a third-century date. Grenfell and Hunt, *Fragment*, 9, and C. H. Roberts, *Manuscript, Society and Belief in Early Christian Egypt* (London: Oxford University Press, 1979) 11, each offer the possibility of a fifth-century date.

Despite the fact that our text is referred to as P.Oxy. 840, it is actually written on parchment and not on papyrus.[13] It is relatively light in colour and has avoided the darkening that is common to many ancient parchment manuscripts. The edges are torn and brittle and there are numerous holes – probably due to worms – along the right side of the recto. The parchment appears shrivelled or wrinkled at points, mostly on the top left margin. Although a large portion of the bottom right corner of the folio is missing, the remaining portion is in quite good condition and the text is easily legible. There are, however, a number of places where the iron gall ink has eaten through the parchment, making some lines difficult to reconstruct (particularly ll. 1, 3, 23, 25).[14] The identification of the recto and the verso has proved to be somewhat difficult due to confusion in terminology. Although the term 'recto' normally refers to the front of a folio and the 'verso' to the back,[15] Grenfell and Hunt refer to the front side of the folio as the 'verso' (instead of the expected 'recto') making it clear that they are using the term simply to refer to the 'hair' side of the manuscript.

One of the most striking features of P.Oxy. 840 is its miniature size: just 7.2 × 8.6 cm.[16] Upon discovery, the tiny dimensions of this manuscript sparked an ongoing debate among scholars over whether it was originally an amulet or miniature codex. Preuschen was one of the first to argue that P.Oxy. 840 was an amulet, followed by Blau and Jeremias.[17] Harnack dissented from these opinions and suggested that P.Oxy. 840 may simply be a miniature codex that was easily carried and hidden.[18] Roberts, Turner and van Haelst all follow

13. Bovon argues that 'the fragment should no longer be called Papyrus Oxyrhynchus 840' ('Fragment Oxyrhynchus 840', 706, n. 2). However, the term 'papyrus' is often used in palaeographical literature to refer to a broader class of written materials (such as parchment) and not just to the papyrus plant itself; see, Roger S. Bagnall, *Reading Papyri, Writing Ancient History* (New York: Routledge, 1995) 9–10. Indeed, this is the very practice of the multi-volume *Oxyrhynchus Papyri* which includes many other parchment fragments beyond P.Oxy. 840 (e.g. P.Oxy. 848, a fragment of Revelation, and P.Oxy. 849, a fragment of the *Acts of Peter*). For further discussion of the significance of parchment and papyrus when evaluating a manuscript, including P.Oxy. 840, see Thomas J. Kraus, '"Pergament oder Papyrus?": Anmerkungen zur Signifikanz des Beschreibstoffes bei der Behandlung von Manuskripten', *NTS* 49 (2003) 425–432.

14. In the course of time, it is not unusual for metallic-based ink to eat through the writing material, as can be seen in the case of Codex Alexandrinus. Such inks were common in the fourth century and later. See T. C. Skeat, 'Early Christian Book-Production', in G. W. H. Lampe (ed.), *The Cambridge History of the Bible*, (Cambridge: Cambridge University Press, 1969) 61.

15. Harry Y. Gamble, *Books and Readers in the Early Church* (New Haven: Yale University Press, 1995) 265, n. 9; E. G. Turner, 'Recto and Verso', *JEA* 40 (1954) 102–106.

16. Grenfell and Hunt arrived at slightly different numbers: 7.4 × 8.8 cm (*Fragment of an Uncanonical Gospel*, 9).

17. Preuschen, 'Das neue Evangelienfragment von Oxyrhynchos', 1; Blau, 'Das neue Evangelienfragment von Oxyrhynchos buch- und zaubergeschichtlich betrachtet nebst sonstigen Bemerkungen', 204–215; Jeremias, *Unknown Sayings of Jesus*, 47.

18. Harnack, 'Ein Neues Evangelienbruchstück', 239–250.

Harnack's lead and place P.Oxy. 840 in the category of miniature codices.[19] I have argued extensively elsewhere that when one examines the features of amulets and compares them to the features of miniature codices, it is quite evident that P.Oxy. 840 is a miniature codex and not an amulet.[20] If so, then not only does this suggest a date no earlier than the late third century (miniature codices were predominantly fourth century and later), the fact that P.Oxy. 840 is a miniature codex makes it more likely to have originally contained a larger collection of Jesus stories. Given what we know about the capacity of other miniature codices – as opposed to the brevity of amulets – it seems possible that P.Oxy. 840 may have been a more fully developed gospel-like book.

The date of P.Oxy. 840 is further clarified by an examination of the scribal hand. The script is a round upright uncial with strokes of even thickness.[21] The text could only be considered 'roughly bilinear' as the scribe often extends letters such as ι, τ, ρ, φ and υ well below the line.[22] The fact that the letters are frequently uneven (note the $\overline{\delta\delta}$ in line 25) and often touch one another (especially lines 25 and 27) shows the scribe to be somewhat informal, though he maintains a competent book-hand.[23] Grenfell and Hunt declared this hand to be 'a type pointing, we think, to a fourth rather than a fifth century date'.[24] The date can be narrowed further – to the early fourth century – when it is recognized that the hand of P.Oxy. 840 is quite similar to Cavallo and Maehler's 'upright pointed majuscule', a style common in the third century but much less common as one moves further into the fourth.[25]

Other notable scribal features include: (1) enlarged first letter (lines 7, 30); (2) the colour red around various forms of punctuation; (3) use of middle points; (4) accents/breathing marks in lines 12, 23 and 36; and (5) frequent use of diaeresis. Not only do such adornments and reader's aids confirm we are dealing with a miniature codex,[26] but also suggest that P.Oxy. 840 may have been quite expensive and thus probably owned by a member of the literate

19. Roberts, *Manuscript*, 11; E. G. Turner, *The Typology of the Early Codex* (Philadelphia: University of Pennsylvania Press, 1977) 30 (Turner clearly labels those documents he considers amulets; for example, P.Oxy. 2065, and P.Lit. Lond. 239); J. van Haelst, *Catalogue des Papyrus Littéraires Juifs et Chrétiens* (Paris: Publications de la Sorbonne, 1976) 583 (V. H. 585).

20. Kruger, 'P.Oxy. 840: Amulet or Miniature Codex?', 81–94; Kruger, *The Gospel of the Savior*, 23–40.

21. Kraus agrees and calls the strokes, 'rund und aufrecht' ('P.Oxy. V 840,' 488).

22. Turner, *Greek Manuscripts of the Ancient World* (2nd edn; London: Institute of Classical Studies, 1987) 3.

23. See Bruce M. Metzger, *Manuscripts of the Bible: An Introduction to Greek Palaeography* (New York: Oxford University Press, 1981) 22; Italo Gallo, *Greek and Latin Papyrology* (London: Institute of Classical Studies, 1986) 83–84.

24. Grenfell and Hunt, *Fragment of an Uncanonical Gospel*, 9.

25. Kruger, *The Gospel of the Savior*, 40–45; G. Cavallo and H. Maehler, *Greek Bookhands of the Early Byzantine Period, A.D. 300–800* (London: Institute of Classical Studies, 1987) 4.

26. Kraus, 'P.Oxy. V 840', 491.

upper class. In addition, the scribe uses the *nomina sacra* for ἄνθρωπος (lines 5, 39), Δαυεὶδ (line 25) and σωτήρ (lines 12, 21, 30). The use of the *nomina sacra* and punctuation confirm the early fourth-century date for P.Oxy. 840.[27]

3. *Text and Translation*

Although P.Oxy. 840 is in relatively good condition, the reconstruction of the text can still prove to be a challenge due to (1) the missing and worn portions of the text, particularly the lower right corner of the folio, and (2) the small size of the scribal hand which makes the individual letters more difficult to decipher. I will offer an English translation here, followed by some brief comments on key textual issues:

> . . . he who intends] beforehand to strike first deviously plans out everything.
>
> But, take care lest you also suffer the same things as them, for not only among the living do evil-doers among men receive judgment, but they also will endure eternal punishment and great torment in the life to come.
>
> And he took them and led them into the place of purification itself and was walking in the temple. A certain Pharisee, a chief priest named Levi, came along and met them and said to the Savior, 'Who allowed you to trample this place of purification and to see these holy vessels, when you have not bathed yourself nor have your disciples washed their feet? But, being defiled, you trampled this temple place which is clean, where no one walks or dares to view these holy vessels except he who has bathed himself and changed his clothes.'
>
> And then the Savior stood with the disciples and answered, 'Are you therefore, being here in this temple, clean?'
>
> He said to him, 'I am clean. For I bathed in the Pool of David, and went down by one staircase and came up by another, and put on white and clean garments, and then I came and looked upon these holy vessels.'
>
> The Savior answered him and said, 'Woe to you blind men who do not see! You have bathed in only these natural waters in which dogs and pigs lay night and day. And having washed, you have wiped the outer skin, which also prostitutes and pipe-girls anoint and wash and wipe and beautify for the lust of men, but the inside of them is full of scorpions and all wickedness. But, I and my disciples, who you say have not bathed, have been bathed in living waters [from heaven] which come from [the Father above]. But, woe to . . .[28]

Textual reconstruction issues are numerous throughout P.Oxy. 840, but I will only address a few of the central ones here:[29]

27. Kruger, *The Gospel of the Savior*, 59–60.
28. English translation from Kruger, *The Gospel of the Savior*, 68.
29. All references to lines in the text are references to the lines of the Greek reconstruction found in Kruger, *The Gospel of the Savior*, 66–68.

1. The opening line is one of the most difficult to reconstruct due to the fact that the ink has eaten through the parchment in places and we only possess the end of a sentence that was begun on a previous page. The preferred option is to consider πρό and ἀδικῆσαι to be one word coming from the root, προαδικέω, which simply means 'to be first in wrong-doing'[30] or in a more contemporary sense 'to strike first'. This word would function as a complementary infinitive that corresponds to an unknown verb on the previous page. If we use βουλόμενος as the hypothetical preceding verb, then we could have something like this: βουλόμενος πρότερον προαδικῆσαι, 'he who intends beforehand to strike first . . .'
2. The verb ἀπολαμβάνουσιν ('they receive') in line 4 lacks the expected object and makes the reader ask, 'receive what?' The manner in which Jesus warns his disciples not to 'suffer' (πάθητε) the same fate as the evil-doers allows the reader to naturally fill in the object for ἀπολαμβάνουσιν: 'judgement'.[31]
3. In the original text, lines 5–6 read, 'For not only among the living do evildoers among men receive [judgement], but they also will endure punishment and great torment . . .' In the original text, the author never fully completes the comparison between the two halves of the sentence. However, given that the sentence is setting up a contrast with the phrase 'among the living', the reader would be expected to add something naturally at the end of the sentence such as 'in the life to come'. In order to capture this contrast in my English translation, I have inserted the adjective 'eternal' before the word 'punishment', and have added 'in the life to come' at the end of the sentence.
4. In line 32, I have translated the phrase χεομένοις ὕδασιν as 'natural waters'. Although this participle, χεομένοις, is defined by Bauer as 'pour out, gush forth',[32] it could be translated as 'waters which are poured' or more simply 'running waters'. When one considers the first-century Jewish context (more on this below) it is clear that Jesus is referring to the Pharisee's preference to bathe in undrawn water, that is, running water or water that occurs naturally. Thus, I have chosen to use the phrase 'natural water' in my translation.
5. In line 44, the word ἐλθοῦσιν ('coming') is still visible, but what precedes it is unclear. Scholars have offered a variety of suggestions; however, all of them assume that the letter before ἐλθοῦσιν is either ς or τ. But, upon close examination, neither of these fit the remaining portion of that letter.

30. Walter Bauer, *A Greek-English Lexicon of the New Testament and Other Early Christian Literature*, trans. William F. Arndt and F. Wilbur Gingrich (Chicago: The University of Chicago Press, 1979) 702.

31. Lagrange, 'Nouveau Fragment', 542.

32. Bauer, *Lexicon*, 881.

Portions of a straight vertical stroke and also the upper right portion of a horizontal stroke are clearly visible, ruling out the ς completely.[33] The τ is more plausible, but the upper right horizontal stroke curves downward and ends in a slight serif, which is never found on another τ in P.Oxy. 840, but occurs frequently with the υ.[34] Thus, we have no choice but to consider a reconstruction that ends in υ. I have offered one for line 44: σιν ἐκ τοῦ οὐρανοῦ ἐλθοῦσιν ἀπὸ τοῦ. The beginning of line 45 is completely lost, but it conceivably could be something such as πατρός ἐπάνω ('father above'). The entire sentence would then read, '. . . have bathed in living waters from heaven, (which) have come down from the Father above . . .'

4. *Historical Problems*

Ever since the initial publication of P.Oxy. 840, most critiques of the fragment have focused on the numerous historical problems it raises. However, a closer look at the historical evidence, in light of another century of research, shows that many of the problematic terms and issues may, after all, be adequately explained in the context of first-century Judaism.

The identification of the Pharisee in P.Oxy. 840 as ἀρχιερεύς ('chief priest') has raised doubts about the fragment because high priests were generally drawn from the Sadducean order, and therefore were not Pharisees. However, the priest-Pharisee combination was not unheard of in the first century.[35] In particular, the Mishnah speaks of Haninah, 'Captain of the Priests' – also known as 'Captain of the Temple' or the *segan* – who was both a chief priest and a Pharisee.[36] That the Captain of the Temple, a chief priest, may have been a Pharisee is a remarkable confirmation of the details of P.Oxy. 840.

The confusion over the identity and location of ἁγνευτήριον ('place of purification') and ἅγια σκεύη ('holy vessels') has been another historical problem for scholars. If the latter term refers to revered articles within the sanctuary (e.g. the candelabrum, the altar of incense and table of showbread), then how would Jesus and his disciples see them since (1) they are normally not visible from the Court of the Israelites, and (2) no laymen were allowed into

33. Grenfell and Hunt acknowledged that the letter may be a τ or an υ (*Fragment of an Uncanonical Gospel*, 22), but then proceeded to use the ς even though there seems to be no evidence for that letter.

34. Note particularly the υ in lines 42 and 43 which aptly demonstrates this characteristic curve in the upper right arm. Such a serif is never found in a τ in this fragment.

35. See Urban C. Von Wahlde, 'The Relationships between the Pharisees and Chief Priests: Some Observations on the Texts in Matthew, John, and Josephus', *NTS* 42 (1996) 506–522.

36. *m. Abot.* 3.2; *m. Pesah.* 1.6. Adolf Büchler, *Die Priester und der Cultus im letzten Jahrzehnt des Jerusalemischen Tempels* (Vienna: Alfred Hölder, 1895) 107–11; Schwartz, 'Viewing the Holy Utensils', 159, n. 33; E. P. Sanders, *Judaism: Practice and Belief 63BCE–66CE* (London: SCM, 1992) 404; Joseph M. Baumgarten, *Studies in Qumran Law* (Leiden: E. J. Brill, 1977) 64.

the sanctuary? A passage in Josephus may provide the solution to this question. Apparently, during certain special times of the year (solemn days or festivals), the restrictions on viewing the vessels were temporarily suspended, and the curtain of the tabernacle was rolled back so that the people could view the interior. Josephus declares that the temple veil could be drawn back 'that then it might be no hindrance to the view of the sanctuary, especially on solemn days'.[37] This custom of periodically allowing the common Israelite to view the sanctuary, and thus the holy vessels, is confirmed in the Talmud which refers to the event several times.[38] This viewing of the sacred areas took place mainly during the Feast of Tabernacles (*Sukkot*) where the Israelites would march around the altar – inside the Court of the Priests – waving willow branches in their hands and praying to God.[39] Thus, it seems most likely that the term ἁγνευτήριον simply refers to the Court of the Israelites or the Court of the Priests where the common Israelite, during the festival, was allowed to view the interior of the tabernacle and to witness the vessels on display.

One of the most criticized aspects of our fragment is the implication that all worshippers (not just priests), prior to entry to the temple, must completely immerse in a bath (whether previously 'clean' or not). This claim has drawn the heaviest fire from critics of the fragment because there is no explicit historical evidence for these practices, and they are not mentioned in the Old Testament purity texts.[40] Although it is true that we have no explicit references of immersion for non-priests, there are good reasons to think that such a custom may have been probable during the period of the Herodian temple. Not only is there a general trend during this time to expand purity laws beyond their original sphere,[41] but also the practice finds support in the express words of *m. Yoma*. 3:3: 'A person does not enter the courtyard for the service, even if he is clean, unless he immerses.'[42] In addition, the location and frequency of *miqva'ot* seem to suggest that the common Israelite immersed more often than OT law would require. Donald Binder declares, 'It is likely that total immersion was the norm for everyone prior to entry [to the temple], as suggested by the large number of pools surrounding the temple mount.'[43] Indeed, the fact that the 'Pool of David'

37. *Ant*. 3.128. Translation is from William Whiston (ed.), *Josephus: The Complete Works* (Nashville: Thomas Nelson, 1998) 103.

38. *b. Yoma*. 54a; *b. Hag*. 26b; *b. Pesah*. 57a; *b. Yom*. 21b; and *b. Men*. 96b.

39. *m. Sukkah*. 4.5; *b. Sukkah*. 43b; *m. Kelim*. 1.8; and similarities with *Jub*. 16.31.

40. Schürer, 'Fragment', 171.

41. Gedaliah Alon, *Jews, Judaism, and the Classical World* (Jerusalem: Magnes Press, 1977) 191; Jacob Neusner, *From Politics to Piety* (Englewood Cliffs, NJ: Prentice Hall, 1973) argues that the *haberim* were concerned to apply priestly rules to the laity (83).

42. See also *y. Yoma*. 3.3 (40b). Thomas Kazen, *Jesus and the Purity Halakhah. Was Jesus Indifferent to Purity?* (Stockholm: Almqvist and Wiksell International, 2002), declares, 'While the context [of m. Yoma. 3.3] is one of priestly service, the saying seems to be general, referring to any visitor in the court assigned for worship' (254, n. 251).

in P.Oxy. 840 is described as having two sets of stairs fits very well with what we know of immersion pools (*miqva'ot*) in the first-century world.[44] The combination of these considerations suggests that there was a strong possibility, if not probability, that common custom required both non-priests and priests to immerse immediately before entrance into the temple.[45]

5. *Relationship to the Canonical Gospels*

Even a cursory reading of P.Oxy. 840 reveals that it shares a number of general similarities with the canonical gospels that require further exploration. Thus, we have three general options before us:

1. *P.Oxy. 840 is literarily dependent upon the canonical gospels.* This view would argue that the author not only possessed and read the canonical gospels but that they were the source from which he drew his material. Thus, on this view, there was a deliberate and conscious effort by the author to use portions from the canonical gospels in his own composition. However, the problem with this position is that there is no extended verbal overlap or significant textual evidence that our author directly used the canonical material.
2. *P.Oxy. 840 is independent of the canonical gospels.* This view would argue that there is no evidence that requires that the author of P.Oxy. 840 knew or used the canonical gospels in the construction of the text and that similarities between P.Oxy. 840 and the canonical gospels are best explained by the use of a common source (whether oral or written). The problem with this position is that there *does* seem to be compelling evidence that P.Oxy. 840 was familiar with the canonical gospels themselves, and not just sources behind them, as will be noted in the next point.
3. *P.Oxy. 840 is* indirectly *dependent upon the canonical gospels.* This view argues that although the author of P.Oxy. 840 knew the canonical gospels, he did not *intentionally* employ them as sources (as option (1) above would suggest), but intended to write his own story. The remaining similarities are explained by the fact that the author was influenced by the cadence and language of the canonical texts and his memory of those texts unconsciously flowed into the composition of P.Oxy. 840. In other words, as our author

43. Donald D. Binder, *Into the Temple Courts: The Place of the Synagogues in the Second Temple Period* (Atlanta: Society of Biblical Literature, 1997) 392–393.

44. Ronny Reich, 'Mishnah, Sheqalim 8:2 and the Archaeological Evidence', in A. Oppenheimer, U. Rappaport, and M. Stern (eds), *Jerusalem in the Second Temple Period: Abraham Schalit Memorial Volume*, (Jerusalem: 1980) 225–256 (Hebrew with English summary); see also Ronny Reich, 'A Miqweh at Isawiya near Jerusalem', *IEJ* 34 (1984) 220–223; Ronny Reich, 'Ritual Baths', *OEANE* 430–431.

45. For my fuller argument, see *The Gospel of the Savior*, 127–134.

sought to compose his story of Jesus it is natural that he would attempt to make it sound like the other stories of Jesus that he was already familiar with in the canonical texts. This third option can explain the obvious connections with the canonical gospels, but can also explain why there is not extended verbal overlap.

The evidence for this last view is found in the fact that P.Oxy. 840 has clear verbal, structural and thematic connections to five passages in the canonical gospels: Lk. 11.37–52; Mt. 23.1–39; Jn 7.1–52; Jn 13.1–30; and Mk 7.1–23. Although there is not room to engage in a detailed analysis of these texts here (I have done so elsewhere[46]), some general observations are in order: (1) A large portion of these connections are with the parts of the canonical gospels most likely due to final redactional activity. In order for the author of P.Oxy. 840 to reflect the redactional work of the evangelists, he must have been influenced by the gospels in their finished form. (2) P.Oxy. 840 has connections with all four of the canonical gospels. Thus, these connections are not just with Q material, but include Mark, M source, L source and the Johannine tradition. When faced with this broad 'spectrum' of connections we are forced to ask a simple question: Is it likely that P.Oxy. 840 could have been influenced by a source prior to the canonical gospels that contained material from such diverse branches of first-century Christianity? The better explanation for this spectrum of influence is that P.Oxy. 840 was influenced by the finished canonical gospels. (3) When we look at these five texts as a whole we see that they are not a random sampling from the canonical gospels but each share three fundamental themes in common: (a) ceremonial washings, (b) inner vs. outer cleanliness and (c) conflict with Jewish authorities.[47] Given that P.Oxy. 840 shares these exact same three themes, we need to ask the following question: If our author knew the canonical gospels and their content resided in his memory, is it not likely that the verbal connections with these five passages are due to the common themes they share with P.Oxy. 840? If so, then the suggestion that P.Oxy. 840 was influenced by the content of the canonical gospels residing in his memory (indirect dependence view) has much explanatory power for helping us understand the author's compositional method.

With all these considerations in mind, there are good reasons to think that P.Oxy. 840 was a production later than the canonical gospels and was influenced by the canonical gospels in their final form.

46. Kruger, *The Gospel of the Savior*, 145–205.

47. Although John 13 may not seem to mention conflict with Jewish authorities, Herold Weiss, 'Foot Washing in the Johannine Community', *NT* 21 (1979) 298–325, has made a convincing case that the chapter deals directly with the upcoming persecution that the disciples (i.e. the church) would face from Jewish authorities. He declares, 'We must interpret the scene of the washing of the disciples' feet in the context of a community facing persecution and martyrdom' (310).

6. *The Place of P.Oxy. 840 within Early Christianity*

In most studies on P.Oxy. 840 the questions of community, date and provenance have received exceptionally little attention. The few studies that even address these issues give a brief one or two sentence suggestion, often focused upon linking P.Oxy. 840 to other known (or unknown) apocryphal gospels. However, further study of the fragment suggests that there may be more to learn about its origins than previously thought. This section will discuss the possible theological and circumstantial environment that may have given rise to such a gospel. Of course, given the brevity of our text and the paucity of information available, any conclusions drawn here must be held tentatively.

As we explore the theological characteristics and tendencies of P.Oxy. 840, one of the most remarkable characteristics of our fragment is that it contains no apparent 'heretical' theology or agenda. Indeed, from the beginning, scholars have noted this characteristic because it seems so rare among known apocryphal material.[48] Thus, rather than looking to fringe groups in early Christianity – like the Naassenes or Manicheans[49] – it seems more fruitful to look in the direction of early Jewish-Christianity.[50] The probable Jewish-Christian origin for P.Oxy. 840 is most vividly seen by noting P.Oxy. 840's most central concern: ritual purity. Numerous factors, some already noted above, corroborate this concern: (1) focus upon access to a holy place and holy objects (the temple and its vessels); (2) description of ceremonial washings in a *miqveh* (which were only done for purity reasons); (3) reference to foot-washing which was also done for purity reasons; (4) conflict centred around what kind of water (running or drawn) really makes one 'clean'; (5) frequent use of the verb λούω which occurs five times in P.Oxy. 840 (lines 14, 19, 24, 32, 37), hardly occurs in the New Testament, but is abundant in the Old Testament texts concerning cultic purity;[51] (6) frequent use of καθαρός[52] and καθαρεύω (lines 18, 23, 24,

48. Grenfell and Hunt, *Fragment of an Uncanonical Gospel*, 13; Goodspeed, 'The New Gospel Fragment', 144; Swete, *Two New Gospel Fragments*, 4.

49. Bovon suggests a Manichean milieu ('Fragment Oxyrhynchus 840', 728), Tripp argues for another Gnostic group, the Naassenes ('Meanings of the Footwashing', 238); and Lagrange links it with the group behind the *Gospel of the Hebrews* (Lagrange, 'Nouveau Fragment', 552).

50. The broad issue of how to define Jewish-Christianity is extremely complex and cannot be fully solved here. Some efforts towards a more precise definition include, S. C. Mimouni, 'Pour une définition nouvelle du judéo-christianisme ancien', *NTS* 38 (1992) 161–186; Raymond Brown, 'Not Jewish Christianity and Gentile Christianity but types of Jewish/Gentile Christianity', *CBQ* 45 (1983) 74–79; Simon Marcel, 'Problèmes du Judéo-Christianisme', in *Aspects du Judéo-Christianisme* (Paris: Presses Universitaires de France, 1965) 1–17.

51. For example, in Leviticus alone: 8.6; 11.40; 14.8, 9; 15.5–8, 10–11, 13, 16, 18, 21–22, 27; 16.4, 24, 26, 28; 17.15–16; 22.6. For more complete discussion see A. Oepke, *TDNT* 4, 295–307, where he even mentions P.Oxy. 840 as an example of such usage. For comparison to νίπτω see F. Hauck, *TDNT* 4, 946–947.

52. The use of this word in OT cultic contexts is so abundant the verses are too many to mention. For more discussion, see F. Hauck, TDNT 3,413–417, and R. Meyer, *TDNT* 3, 418–423.

28) to refer to ceremonial 'cleaning'; (7) reference to 'dogs and pigs' which are the height of Jewish ritual impurity;[53] (8) P.Oxy. 840 shows 'indirect dependence' upon five canonical passages which themselves deal with the issue of ritual purity and internal/external cleanliness: Lk. 11.37–52; Mt. 23.13–32; Jn 7.1–52; Jn 13.10; and Mk 7.1–23. Of course, given that issues of ritual purity are a distinctively Jewish concern, it seems very likely that P.Oxy. 840 originated from a Jewish-Christian setting.

I have argued elsewhere that the characteristics of P.Oxy. 840's Jewish Christianity may fit with the historical Jewish-Christian sect of the Nazarenes.[54] Both were 'orthodox' Jewish-Christian groups, had intimate knowledge of the temple cult, were in conflict with Rabbinic Judaism and were pro-Paul in their approach to whether ritual purity laws should be required for entrance into the covenant community. In addition, a possible connection between the community of P.Oxy. 840 and the Nazarene community is suggested by the fact that the *Gospel of the Nazarenes* also uses the distinctive phrase 'harlots and pipe-girls'.[55] This connection does not prove that P.Oxy. 840 is actually part of the *Gospel of the Nazarenes*, but is mentioned simply to show that each community knew and used this phrase in its production of gospel stories, raising the possibility that P.Oxy. 840 may have originated within the Nazarene community.

If the above analysis is correct, then the composition of the story in P.Oxy. 840 can be dated after the canonical gospels and yet also when the Nazarenes were seriously in conflict with Rabbinic Judaism. This would suggest a time in the early to middle second century, perhaps AD c. 125–c. 150. But, again, the evidence is too slight to rest on this date or provenance with any assurance.

7. *Conclusion*

In conclusion, P.Oxy. 840 is an apocryphal gospel fragment of great value to scholars in their studies of early Christianity. Not only is it relatively well-preserved, but its format (miniature codex) suggests that it was likely a portion of a longer gospel-like book used by well-to-do Christians during their travels and studies. The historical problems of the fragment, once formidable obstacles to its early acceptance by scholars, seem to be less and less troubling as we compare it to the detailed evidence of first-century Judaism. Thus, P.Oxy. 840

53. The term 'dog' is used to refer to Gentiles/pagans (Deut. 23.18; Mt. 15.26–27), wicked men in general (Rev. 22.15) and a broad term of reproach (1 Sam. 17.43; 24.14; 2 Sam. 9.8; 16.9). Pigs, of course, were unclean food (Lev. 11.7; Deut. 14.18; Isa. 65.4), and generally seen as negative (Isa. 66.17; Mt. 8.30–32).

54. Kruger, *The Gospel of the Savior*, 206–247. For a survey of the Nazarenes, see R.A. Pritz, *Nazarene Jewish Christianity: From the End of the New Testament Period to Its Disappearance in the Fourth Century* (Leiden: E.J. Brill, 1988).

55. Eusebius, *Theophania* 4.22.

stands before us not only as yet another example of an apocryphal gospel somewhat dependent upon the canonical gospels, but as a possible window into the world of early Jewish Christianity (and the Nazarenes in particular). As such, P.Oxy. 840 proves to be an apocryphal gospel worthy of further and deeper study by the next generation of scholars.

Bibliography

L. Blau, 'Das neue Evangelienfragment von Oxyrhynchos buch- und zaubergeschichtlich betrachtet nebst sonstigen Bemerkungen', *ZNW* 9 (1908) 204–215.

F. Bovon, 'Fragment Oxyrhynchus 840, Fragment of a Lost Gospel, Witness of an Early Christian Controversy Over Purity', *JBL* 119 (2000) 705–728.

A. Büchler, 'The New "Fragment of an Uncanonical Gospel"', *JQR* 20 (1908) 330–346.

B. P. Grenfell and A. S. Hunt, *Fragment of an Uncanonical Gospel* (London: Oxford University Press, 1908).

A. von Harnack, 'Ein neues Evangelienbruchstück', in *Aus Wissenschaft und Leben, Band II*, (Giessen: Alfred Töpelmann, 1911) 239–250.

J. Jeremias, 'Der Zusammenstoss Jesu mit dem pharisäischen Oberpriester auf den Tempelplatz. Zu Pap. Ox V 840', *Coni. Neotest.* 2 (1947) 97–108.

M. J. Kruger, *The Gospel of the Savior: An Analysis of P.Oxy. 840 and Its Place in the Gospel Traditions of Early Christianity* (Leiden: Brill, 2005).

E. Preuschen, 'Das neue Evangelienfragment von Oxyrhynchos', *ZNW* 9 (1908) 1–11.

H. B. Swete, *Two New Gospel Fragments* (Cambridge: Deighton, Bell & Co., 1908).

Chapter 14

Secret Mark

Paul Foster

Secret Mark remains one of the most controversial and enigmatic texts relating to the New Testament that has been discovered in the last century. Accusations of forgery as well as acrimonious debate have often characterized the discussion. For many years the only book-length treatments of this text were the two volumes published by Morton Smith the putative discoverer of the text. However, in the last few years there has been a renewed flurry of interest with three important books appearing. Two of these claim that the text is either a forgery or a hoax, while the other strongly defends the authenticity of the text. It is this minefield of academic claim and counterclaim that those interested in *Secret Mark* must cautiously navigate.

1. *Discovery?*

For those who enjoy a good conspiracy theory, the discovery of the text known as *Secret Mark* seems to have all the necessary ingredients: a dusty manuscript unearthed in the back of a seventeenth-century book; in an Orthodox monastery in the Holy Land, by one of the most controversial New Testament scholars of the twentieth century. The discussion that followed the publication of the manuscript is shrouded in accusations of forgery and claims that it undermines the traditional account of Christian origins. Then, perhaps 30 years after the discovery, the manuscript disappeared. One may well think that this even has the potential to become a Hollywood script, but perhaps here is a case where the fiction surrounding *Secret Mark* is actually stranger than the fact.

The discoverer of *Secret Mark*, Morton Smith, had first visited what was then Palestine in 1941, as the recipient of a travelling fellowship from Harvard Divinity School.[1] American involvement in the Second World War and heightened hostilities in the Mediterranean resulted in Smith being stranded in the Holy Land until the end of the war. During this time Smith became enamoured with Orthodox Christianity, and his acquaintance with Archimandrite Kyriakos

1. B. Ehrman, *Lost Christianities*, 71.

Spyridonides resulted in him being invited to the monastery of Mar Saba, approximately 20 km south-east of Jerusalem. More than a decade later these relationships were to prove instrumental in gaining Smith access to the monastery, to catalogue the contents of its library.[2]

During this return visit in 1958 to Mar Saba, Smith found a number of important manuscripts including two hitherto unknown 'folia of a fifteenth-century manuscript of Sophocles' which 'had been used as end papers for an eighteenth-century Venice edition of the evening and morning prayers'.[3] In addition, Smith noted that many of the books contained handwritten notes, mainly in seventeenth- to nineteenth-century hands. The authenticity of these finds has not been disputed. Towards the end of his stay, Smith examined what turned out to be a copy of a 1646 edition of the Letters of Ignatius of Antioch by the Dutch scholar Isaac Voss. Later Smith described how he discovered a letter from Clement of Alexandria to a certain figure named Theodore, written 'over both sides of the last page [which was blank] of the original book and over half the recto of a sheet of binder's paper'.[4] The excitement and importance of discovering a letter from Clement led Smith to photograph the text.[5] With his stay coming to an end, Smith did not engage in detailed analysis or even translation of the text, instead he returned to the task of cataloguing the collection.

2. *Contents*

When the photographs were processed, the works of transcription and translation were commenced. The correspondence contained in this letter of Clement was in response to an enquiry made by Theodore concerning a group known as the Carpocratians,[6] who have been characterized by the Church Fathers as a libertine group, with a particularly relaxed attitude towards sexual practices. The text of the letter itself describes the Carpocratians as those who have 'become slaves to servile desires' (I.7).[7] The enquiry, to which the letter responded, did not centre upon the behaviour of this group, but rather the veracity of their claim to possess an alternative, but nonetheless genuine, version of Mark's Gospel which validated their own beliefs and practices. In response, Clement did not deny such claims out of hand. Instead, he recounted

2. S. Brown, *Mark's Other Gospel*, 36.

3. M. Smith, *The Secret Gospel*, 12.

4. See M. Smith, *Clement of Alexandria and a Secret Gospel of Mark*, 1. Images are available online at http://www-user.uni-bremen.de/~wie/Secret/secmark_home.html (last accessed on 26 March 2008).

5. Smith, *The Secret Gospel*, 12–13.

6. In appendix B of *Clement of Alexandria and a Secret Gospel of Mark*, Smith provides an extensive collection of Patristic texts referring to the Carpocratians. See 295–350.

7. The division of the text and reference numbers were devised by Smith. See Smith, *Clement of Alexandria and a Secret Gospel of Mark*, 6–120. For convenience, this text is helpfully set out in Brown, *Mark's Other Gospel*, xvii–xxii.

a compositional history of the gospel that involves three versions, two of which he states are genuinely Markan, the other a Carpocratian fabrication. According to the letter, Mark composed his initial version of the Gospel in Rome during Peter's lifetime drawing on the apostle's recollections and other sources of information. Upon Peter's death, Mark relocated to Alexandria where he brought, according to the letter, 'both his own notes and those of Peter, from which he transferred to his former book the things suitable to whatever makes for progress towards knowledge. Thus he composed a more spiritual gospel for the use of those who were being perfected' (I.19–22). This second version was not for general circulation, but Carpocrates, using what Clement depicts as nefarious means, obtained a copy of this expanded spiritual gospel and inserted some of his own teachings into the text.

In order to demonstrate that the second edition composed in Alexandria did not support Carpocratian teachings, Clement cited two passages from it for Theodore's benefit and perhaps also for his peace of mind. The first recounts a miracle story reminiscent of the raising of Lazarus, but without named characters and lacking any distinctively Johannine vocabulary. According to Clement this was inserted after Mk 10.34.

> And they come to Bethany. And there was there a certain woman whose brother of hers had died. And coming, she prostrated before Jesus and says to him, 'Son of David have mercy on me.' But the disciples rebuked her. And having become angry Jesus went away with her into the garden where the tomb was. And immediately was heard from the tomb a great cry. And approaching, Jesus rolled the stone from the door of the tomb, and going in immediately where the young man was, he stretched out his hand and raised him, having grasped the hand. But the young man, having looked upon him, loved him and began to beg him that he might be with him. And going out of the tomb they went into the house of the young man; for he was rich.
>
> And after six days Jesus gave charge to him; and when it was evening the young man comes to him donning a linen sheet upon his naked body, and he remained with him that night; for Jesus was teaching him the mystery of the kingdom of God. Now rising, he returned from there to the other side of the Jordan.

The second passage is much shorter, and according to the Clementine letter was inserted after the first two clauses in Mk 10.46.

> And there were there the sister of the young man whom Jesus loved him and his mother and Salome, and Jesus did not receive them.

It appears that Clement had selected these two passages relating to the young man to assure Theodore that the expanded gospel did not support the reading of 'naked man with naked man' (III.13) as claimed by the Carpocratians. In effect, citation of these two pericopae was an attempt to rebut libertine interpretations of the Jesus tradition.

3. *Response to the Text*

At the Society of Biblical Literature meeting in 1960 Smith announced the discovery of the letter. His detailed analysis of the text was largely completed by 1966, but for reasons that are not totally obvious[8] the work was not published until 1973.[9] This coincided with the publication of his more popular account of the discovery and contents of the letter, *The Secret Gospel*. Scholarly reaction to the publication was mixed and at times overly heated. In 1974, F. F. Bruce,[10] Raymond Brown[11] and Robert Grant[12] suggested that the text was dependent on existing canonical material, or even a pastiche of traditions derived from all four gospels. This interpretation has been followed by a number subsequent scholars, such as Frans Neirynck.[13] The implication was that this 'collage' of texts drawn from the canonical accounts reflected the literary forms known from the corpus of apocryphal gospels. Thus Robert Gundry stated that it represented 'expansions of the sort we find everywhere in apocryphal literature'.[14] At this stage the main accusation against the text centred on the authenticity of the two gospel fragments it cited. No attempt was made to impugn Smith's integrity; rather there was scepticism directed towards some of his scholarly judgements.

This was to change with the publication of Quentin Quesnell's *CBQ* article that appeared in 1975.[15] One of his main complaints about Smith's two books is that they provide little information about the physical characteristics of the manuscript, or the means to validate its authenticity. Quesnell dismisses the quality of the images of the manuscript provided in the books, stating that 'Smith's photographs are less than satisfactory.'[16] Further, he describes limitations in Smith's description of the work carried out by palaeographers in dating the handwriting. In section two, titled 'The Unavoidable Next Question', he goes on to state, 'When adequate physical evidence for determining

8. Joseph Fitzmyer suggested that the technical treatment was delayed in order that its sales might be boosted by the circulation of the more popular volume. See J. A. Fitzmyer, 'Reply to Morton Smith', *America* 129 (4 August 1973) 65. Smith indicated that the book was 'going through the press' in 1966, Smith, *The Secret Gospel*, 76.

9. For further details see Brown, *Mark's Other Gospel*, 6.

10. F. F. Bruce, *The Secret Gospel of Mark*, Ethel Wood Lecture, 11 February 1974. Most conveniently reprinted in a slightly amended form as Appendix 1 in *The Canon of Scripture* (Downers Grover: IVP, 1988).

11. R. E. Brown, 'The Relation of "The Secret Gospel of Mark" to the Fourth Gospel', *CBQ* 36 (1974) 466–485.

12. R. M. Grant, 'Morton Smith's Two Books', *ATR* 56 (1974) 58–64.

13. F. Neirynck, 'La fuite du jeune home en Mc 14, 51–52', *ETL* 55 (1979) 43–66.

14. R. H. Gundry, 'Excursus on the Secret Gospel of Mark' in *Mark: A Commentary on His Apology for the Cross* (Grand Rapids: Eerdmans, 1993) 612.

15. Q. Quesnell, 'The Mar Saba Clementine: A Question of Evidence', *CBQ* 37 (1975) 48–67.

16. Q. Quesnell, 'The Mar Saba Clementine: A Question of Evidence', 50.

a document's age has not been provided, the scientific inquirer is forced to go on to ask about the possibilities of forgery.'[17] For Quesnell, one of the most significant factors in answering this question was recognition of the fact that in 1936 Stählin published the fourth volume of his edition of Clement's works, which contained a concordance of that Church Father's vocabulary. This register of Clementine terminology spanned more than 600 pages of printed text.[18] According to Quesnell it was just the kind of tool a potential forger would require in order to produce a letter of the type discovered by Smith. In his conclusion to this section he states, 'Until the standard physical evidence is produced, the possibility remains wide open that the document was produced sometime between 1936 and 1958.'[19]

It is worth noting that Smith wrote a response in the same journal in 1976 in which he states, 'Quesnell insinuates that I forged the MS. Such accusations are customary when important MSS are discovered.'[20] Quesnell was allowed a response to Smith's comments in the same issue in which he denies that he had accused Smith of forging the letter. He replied,

> Dr. Smith feels the point of my article was to prove that he forged the Clement text. If that had been my point, I would have stated it clearly. He would not have had to compose his reply in terms like 'insinuates . . . suggests . . . insinuation . . . suspicion . . . etc.'[21]

Admittedly, Quesnell nowhere directly states that Smith was the putative forger: in fact he refers to 'many others besides Smith' who might have set this up as a controlled experiment to see how the scholarly world responded, but nonetheless the reader is given a strong impression of who should be considered the prime suspect.

A particularly acrimonious chapter in this tale of reactions to *Secret Mark* involves one of Smith's former doctoral students, Jacob Neusner, now known for his prolific writing on Judaism in the late Second Temple and Tannaitic periods. Neusner was initially positive about Smith's discovery. When he penned the dust jacket endorsement for *The Secret Gospel* he described it in laudatory terms as 'a brilliant account of how Morton Smith reached a major discovery in the study of first-century Christianity'.[22] For a variety of reasons, many of which have been documented elsewhere,[23] relations between Smith

17. Q. Quesnell, 'The Mar Saba Clementine: A Question of Evidence', 53–54.

18. O. Stählin, *Clemens Alexandrinus* IV (GCS 39; Leipzig, 1936).

19. Q. Quesnell, 'The Mar Saba Clementine: A Question of Evidence', 58.

20. M. Smith, 'On the Authenticity of the Mar Saba Letter of Clement', *CBQ* 38 (1976) 196–199.

21. Q. Quesnell, 'A Reply to Morton Smith', *CBQ* 38 (1976) 200–203.

22. See Smith, *The Secret Gospel*.

23. H. Shanks, 'Annual Meetings Offer Intellectual Bazaar and Moments of High Drama', *BAR* 11.2 (1985) 16. Brown, *Mark's Other Gospel*, 39–45.

and Neusner deteriorated with both calling into question the quality of the scholarship produced by the other, at times in the most vitriolic terms. After Smith's death, Neusner described him as 'a charlatan and a fraud' and he continued by depicting *Secret Mark* as 'the forgery of the century'.[24]

Such reactions may well leave the general reader somewhat confused, with little sense of how to assess the merits of this vitriolic series of claim and counterclaim. First, it should be stated that, contrary to some accounts, Morton Smith was not the only person ever to view the text. In 1976 the book containing *Secret Mark* was transferred from the library at Mar Saba to the Jerusalem Patriarchate library. The then librarian, Father Kallistos Dourvas, cut the pages containing the text out of the book, and took colour photographs.[25] These were published by Charles Hedrick in 2000.[26] The story of the transfer of the book is elucidated by Guy Stroumsa. He recounts a trip he took from Jerusalem to Mar Saba. He was accompanied by three others, now deceased, Prof David Flusser, Prof Shlomo Pines and Archimandrite Meliton. Apparently, because of thefts from the library the party was not optimistic of success. Stroumsa describes the search for the book by a young monk.

> We did not put our expectations too high, but at some point, the monk did find the book, with 'Smith 65' inscribed on its front page, and the three manuscript pages of Clement's letter written on the blank pages at the end of the book, exactly as described by Smith. The book had obviously remained where Smith had found it and had replaced it, after having photographed the manuscript letter. It was obvious to all of us that the precious book should not be left in place, but rather be deposited in the library of the Patriarchate. So we took the book back to Jerusalem, and Father Meliton brought it to the library.[27]

The existence of a second set of photographs and the testimony of Stroumsa should finally quiet any doubts that the manuscript existed or that Smith controlled access to it. Unfortunately, subsequent to its transferral to the Patriarchate library in Jerusalem the whereabouts of the manuscript has become uncertain. Perhaps it was lost, misplaced, stolen, sequestered or sold on the antiquities market.[28]

24. J. Neusner and N. Neusner, *The Price of Excellence: Universities in Conflict during the Cold War Era* (New York: Continuum, 1995) 78.

25. C. Hedrick, 'The Secret Gospel of Mark: Stalemate in the Academy', *JECS* 11 (2003) 140.

26. C. Hedrick, 'Secret Mark: New Photographs, New Witnesses', *The Fourth R* 13.5 (2000) 3–11; 14–16.

27. G. Stroumsa, 'Comments on Charles Hedrick's Article: A Testimony', *JECS* 11 (2003) 147–148.

28. Hedrick, 'The Secret Gospel of Mark: Stalemate in the Academy', 140.

4. *Current State of Research*

Given the information surrounding the discovery of the manuscript and the initial reactions in the years following its publication, what can now be said about this enigmatic document? Basically the options articulated by Morton Smith and the initial reviewers still remain the positions that are being debated. Opinion is divided between those who see the text as authentic, and those who are more convinced by the arguments suggesting that the document is a forgery. Yet, even here, the options subdivide, creating at least five main alternatives:

1. Authentic
   a. A genuine letter of Clement and conveying accurate information about multiple editions of Mark's Gospel.[29]
   b. A genuine letter of Clement, but misinformed about Markan authorship of an alternative version of the gospel.[30]
2. Forgery
   a. An ancient forgery, written in Clement's name to legitimize an alternative version of the gospel.
   b. An eighteenth-century forgery, created for uncertain reasons.
   c. A twentieth-century forgery, most likely by Morton Smith, the motivation could be to fool members of the academic community, to provide legitimization of homosexual practice, or to enhance personal fame and scholarly reputation.[31]

None of these possibilities is without problems. If this is a genuine letter containing accurate information, why do the two passages from Mark look like a composite of phrases from canonical accounts? If this is a misinformed letter by the historical Clement, what led him to believe and perpetuate this erroneous information? The forgery explanations are also not without problems. If the letter were an ancient forgery, what did it gain for its author by supporting the existence of an alternative form of Mark, but refuting the claims of the Carpocratians? The possibility of an eighteenth-century forgery is the most perplexing alternative. What plausible motive can be attributed to the monastic(?) scribe who hid his work away in the library? Finally, the suggestion that

29. This is the option favoured by Scott Brown in his recent treatment, *Mark's Other Gospel*.

30. This would appear to be the position of many scholars who view *Secret Mark* as a second-century pastiche of canonical traditions. See Gundry, 'Excursus on the Secret Gospel of Mark' 603–623.

31. S. Carlson argues that analysis of the manuscripts reveals the flaws that occur with imitation of an unfamiliar handwriting style. This would only be the case if a twentieth-century forger was trying to imitate eighteenth-century Greek script.

the text was a modern forgery raises the question of whether Morton Smith, or another figure with access to the library, had the technical skills to create this hoax. Carlson provides startling new evidence that suggests this was within Smith's range of competence.[32] Yet one is forced to speculate on Smith's motivation, as well as the plausibility of Smith spending 15 years (1958–1973) analysing and preparing an edition of what he knew to be a spurious text for publication. While none of these alternatives is impossible, each has complications that mean that no suggestion is entirely compelling.

Some of those who see Smith as the author of the manuscript argue that it contains a homosexual subtext. Smith himself saw the first passage cited from *Secret Mark* as part of a baptismal initiation story. In this context he stated 'In this baptism the disciple was united with Jesus. The union may have been physical (. . . there is no telling how far symbolism went in Jesus' rite), but the essential thing was that the disciple was possessed by Jesus' spirit.'[33] Hedrick views the possibility of a homosexual subtext as a non-issue, since Smith himself argued that speculation was inconclusive. He observes, 'Not even Smith pursued that line of thinking in his analysis of the text.'[34] Not all, however, were convinced by Hedrick's rebuttal. Ehrman argues that the 'homoerotic emphasis was not imported into Smith's view from outside, by homophobic voyeurs in the guild. It is all right there, plain to see, at the climactic moment of the narrative.'[35] He finds support for this assessment in statements contained in Smith's more popular account. Chief among these is 'Freedom from the law may have resulted in completion of the spiritual union by physical union.'[36] Furthermore, Ehrman draws attention to another piece of evidence in a footnote from the same book.

> In possibly the most telling footnote of the book, Smith makes a suggestion about what these 'unknown ceremonies' may have entailed: 'manipulation too was probably involved; the stories of Jesus' miracles give a large place to the use of his hands.' Indeed.[37]

It does appear that Ehrman has the stronger argument here. Regardless of the original intention of the text (if it was not produced by Smith) there seems little doubt that Smith saw the potential to recognize in the text homoerotic tendencies, specifically in the first passage that Clement cites from the longer version of Mark's Gospel.

32. S. C. Carlson, *The Gospel Hoax: Morton Smith's Invention of Secret Mark* (Waco, TX: Baylor University Press, 2005).

33. Smith, *Clement of Alexandria and a Secret Gospel of Mark*, 251.

34. Hedrick, 'The Secret Gospel of Mark: Stalemate in the Academy', 142.

35. Ehrman, 'Response to Charles Hedrick's Stalemate', *JECS* 11 (2003) 157.

36. See Smith, *The Secret Gospel*, 114.

37. Ehrman, 'Response to Charles Hedrick's Stalemate', 157, referring to Smith, *The Secret Gospel*, 113, n. 12.

Secret Mark has also been used as a key text in certain discussions surrounding synoptic relationships and the instability of the text of the gospels. Helmet Koester proposed the priority of the longer form, with canonical Mark being an abbreviation of this text.[38] Yet *Secret Mark* itself was not the first stage of the evolution of the Markan tradition, for, according to Koester, a proto-Gospel of Mark was expanded into the longer form evidenced by Clement, and this in turn was abbreviated to produce what we now know as the *Gospel of Mark*.[39] These extracts from the theory give an indication of its postulates:

> A large number of features which distinguish *Canonical Mark* from Proto-Mark are so closely related to the special material of *Secret Mark* quoted by Clement of Alexandria that the conclusion is unavoidable: Canonical Mark is derived from Secret Mark . . . The redaction of Mark which produced the *Secret Gospel* must have taken place early in the 2nd century . . . 'Canonical Mark' would have been written some time thereafter, but before Clement of Alexandria. The Carpocratians, however, based their new edition of Mark upon the full and unabbreviated text of the *Secret Gospel*. Clement of Alexandria believed that Mark first wrote the 'canonical' (or 'public') Gospel, and later produced the 'secret' version of this writing. My observations, however, lead to the conclusion that 'canonical' Mark was a purified version of that 'secret' Gospel, because the traces of the author of *Secret Mark* are still visible in the canonical Gospel of Mark.[40]

The speculative nature of this thesis has prevented it from gaining widespread acceptance.[41]

Many scholars have also seen the text depicting a baptismal rite, perhaps from the second century, and hence feel that it reflects more about forms of Christian initiation than it does about the practices of the Historical Jesus. This idea was first suggested by Smith himself, who, in relation to Clement's first extract from longer Mark, stated, 'the pericope may have been read at the baptismal service preceding the pascha.'[42] Similarly, Crossan sees the text functioning in a cultic setting: 'it was probably used in the nude baptismal practices of his [i.e. Clement's] community and thereby received an erotic interpretation among some believers.'[43] Despite the popularity of this interpretation,

38. H. Koester, *Introduction to the New Testament: Volume 2, History and Literature of Early Christianity* (Philadelphia: Fortress, 1982) 168–169.

39. H. Koester, 'History and Development of Mark's Gospel (From Mark to *Secret Mark* and "Canonical" Mark', in B. Corley (ed.), *Colloquy on New Testament Studies: A Time for Reappraisal and Fresh Approaches* (Macon, GA: Mercer University Press, 1983) 35–57.

40. Koester, 'History and Development of Mark's Gospel (From Mark to *Secret Mark* and "Canonical" Mark', 56–57.

41. A similar theory is advanced by J. D. Crossan, *The Historical Jesus: The Life of a Mediterranean Jewish Peasant* (New York: HarperCollins, 1991) 329. His theory differs from that of Koester in that he dispenses with the proto-Gospel and places the longer version of Mark first. This is then abbreviated to form the canonical account.

42. Smith, *Clement of Alexandria and a Secret Gospel of Mark*, 168.

43. Crossan, *The Historical Jesus*, 329.

Brown points out the lack of any reference to water in the passage from longer Mark, which one may consider an essential ingredient in a baptism story![44] Also, it may be significant to note that *Secret Mark* is not the only non-canonical gospel text that has been viewed as related to early Christian baptismal practices.[45]

5. *Conclusion*

Debate about *Secret Mark* has not divided New Testament scholars along pre-conceived party lines. The Jesus Seminar, noted (perhaps not entirely accurately) for its preference of apocryphal traditions over canonical gospels for reconstructing the Historical Jesus, was not convinced that the material in *Secret Mark* was historically reliable.[46] This of course is different from saying the document was a forgery. The debate about the genuineness of *Secret Mark* continues, and understandably many scholars are unwilling to invest time in studying two short *pericopae* which may turn out to be part of a twentieth-century hoax. This impasse surrounding the foundational issue of authenticity has resulted, by and large, in *Secret Mark* being omitted from discussions surrounding the teaching of the Historical Jesus or the nature of the diversity in nascent Christianity. This is not motivated by a desire to present Christianity as an originally pristine orthodox faith from which heretics later deviated. A scholar such as Ehrman, who is a strong advocate of Bauer's thesis (of diverse strands emerging in early Christianity the majority of which were later deemed heretical by those who labelled themselves the orthodox party),[47] nonetheless rejects the authenticity of *Secret Mark* even though it would apparently support the diversity thesis. The reason is that Ehrman simply is not persuaded that the document published by Smith is an ancient source. Thus he states,

> At the end of the day, I don't think we can say whether or not Smith forged the letter. We won't know until, if ever, the manuscript is found and subjected to a rigorous investigation, including the testing of the ink. Until that happens, some will continue treating the piece as authentic, others will have their doubts.[48]

This final sentence exemplifies the perspectives of the three most recent works analysing *Secret Mark*. Scott Brown is convinced by arguments for the

44. He notes, 'The story is strangely unclear about what is transpiring between Jesus and the young man. There is no mention of water or depiction of a baptism.' Brown, *Mark's Other Gospel*, 145.

45. F. Bovon, '*Fragment Oxyrhynchus 840*, Fragment of a Lost Gospel, Witness of an Early Christian Controversy over Purity', *JBL* (2000) 705–728.

46. This point is also made by Scott Brown in *Mark's Other Gospel*, 17, 18, 46.

47. See W. Bauer, *Orthodoxy and Heresy in Earliest Christianity* (Eng. trans.; London: SCM, 1972).

48. Ehrman, 'Response to Charles Hedrick's Stalemate', 162–163.

authenticity of the longer version of the *Gospel of Mark*.[49] He carefully examines, and at times rejects, many of Smith's interpretations of the text. Yet from his positive assessment of the authenticity of both the Clementine letter and the two fragments excerpted from longer Mark he offers a number of fresh and stimulating insights. By contrast, Carlson brings his analytical skills to bear on the actual photographic images of the text.[50] He argues strongly that the handwriting itself preserves features which suggest the manuscript is a modern forgery. Most recently, Peter Jeffery has, like Carlson, rejected the authenticity of the document albeit for different reasons.[51] He sees the text operating as a cipher for Smith's own proclivities in relation to his religious understandings and sexual orientation. Thus, according to Jeffery, the Carpocratian or 'Gnostic' perspective is supportive of Smith's own spiritual journey away from mainstream Christianity.[52] Moreover, the type of homosexuality portrayed in the text, according to Jeffery is not reflective of ancient practice. Thus it is suggested that in the ancient world homosexual practice worked in parallel with men engaging in heterosexual relationships to produce heirs. By contrast, it is argued that the homosexuality enshrined in *Secret Mark* (if that is what the text is denoting) represents 'the "Uranian" homosexual subculture of nineteenth-century English universities'.[53] This is seen as being far more misogynistic, and it is seen as inconceivable in antiquity that the young man could approach Jesus thereby breaking hierarchical status relationships to initiate sexual contact.

It is yet to be seen if any of these recent works will lead to the emergence of a consensus position, or whether competing opinions will become even more polarized. One can but hope that debate will remain respectful and attentive to alternative points of view. If, however, previous debate on *Secret Mark* is any indicator, this is probably a vain hope.

49. Brown, *Mark's Other Gospel*.

50. S. C. Carlson, *The Gospel Hoax Morton Smith's Invention of* Secret Mark (Waco: Baylor University Press, 2005).

51. P. Jeffery, *The Secret Gospel of Mark Unveiled: Imagined Rituals of Sex, Death, and Madness in a Biblical Forgery* (Yale: Yale University Press, 2007).

52. The way in which Jeffery attempts to make this point at times verges on a personal attack on Smith rather than remaining an objective assessment of the motivations behind the supposed forgery of the document. 'The tragic paradox of the man who thought he had exchanged Christianity for a latter-day Carpocratian Gnosticism is not that he wasn't a good Christian, but that he wasn't even a very good Gnostic. Despite all his priestly experience, his visits to monasteries, his two doctorates, his enviable skill with ancient languages, his prestigious research grants and access to world famous libraries, he wrote what he did not know.' Jeffery, *The Secret Gospel of Mark Unveiled*, 251.

53. Jeffery, *The Secret Gospel of Mark Unveiled*, 225.

Bibliography

A. J. Pantuck and S. G. Brown, 'Morton Smith as M. Madiotes: Stephen Carlson's Attribution of *Secret Mark* to a Bald Swindler', *JSHJ* 6 (2008) 106–125.

S. Brown, *Mark's Other Gospel: Rethinking Morton Smith's Controversial Discovery* (ESCJ 15; Waterloo: Wilfrid Laurier University Press, 2005).

S. C. Carlson, *The Gospel Hoax: Morton Smith's Invention of* Secret Mark (Waco: Baylor University Press, 2005).

B. Ehrman, 'The Forgery of an Ancient Discovery? Morton Smith and the Secret Gospel of Mark', in *Lost Christianities* (Oxford: Oxford University Press, 2003) 67–89.

B. Ehrman, 'Response to Charles Hedrick's Stalemate', *JECS* 11 (2003) 155–163.

C. Hedrick, 'Secret Mark: New Photographs, New Witnesses', *The Fourth R* 13.5 (2000) 3–11, 14–16.

C. Hedrick, 'The Secret Gospel of Mark: Stalemate in the Academy', *JECS* 11 (2003) 133–145.

P. Jeffery, *The Secret Gospel of Mark Unveiled: Imagined Rituals of Sex, Death, and Madness in a Biblical Forgery* (Yale: Yale University Press, 2007).

H. Koester, 'History and Development of Mark's Gospel (From Mark to *Secret Mark* and "Canonical") Mark', in B. Corley (ed.), *Colloquy on New Testament Studies: A Time for Reappraisal and Fresh Approaches* (Macon: Mercer University Press, 1983) 35–57.

M. Meyer, *Secret Gospels: Essays on Thomas and the Secret Gospel of Mark* (Harrisburg: TPI – A Continuum Imprint, 2003).

Q. Quesnell, 'The Mar Saba Clementine: A Question of Evidence', *CBQ* 37 (1975) 48–67.

Q. Quesnell, 'A Reply to Morton Smith', *CBQ* 38 (1976) 200–203.

M. Smith, *Clement of Alexandria and a Secret Gospel of Mark* (Cambridge, MA: Harvard University Press, 1973).

M. Smith, *The Secret Gospel: The Discovery and Interpretation of the Secret Gospel* (New York/London: Harper and Row/Victor Gollancz, 1973/1974).

M. Smith, 'On the Authenticity of the Mar Saba Letter of Clement', *CBQ* 38 (1976) 196–199.

G. Stroumsa, 'Comments on Charles Hedrick's Article: A Testimony', *JECS* 11 (2003) 147–153.

Author Index

Reference Index

Old Testament

Rabbinic Works

Other Texts

Subject Index

MIX
Papier aus verantwortungsvollen Quellen
Paper from responsible sources
FSC® C105338

Printed by Books on Demand GmbH, Norderstedt / Germany

More Books!

I want morebooks!

Buy your books fast and straightforward online - at one of world's fastest growing online book stores! Environmentally sound due to Print-on-Demand technologies.

Buy your books online at
www.morebooks.shop

¡Compre sus libros rápido y directo en internet, en una de las librerías en línea con mayor crecimiento en el mundo! Producción que protege el medio ambiente a través de las tecnologías de impresión bajo demanda.

Compre sus libros online en
www.morebooks.shop

KS OmniScriptum Publishing
Brivibas gatve 197
LV-1039 Riga, Latvia
Telefax: +371 686 204 55

info@omniscriptum.com
www.omniscriptum.com

OMNIScriptum